TRANSATLANTIC SHELL SHOCK

British and American Literatures of World War I Trauma

Edited by Austin Riede

UNIVERSITY of NORTH GEORGIA™
UNIVERSITY PRESS

Blue Ridge | Cumming | Dahlonega | Gainesville | Oconee

Copyright © 2019 by University of North Georgia Press

All rights reserved. No part of this book may be reproduced in whole or in part without written permission from the publisher, except by reviewers who may quote brief excerpts in connections with a review in newspaper, magazine, or electronic publications; nor may any part of this book be reproduced, stored in a retrieval system, or transmitted in any form or by any means electronic, mechanical, photocopying, recording, or other, without the written permission from the publisher.

Published by:
University of North Georgia Press
Dahlonega, Georgia

Printing Support by:
Lightning Source Inc.
La Vergne, Tennessee

Cover image: *Flower of Death—The Bursting of a Heavy Shell—Not as It Looks, but as It Feels and Sounds and Smells*, Claggett Wilson, WWI veteran, 1919.

Cover and book design by Corey Parson.

ISBN: 978-1-940771-65-6

Printed in the United States of America
For more information, please visit: http://ung.edu/university-press
Or e-mail: ungpress@ung.edu

CONTENTS

1 | Transatlantic Shell Shock: An Introduction — 1
Austin Riede

2 | "Strange Hells": Shell Shock, Trauma, and Transatlantic Poetry of the First World War — 38
Argha Banerjee

3 | "Flesh and blood is weak and frail, Susceptible to nervous shock": T. S. Eliot, Shell Shock, and the First World War — 74
Qiang Huang

4 | "It Still Haunts Me": Trauma and Shell Shock in the Writings of the Nurses of the First World War — 95
Samraghni Bonnerjee

5 | Troping Shell Shock: The Anti-Sublime in American and British Women's Great War Narratives — 125
Iro Filippaki

6 | Reporting From the Neuropathic Ward: Eugène Jolas, *transition*, and Psychological Refuge — 153
Jason Parks

7 | Modernism, Shell Shock, and Transatlantic Periodicals — 182
Louise Kane

8	No Way Back: War Trauma in Richard Aldington and Virginia Woolf	208
	Elisa Bolchi	
9	Three Iterations of Shell Shock: Mary Butts and Modern Violence in Interwar Dorset	232
	Ria Banerjee	
10	"A Walking Personification of the Negative": African-American World War I Veterans in Ralph Ellison's *Invisible Man* and Toni Morrison's *Sula*	260
	Jill Goad	
11	Punitive/Analytic Dichotomy and Antiwar Complexes in Pat Barker's *Regeneration* and Dalton Trumbo's *Johnny Got His Gun*	292
	Arsev Ayşen Arslanoğlu Yıldıran	

TRANSATLANTIC SHELL SHOCK

An Introduction

Austin Riede

SEPTIMUS Smith, the shell-shocked soldier who haunts the pages of Virginia Woolf's *Mrs. Dalloway* (1925), is probably the most famous invented literary character to suffer from the enigmatic condition. He is a madman, a threat, a warning, a cursed reminder of a war the Londoners of the novel would rather forget, a danger to society, to his wife, and to himself. He is also a visionary, an artist, a poet who expresses post Great War alienation, a witness to that conflict's degradation of humanity and to the hypocrisy of a society in denial over what the war has revealed about the fundamental fragility of the human mind and the animal aspects of human experience.[1]

Across the Atlantic, and in entirely different circumstances, another modernist madman torments those around him and questions the morality of both his family and his society: Darl Bundren, the moral center of William

---

[1] Vara Neverow traces the real-life inspirations for Septimus, which include T. S. Eliot and argues that, despite the narrator's derision, Septimus has all the makings of a successful modernist war poet. *Septimus Smith: Modernist and War Poet: a Closer Reading* (London: The Bloomsbury Heritage Series, 2015).

Faulkner's *As I Lay Dying*. Like Septimus, Darl has been to the war in France. Also like Septimus, he has become a visionary who speaks in enigmatic riddles, although his powers surpass even those of Septimus, for within the logic of the novel, Darl's telepathy seems more than a mere delusion. While Septimus gains his terrible freedom in his very public suicide, the climax of the novel and the event that finally brings him and Clarissa Dalloway together, Darl ends up in a madhouse, isolated from society, his visions and his warnings unheeded. This separation, though, is thought to be for the best. Although his older brother Cash questions the morality of Darl's isolation, he concludes that "it is better for him. This world is not his world; this life his life."[2]

Septimus and Darl have a lot in common, despite their obvious superficial differences. Septimus is an autodidact and would-be poet who had taken a job as a clerk, a Londoner who has become cosmopolitan as a result of the war, returning with an Italian bride and a head full of what he considers to be very important ideas about the meaning of love. Although he is occasionally treated with some scorn by his narrator, there is nothing to indicate that Septimus is exceptional in his intellectual and social strivings before the war. His aspirations are similar to those of Hardy's Jude Fawley and Forster's Leonard Bast. Darl Bundren, however, an impoverished rural inhabitant of Faulkner's Yoknapatawpha County, has no such pretensions. There is no way in which Darl could or would think of speaking for his society or his nation. Though he is a destructive force in the novel in many ways, his violence works towards respecting death by disposing of his mother's rotting corpse. Unlike Septimus, he narrates himself.

One of the biggest differences in these transatlantic representations of shell shock is the degree to which the condition of the subject is associated with or linked to the war. Within Woolf's indirect freestyle, Septimus is

---

[2] William Faulkner, *As I Lay Dying* (New York: Vintage books, 1990), 261.

constantly linked with the war. The war defines the character. Hardly any part of the novel that focuses on him does not consider him in the light of his war experience, and his madness is directly attributed to that experience by the imposing Dr. Bradshaw, who refers to his condition directly as shell shock.[3] Throughout, Septimus is haunted by memories of the war. It has prevented him from feeling, he thinks, and he is tormented by the memory of an officer named Evans, with whom he may have been romantically involved, and with whose violent destruction Septimus's troubles seem to begin.

For Darl Bundren, on the other hand, the war is only mentioned once, as a kind of afterthought. Though his having been "at the war" is crucial to understanding Darl, Faulkner seems to suggest that it is not an experience that would be recognized by those around him as contributing to the character's idiosyncrasies. The monumental experience of his service in the war, in whatever capacity (what he was doing "at the war" is never made clear), must have meant a great deal to him and his family, yet the entire experience is shut away and elided. Darl is simply problematic to his family; his morality and his insistences interfering with their worldly pursuits.[4] Only when Darl is being put on the train to be taken to the asylum in Jackson do we learn about this crucial missing part of his experience, and we learn about it only through the detail of a lewd souvenir: "Darl had a little spy-glass he got in France at the war. In it it had a woman and a pig with two backs and no face."[5]

The ubiquity of the war in reference to Septimus, and its near total absence in reference to Darl, demonstrate a lot about the ways in which writers in the U.K. and the U.S. understood shell shock in the years immediately

---

3   Virginia Woolf, *Mrs. Dalloway* (Orlando: Harcourt Books, 2005), 179.

4   For each of the other Bundrens, the journey to bury Addie's corpse is an occasion to get something else, whereas only Darl seems to be primarily devoted to respecting the corpse by getting it out of the sight of human society, through fire, flood, or burial.

5   Faulkner, 254

following the war. In the U.K., it had been a very open subject for public debate. The problem arose before any apparatuses of state power could contain it. It spilled over and blurred the neatly drawn divisions between military and civilian life. It had come seemingly from out of nowhere, and, like Septimus, it haunted the public spaces of British discourse during the interwar yeas. A subject such as Septimus was a lamentable, but not unsurprising spectacle. In the U.S., however, the American military and medical authorities had been forewarned of this strange new malady and had done all they could to prevent its occurrence. Some denial, therefore, would surface when veterans demonstrated symptoms of the disease, and an almost total lack of knowledge about shell shock would not be surprising in the impoverished Mississippi of Faulkner's fiction.

As brief as the mention of Darl's war experience is, however, it does share with Septimus's experiences an important trait that I will explore further in this introduction. Beyond its obscenity, the frank depiction of bestiality in Darl's spy-glass suggests something about the limits between the human and the animal that is central to the medical and psychological understandings of shell shock that emerged during and after the war years. Septimus, too, has visions that blur this constitutive boundary as he tries to gather his thoughts on human love: "No crime; love; he repeated, fumbling for his card and pencil, when a Skye terrier snuffed his trousers and he started in an agony of fear. It was turning into a man! He could not watch it happen! It was horrible, terrible to see a dog become a man! At once the dog trotted away."[6]

However far apart in terms of social status and nationality, these two characters' experience of shell shock both demonstrate that even those who did not serve directly in the war, like Woolf and Faulkner, could see that the global phenomenon of shell shock put at stake the very meaning of humanity.

---

6   Woolf, 66.

In their literary way, Woolf and Faulkner grasp towards an idea that the medical and psychological authorities of their time debated: did this failure of nerve constitute a failure of masculinity? Or of humanity? Was it a mental or a physical problem? Was it even a real problem at all, or an elaborate fraud? What did this enigmatic malady signify for society? For humanity?

Long before Septimus and Darl were conceived in their authors' minds, the literature of shell shock had its beginning with Wilfred Owen and Siegfried Sassoon, who wrote their war poetry both in the trenches and while being treated for mental breakdown in the Craiglockhart War Hospital. Since those poems were published, shell shock has been central to British literature about the experience of the Great War. It plays a major factor in the most enduring memoirs and war books of those who served in the war, and in the years following, it profoundly influenced interwar modernism, becoming a metonym for the larger social upheavals and fragmentation the war produced. Along with scenes from the trenches, the cratered and corpse-strewn images of No Man's Land, the burnt forests and bombed cathedrals of Northern France, the shell-shocked soldier's blank gaze is an iconic symbol of the war, and is crucial to our contemporary constructions of a war that, as of recently, no longer lives in modern memory.

Many more accounts of shell shock were published in Great Britain than survive in popular culture. The archives of the Imperial War Museum in London are full of unpublished diaries and correspondences that recount patients' suffering, and many monographs were published on the subject by sufferers. There is extensive medical and scientific literature on shell shock from the period, most famously the accounts of W. H. R. Rivers, who treated Sassoon with psychoanalytic techniques, and Lewis Yealland, whose methods, including electric shocks and the application of lit cigarettes to mute soldiers' tongues, more closely resemble torture than therapy. Both doctors' techniques are described by Elaine Showalter in her influential reading of shell shock in *The Female Malady* (1985), and are fictionalized in Pat Barker's Booker prize winning *Regeneration* Trilogy (1990-95).[7]

In British literary studies, the literature of World War I has long been recognized as its own field of study. Paul Fussell's enormously popular study *The Great War and Modern Memory* (1975) which includes a chapter entitled "Oh, What a Literary War!" popularized the study of Great War literature in 1975, and remains a staple and obvious beginning point for anybody new to the field. It focuses largely on representations of shell shock in the poetry and memoirs of British soldiers. In American literary studies, on the other hand, there is not nearly as extensively recognized a field of World War I literature, let alone of shell shock. Although there are canonical novels dealing with World War I, the war itself is often either peripheral in those novels, or to that author's *oeuvre*, as with Hemingway, Faulkner, Cather, and Cummings. Scott D. Emmert and Steven Trout's anthology of American short fiction about the war, published in 2014, is the first such collection.[8] Because American soldiers and nurses worked alongside the British military in a common language, comparative works such as this volume of essays can help us understand the qualitative differences between the canonized body of British shell shock literature, and an emerging field of inquiry into American literary engagements with shell shock.

Trevor Dodman's *Shell Shock, Memory, and the Novel in the Wake of World War I* (2015) is primarily meant as a corrective to the elision of the novel in the study of shell shock in Great War literature, but it is also a transatlantic study, as it examines prose not only from the U.K. and the U.S., but also from the Indian army. Dodman asserts that, "[d]espite its cultural visibility, we continue to misunderstand and misrepresent shell

---

7   *The Female Malady: Women, Madness and English Culture, 1830-1980* (New York: Virago 1987).

8   Scott D. Emmert and Steven Trout, editors. *World War I in American Fiction: An Anthology* (Kent, OH: Kent State University Press, 2014).

shock in significant ways."⁹ Dodman primarily redresses our failure to look beyond poetry and memoir to the shell shock represented in novels, but his work also explicitly states that shell shock was a phenomenon that extends well beyond the experience of soldiers in the trenches of Northern France.

This collection is very much in the spirit of Dodman's work, as it examines representations of shell shock in a variety of novels, by both authors who lived through the war and those who knew it only as history. Half of the essays in this collection, those by Arsev Ayşen Arslanoğlu Yıldıran, Ria Banerjee, Elisa Bolchi, Iro Filippaki, and Jill Goad, examine shell shock in British and American novels, including novels that address the African-American experience of shell shock, which Dodman elucidates. These novelists include Richard Aldington, Pat Barker, Mary Borden, Mary Butts, Ralph Ellison, Toni Morrison, Evadne Price, Dalton Trumbo, and Virginia Woolf. Significantly, the number of female novelists under consideration in the essays here collected is greater than that of male authors, demonstrating that the supposed purview of shell shock has shifted in multiple ways. While it has formally been the domain primarily of white male British officers, we have begun to consider its effects on a much broader and much more diverse population.

The collection contains analysis, too, of poetry and memoir, the more traditionally recognized forms of shell shock representation. Argha Banerjee examines the competing impulses in the canonical shell shock poems of Owen and Sassoon, and the lesser known American poets, Joyce Kilmer and Alan Seeger, while Qiang Huang's essay seeks out war trauma in the poems of the always transatlantic T. S. Eliot. Samraghni Bonnerjee examines memoir, but shifts the focus, and in some way the "ownership" of war trauma from male combatants to female volunteer nurses. Another form represented in

---

9   Trevor Dodman, *Shell Shock, Memory, and the Novel in the Wake of World War I* (Cambridge: Cambridge University Press, 2015), 5.

this collection is the periodical. Both Jason Parks and Louise Kane examine the representation of shell shock (or its striking absence) in periodicals that appeared on either side of the Atlantic both during and after the war.

In this introduction to the collection, I will offer a brief history of the slippery term shell shock, which, as Dodman and others have pointed out, is useful to us now as a historical term. I will then briefly examine some archival first-hand accounts from sufferers of both sexes on both sides of the Atlantic before moving onto a comparative analysis first of how shell shock was received in the United Kingdom, and then how shell shock was anticipated and prepared for in the United States.

Physical or Mental War Trauma? Shell Shock and its Antecedents

The term shell shock has been debated ever since it was first coined in the Great War. It is no longer used to describe psychological war trauma, having been replaced by the term "Post Traumatic Stress Disorder," which was introduced in the DSM in 1980 and has, since then, achieved mainstream recognition as a condition that often derives from, but is not exclusive to, combat.[10] Shell shock, on the other hand, implies that the sufferer has an injury that results from a kind of mental wound sustained in or because of the conditions of combat, although clearly soldiers suffered from mental trauma that was not related to loud noises or the proximity of exploding shells.

Even during the war, many doctors and observers recognized "shell shock" as a misnomer, a catch-all phrase for a variety of mental conditions. In retrospect, it is clear that it is also a misnomer overladen with assumptions and ideological desires about bravery, masculinity, and honor. However, the

---

10   Edgar Jones and Simon Wessely. *Shell Shock to PTSD: Military Psychiatry from 1900 to the Gulf War* (Hove: Psychology Press, 2005), xvi.

term shell shock has come to have a very specific value, because and despite the misperceptions about war-related mental trauma that it carries. It refers not only to mental trauma incurred by both men and women who served in the Great War, but also as serves as a shorthand for the entire global phenomenon of World War I mental trauma; as such, the frustratingly vague term coined more than a century ago has transformed into a helpful way to address the specificities of a historical mass phenomenon. As Dodman writes, "we must consider PTSD today and shell shock in the wartime and postwar period as discursively and culturally produced entities derived from and shaped by the historically specific contexts in which they arise."[11]

While the term is unique to the World Wars, surviving with increasing skepticism into the later twentieth century, it is one of many steps on the way to our current (and no doubt tentative) understanding of war trauma. The weaponry and techniques of World War I were novel and unprecedented, but war trauma is obviously as old as humanity itself. Anthony Babington notes that Herodotus, in a description of the Battle of Marathon in 490 BC, records the blinding of a soldier who was not physically wounded, which is the kind of psychosomatic disability that became so common during the Great War.[12] The frustration that gave rise to the term came from doctors seeing shattered soldiers who could not walk properly, or speak, unable to go on, but with no discernible physical injuries.

Babington goes on to describe the forms of war neurosis and their various appellations in modern times, beginning with Nostalgia, a term coined by the Swiss physician Johannes Hofer in 1678.[13] This term, which described a melancholy and homesickness among soldiers so strong that it could lead

---

11 Dodman, 7.

12 Anthony Babington, *Shell-Shock: A History of the Changing Attitudes to War Neurosis* (London: Leo Cooper, 1997), 7.

13 Ibid.

to death, was remarkably persistent, and was still in circulation by the time of the American Civil War. Although the Civil War is not remembered in conjunction with mental disorder to the extent that the Great War has been, Babington calls attention to a significant degree of war neurosis during that conflict. Afflicted soldiers, if not diagnosed with "nostalgia," may have been diagnosed with "soldier's heart," or "irritable heart," a condition through which seemingly healthy soldiers would develop weakness and heart palpitations with even slight exertion. This condition, which resulted in casualties, was considered entirely physical, and was ascribed to "overstrain and poor feeding."[14]

Shell shock's most immediate precedent in regards to its confusion of physical and mental trauma sustained during combat was the phenomenon of "windage," which also arose during the American Civil War. The concept underlying windage, like that behind shell shock, was that the explosion of a shell in close proximity could cause physical damage to the nervous system with no outward physical indications of injury or trauma.[15]

While the windage hypothesis has been discredited, it is important to note how appealing such an idea would be to a genuinely impaired soldier who needed to find some cause for his impairment that did not taint him with the cowardice or shirking related to "neurasthenia," the nineteenth century term that described weakness of nerves. As I will demonstrate, the primary British debate around shell shock, once it was determined to be a legitimate problem (both for the individual and for the state that depended on able fighting men), focused on whether the condition was mental or physical. Throughout and after the war, many afflicted soldiers insisted on the physicality of their disorder, as a mental disorder would clearly impugn their honor and masculinity.

---

14   Ibid., 16.

15   Ibid., 17.

Shell shock and the anxiety surrounding it are always wrapped up in notions of masculinity. But if shell shock is read as either a fundamental failing of masculine traits, or their painful erasure, what can or does shell shock mean for women, who also experienced incredible strain, hardship, and loss during the war? As shell shock has become a catch all term for the war's trauma, it is necessary to reconsider the manifestations of trauma in the women who suffered in direct proximity and as constant witnesses to the war's violence. While trauma manifests itself in women in a number of ways that are similar to the trauma of men, their experiences reveal the precariousness of basing an understanding of trauma, as doctors so often did at the time, on notions of immutably stable gender traits. As so many narratives show, the dependence on gender norms to explain or diagnose trauma could be as damaging as the insistence on its entirely physical nature.[16]

This insistence on shell shock's physicality is compellingly distilled in a self-help book by British veteran Joseph Snowball Milne, *Shell-shock, Neurasthenia, and a New Life* (1918), which is fraught with anxiety about what his condition may suggest about his masculinity and his status as a political subject.[17] In his insistence on the physicality of his condition, Milne reveals less about the physical and psychological trauma caused by combat than about the emotional trauma caused by its treatment. His righteous insistence that he was misdiagnosed with neurasthenia, and actually suffered from shell shock (which he considers entirely physical), is predicated on his refusal to consider his problem as psychological. He uses the term shell shock to *validate* his condition, over which he insists he has no control,

---

16   One instance of a woman's war trauma manifesting in a surprisingly gendered way is Vera Brittain's delusion, recorded in *Testament of Youth*, that she is growing a beard: "I looked one evening into my bedroom glass and thought, with a sense of incommunicable horror, that I detected in my face the signs of some sinister and peculiar change. A dark shadow seemed to lie across my chin; was I beginning to grow a beard, like a witch?" In this case, the identity of a witch seems to save Brittain from identifying as male. Vera Brittain, *Testament of Youth*, (New York: The MacMillan Company, 1933), 484.

17   Joseph Snowball Milne, *Neurasthenia, Shell-shock, and a New Life* (Newcastle-on-Tyne, 1918).

whereas the sufferer of neurasthenia, he believes, has worn out what was not a strong mental constitution to begin with.[18] Milne writes:

> I have been led to read of Neurasthenia, for that is the diagnosis or verdict concerning my case, by specialists who have examined me. While that is the verdict, yet, on consideration of what I now struggle to read and write, I believe that where my condition may be Neurasthenia, of Shell-shock nature, it might well have been called something more like itself,—and especially after reading Dr. Hartenberg's conclusions on symptoms of Neurasthenia without the Special Manias. Neurasthenical patients are credited with certain manias of the imagination etc., but when one of the sufferers "struggles to get better" for at least eighteen months under this condition of Shell-shock trouble, it must indicate that he has no such mania. He has a severe injury which needs at least to be repaired, or rather, as I have already stated, something needs to be "re-created."[19]

Milne's assertion of the total physicality of shell shock portends the general consensus in the later Parliament requisitioned *Report of the War Office Committee of Enquiry into "Shell-Shock"* (1922) that a sufferer of emotional, rather than commotional, war neurosis must have been previously mentally or emotionally weak.[20] For Milne, shell shock is as physical as a bullet

---

18 The source of Milne's and Northfield's neurasthenia was novel, but their rhetoric reflects the widespread diagnoses of neurasthenia in the decades before the war, and concerns that neurasthenia reflected a degeneration of masculinity and virility that would affect England's ability to sustain itself as both an Empire and a nation.

19 Ibid., 44.

20 *Report of the War Office Committee of Enquiry into Shell-Shock* (London: H.M. Stationery Office, 1922), 14. The report contains expert testimony of 59 witnesses, many of whom affirm this belief. Although the inquiry reads the existence of shell shock as clear grounds for suspicion of the sufferers' honesty, at worst, or general constitution and intellectual ability, at best, the designation of shell shock was not merely applied to those who complained of their condition. As soon as it had been epistemologically

wound, and must be overcome, like any other invalided soldier's injury, through physical therapy. To this way of thinking, the distinction between medical cases and mental cases can be made based on the strength of the patient's willpower.

Although the therapies imposed on Milne did not work, he develops his own strategies, ingeniously re-inscribing himself into the social space of power he has been forced to abdicate as a patient. It is apparent in his use of the word "verdict" that he feels an unjust sentence has been passed against him, rather than a medical diagnosis. He masters his guilt and demonstrates to his doctors that, through an Olympian act of will, *he* can succeed where *they* have failed. He rejects the disciplinary devices, masquerading as therapies, which have been used against him: electricity and cold baths, although physical, would locate his cure outside himself and on someone else's authority. Rather, he reaches his own physical remedy by stooping forward and "pressing the blood to [his] head," so he can feel the brain "lifting" in his head. This physical cure demonstrates the extent to which he refuses a psychological one: "Now I can imagine that my brain must have been low down in my head [. . .] My brain must have been torn down from behind almost to the forehead."[21] By finding or fabricating this physical source for his disorder, Milne asserts the honorable nature of his injury and rescues his self-esteem and (what is more or less the same thing) his masculinity.

As these scientifically dubious solutions demonstrate, recovering from shell shock through a physical intervention into the body was a way to displace its damaging effect from the socialized human onto the corporeal

---

constituted, it could also be used *by* the state, in conjunction with psychiatry, for the benefit of military operations. Consider, for example, the case of a young Lieutenant who was sent to Craiglockhart War Hospital against his will. His letters to a friend reveal that the ruling came as a surprise, as he felt healthy, and would mean the loss of his pension. The unfortunate case of this lieutenant demonstrates that shell shock, almost as soon as it was defined, could also be used against soldiers.

21 Milne, *New Life*, 16-17.

animal. Historically speaking, mental trauma suffered through warfare has lost some of its social stigma in the ceaselessly violent years since World War I (although sufferers have constantly had to fight for government aid and recognition). When this phenomenon was new and recognizable for the first time on a large scale, however, it posed a fundamental question to British civil society and the state about what constituted the cultural, political, and social identity of its subjects.

A similar example from an American in a far different context shows how pervasive the fear of a stigmatizing diagnosis of "neurasthenia" had become. Alta Mae Andrews Sharp served throughout the war as a nurse, and she later formed her diary and her letters into an unpublished memoir. Her memoir is fascinating for its details about her experience and her generally unflagging optimism throughout the war. The only moment in her experience when she is really demoralized is at the end of her service, when she is going to be discharged. Although she insists that she is suffering from trouble with her ear, the military doctor who diagnoses her does not find a problem, and gives her instead a diagnosis that enrages her:

> All during sixteen months of service, nothing has been encountered which has precipitated a greater state of despondency and resentment than having this damning stigma attached to my record! Neurasthenia! It has but one interpretation to the "Medics"—gold-bricking! It has been a cruel thorn whose torment is gradually sweeping away any existing glamour which may have remained in my career as an army nurse![22]

Sharp's torment is short-lived, however, because she is soon exonerated from her shameful diagnosis by a female medical officer, who understands

---

22 Alta May Andrews Sharp. Unpublished memoirs, 390. Courtesy of the National World War I Museum, Kansas City, Missouri.

immediately the dishonor the diagnosis means, not only for Sharp, but for anybody who has served. Sharp writes that the doctor tells her "My dear girl—no one who has been in service over here is going through my hands as a "neurasthenic!" There is just cause for all this nervousness [. . .] That diagnosis means absolutely nothing to me! It comes off today! You are an "ear case" and that is how you are going home!"[23]

As a nurse, Sharp was not often exposed to the immediate proximity of violent explosions that might have earned her a diagnosis of shell shock rather than neurasthenia, or "neurasthenia of shell shock nature," as Milne puts it. However, her horror at a mental rather than physical diagnosis, and the doctor's affirmation of the shame attaching to mental diagnoses, demonstrate how thoroughly invested both men and women at every level of service were in the honorably *physical* nature of any impairment. Indeed, the medical officer, and Sharp's own accounting of the event, betray her actual condition. The officer's statement that "there is just cause for all this nervousness" demonstrates her understanding that Sharp's condition is largely mental, but is nevertheless as valid as a physical injury, although it cannot be spoken of as such. The ear diagnosis is a cover to preserve dignity and appearances, but one that Sharp has earned and deserves through her real suffering. Sharp's intense relief at this reprieve, which validates her service, is entirely understandable under such circumstances.

Shell Shock in Great Britain: Sickness, Psychology, and the State

"I remember when I was very ill, I used to say to myself, 'While there's life, there's hope; and when there's no hope, there's rope.' But that was only

---

23   Ibid., 391-2.

jocularly. I was only trying to recapture my lost sense of humour."²⁴ So writes recovered shell shock sufferer Wilfrid Northfield in the preface to his giddily confident self-help book *Conquest of Nerves* (1933), which was, like Milne's book, directed at England's burgeoning population of "neurasthenics" in the inter-war period. This grim jocularity alone may not console his suffering readers, however, and Northfield is quick to assure them that he has suffered like them "and triumphed, and having triumphed is out to help [them] to do likewise."²⁵ These prefatory assertions emphasize three generic aspects of British interwar fictional and non-fictional shell shock narratives:

First: there is a constant oscillation between attraction to death, on one hand, the inherent privacy of which offers relief from the explicitly social field of suffering, and the need to face up to one's social duty on the other hand. Like Northfield and others who documented their recovery processes, literary representations of shell-shocked sufferers, such as Rebecca West's Chris Baldry, Virginia Woolf's Septimus Smith, Ford Madox Ford's Christopher Tietjens, Richard Aldington's George Winterbourne, and David Jones' and Vera Brittain's recollections of their shell-shocked selves, among others, share this characteristic.²⁶ Sufferers alternate between exhausted attraction to death as a private release from suffering and a social sense of duty to carry on.

Second: the sufferers' recoveries depend on their recognition and distancing of themselves from their symptoms and, in the case of self-help books such as Northfield's and Milne's, the re-creation of their precise conditions in the suffering reader, over whom the author thereby gains a

---

24 *Conquest of Nerves: The Inspiring Record of a Personal Triumph Over Neurasthenia* (London: The Fenland Press, 1933), 15.

25 Ibid., 16.

26 West's *The Return of the Soldier* (1918), Woolf's *Mrs. Dalloway* (1925), Ford's *Parade's End* Tetralogy (1924-28), Aldington's *The Death of a Hero* (1929), Jones's *In Parenthesis* (1937), and Brittain's *Testament of Youth* (1933).

feeling of control. Northfield writes his own erstwhile symptoms onto his imagined readers with insouciance to demonstrate how fully he is cured, and to reiterate to the reader that he or she, too, can be cured by simply "getting the right idea."[27] What determines recovery is the ability to re-constitute oneself as a social subject and object of power.

Third: the sufferer only recovers through submission to a larger, social, and ultimately paternalistic external force. In the end, he recovers or not depending on his submission to foundational social rules and his ability to overlook the ideological aporias that war trauma has revealed. In *The Return of the Soldier* (1918), Chris Baldry can be returned to warfare when he submits to psychoanalytic treatment, for example, whereas Septimus Smith takes his own life in order to avoid it.

British shell shock literature shows how war trauma irrevocably transformed the British state's relationship to its subjects through psychological state interventions. Although "shell shock" as a medical category had its roots in prewar anxieties about neurasthenia, it also exposed the tenuousness and exhaustion of national paradigms of character and control; the return of traumatized soldiers impacted social and political discourses of psychology, science, race, gender, sexuality, empire, and class, unsettling essentialist and nationalist ideologies that were central to war mobilization and propaganda. Because it affected previously hardy and resourceful Englishmen, pervasive shell shock implied two things: English manhood was not as unbreakable in its taciturn reserve and self-control as myths of national character had promoted, and hysterical breakdown was not the exclusive province of women and the emotionally or culturally delicate. Rather, the prevalence of mental breakdown suggested to many doctors that the pre-social and animalistic desires of the individual, even at the height of Edwardian socialization, lingered beneath the cultivated social surfaces. Though this emotional

---

27 Northfield, 60.

breakdown was widespread in the armies of all heavily involved nations, it posed a particular crisis to English state power and national identity. England had long defined itself in opposition to the continent in general, opposing its Protestant reserve and famous "stiff upper lip" to dissolute and emotional continental (and Irish) Catholicism.[28]

Perhaps because the English understood themselves to be particularly stoic, many British wartime medical and military authorities explicitly described shell shock as the subject's regression to animal instinct, the triumph of the latent, pre-contractual animal over the socialized human. Shell shock and its treatment present a juridical problem of sovereignty that concerns the two modes of power that characterize much of Michel Foucault's work, specifically on biopower: power directed at the subject through state institutions, such as the madhouse or the prison, and the more subtle structures of ideological and epistemological power that address themselves to the self, as distinct from the subject of the state.[29] As England's reaction to shell shock demonstrates, these are not necessarily two unidirectional modes of power, but rather two separate manifestations of power. They are different manifestations of the same necessity to subordinate the individual to the social, a necessity revealed through the common characteristic of paternalism and paternal authority in state power apparatuses (such as the military itself) as well as in social or civic power structures directed towards the individual self and its cultivation, such as discourses of family and religion presented through self-help books and private counseling.

During and immediately after the war, Tracy Loughran has shown, the biopolitical implications of shell shock were evident in two distinct ways.[30] Shell shock clearly represented a breaking of the shell-shocked soldier's

---

28 Linda Colley, *Britons: Forging the Nation, 1707-1837* (New Haven: Yale University Press, 1992).

29 Michel Foucault, *History of Sexuality, Volume I,* trans. Robert Hurley, (New York: Vintage Books, 1990).

30 Tracy Loughran, "Evolution, Regression, and Shell-shock: Emotion and Instinct in Theories of the War Neuroses, C. 1914-1918." (Manchester Papers in Economic and Social History 58, September 2007).

military and official pact with his sovereign state, as well as his unofficial social pact in the contractarian sense: he had either regressed willfully to an animalistic state of nature through cowardice, or he had lost his ability to adhere to his social contract, as he willed.[31] The effects of this epidemic constituted, as Loughran points out, a "national emergency" by 1917, when the outcome of the war was unpredictable, and the immediate necessity of containing and preventing the problem was obvious.[32] Its solution, therefore, was an immediate legal and political concern. No doubt many genuinely impaired soldiers were punished, but the punitive solution went against the state's ostensible role as the preserver of the species and its way of life.[33] Because shell-shocked soldiers were often violently punished while injured, shell shock quickly became a useful symbol of the barbarity of war to pacifists and the anti-war movement, while it was a symbol of cowardice and dishonesty to jingoists.[34] The problem shell shock posed was about the limits of state power, and where state power had to resign and let other cultural forces—in this case psychology—take over.

This bafflement of state power and its limits was a matter of public knowledge and debate, but the juridical conundrum it presented was not formally investigated by parliament until April 1920, when the parliamentary investigation into shell shock was first proposed.[35] At this

---

31 Conscientious objectors, equally subject to state intervention, although not to capital punishment, also pose a problem to state power, but not so fundamentally. Though they occupy a similarly ambiguous space between criminality and legality, they pose no threat to the biopolitical exercise of sovereignty. They willfully defy, and can simply be punished, the only question being the type of punishment fitting this transgression.

32 Loughran, 17.

33 Foucault, *History of Sexuality I*, 137.

34 The shell-shocked poets Sassoon and Owen spent many years of the war writing popular and effective anti-war propaganda poems chronicling the soldier's suffering, frequently from Craiglockhart War Hospital. In Ford Madox Ford's *Parade's End*, however, the rich Sylvia Tietjens and her set "cynically approved" of what they see as the "wangle" of shell shock. Ford Madox Ford, *Some Do Not . . .* (Manchester: Carcanet, 2010), 207.

35 In proposing the investigation into shell-shock, Lord Southborough stated "If it is the fact that a true identification of the disorder was wanting in the early months of the war, then I fear that, through

point the threat of war was contained and the emergency was considered over, despite the abundance of shell-shocked veterans. The commission gathered and interpreted expert medical accounts of shell shock from both army and private doctors for the purpose of finding "some scientific method of guarding against its occurrence" in the future.[36] The commission suggested two sources for the medical and legal difficulties of categorizing shell shock: first, the state's dual goal to send every able-bodied man, but to protect the incapacitated; second, the obvious opportunity shell shock presented for shirking duty and exploiting the state—for "such was the appeal of the term 'shell-shock' [. . .] that it became a most desirable complaint from which to suffer."[37] The term's potential to mask or conceal was clearly a threat to state sovereignty, and although it genuinely was misleading for many of the reasons the commission lists, the commission's interest in debunking it at the level of language indicates an interest in debunking it as any coherent circumstance, or set of circumstances, that permitted the release from duty to the state. The inquiry's origin as an army report, requested by parliament, may have guided it to the findings most beneficial to state power.

As the commission's report and the narratives of sufferers and specialists reveal, shell shock changed mass culture's relation to psychiatry, even as it coincided with changes in official psychiatric discourse. The received story is of a gradual change from physiological explanations of neuroses to psychological explanations, as the problem's scale and the lack of progress with physiological cures impelled an acceptance of the talking cures and psychoanalysis that had been popular only among a small, continentally-

---

inadvertence and want of knowledge, dreadful things may have happened to unfortunate men who had in fact become irresponsible for their actions" (*Parliamentary Debates, House of Lords* [Wed. April 28 1920, vol. 39. Number 29], 1096).

36   *War Office Enquiry*, 3.

37   Ibid., 6.

inflected *avant-garde* before the war.[38] Ben Shephard, accepting this old narrative, has defined physiologists as shell shock's realists, in contrast to psychologists, its dramatists. Shephard seeks to purify discourses of shell shock from "modern baggage derived from the women's movement" and cordon it off from culture, gender, or sexual studies.[39] Generally, Shephard's account is a reactionary attempt to restore representations of the lower class British Tommy as prone to malingering. Conversely, Loughran convincingly demonstrates that this separation of physiological and psychological wartime explanations of shell shock is misguided and historically inaccurate. Shephard argues against Elaine Showalter, who offers a hagiographic reading of W. H. R. Rivers, the ostensibly Freudian doctor of Craiglockhart War Hospital. Showalter misrepresents him as thoroughly psychoanalytic, however, whereas Loughran demonstrates that he remained at least partially committed to physiological explanations even after the war.[40]

Loughran is correct that the extent of Rivers's commitment to psychoanalysis is not as great as Showalter's historiography or Pat Barker's fictional account make it appear. Archival records, however, demonstrate that analytic questions that now seem commonplace in diagnosing sufferers of mental breakdown struck soldiers during the war as unusual. One soldier who stayed at Craiglockhart War Hospital wrote to a close friend about his first encounter with his doctor, who may well have been Rivers:

> he is a clever man, a bit of a philosopher, an eminent nerve specialist and somewhat of a crank. He extracts from you your life history with such questions as:—is there any nervous trouble in your family? Have you been ill as a boy? Where were you at school? Do you smoke much?

---

38 Loughran, "Evolution, Regression, and Shell-shock," 2.
39 Ben Shephard, *A War of Nerves* (Harvard UP: Cambridge, 2001), xx-xxii.
40 Loughran, "Evolution, Regression, and Shell-shock," 18

Etc. etc. His great idea, as I had been previously warned, is to get you to take up a hobby. He asked me what hobbies I had. I said that I played tennis and bridge. He said the 1st was all right but that the latter tended to keep you too much in the house.[41]

Although the doctor is motivated by psychoanalytic inquiry, he seems just as concerned with attending to his patient's trauma through physical exercise of the sort recommended by Milne and especially Northfield, who puts more curative faith in golf than in any of his other recommendations for his suffering readers. The treatment proposed by this eminent nerve specialist is neither wholly psychological nor wholly physical, but a combination of both.

Loughran further argues that the physiological understanding allowed English psychiatry to subsume shell shock into a larger Darwinian narrative, reducing it to the defeat of human will by instinct, and so marking its victims as degenerates who had regressed to an animal state. The fault of breakdown therefore lay with the sufferer, not the state, and this convenient way of coping with the problem lasted throughout the war. The psychologization of shell shock, which would imply more than acceptance of Freudian thought by the English medical establishment, but, in fact, its radical progression, did not come until later.[42] Loughran's thesis that "[t]here was no straightforward transition to a psychological understanding of the war neuroses" is useful and correct. For the psychiatrists who defined it, shell shock may have been, as Loughran says, "a horrifying revelation of the survival of animal origins within civilization."[43]

---

41   Private letter of James Butlin (Imperial War Museum). These letters, written on Craiglockhart stationary, are quite literate and amusing; Butlin and his dear friend Basil were primarily preoccupied with bridge, flappers, and dissipation. A coded discussion of venereal disease runs throughout their correspondence.

42   Showalter is right that Rivers did radically champion Freud and the use of his work in dealing with neurosis, but he did not apply Freudian psychoanalysis as exclusively as she claims (*The Female Malady*, 189). Freud himself was still committed to mapping psychoanalytic theory onto the physical brain.

43   Loughran, "Evolution, Regression, and Shell-shock," 2.

Though the scale of psychiatric intervention into state power was new, the phenomenon was not. Foucault has demonstrated that, beginning in the eighteenth century, in France and elsewhere, the state had increasingly relied on medical experts to provide the grounds on which to decide punishment for crime, and pretending to be disabled to get out of military duty would surely be a crime.[44] Psychologists and experts were called into courts more frequently, not so much to explain a suspect's actions as to explain her or his psychological identity. But the way in which expert testimony on the mental conditions of defendants was (and is) used is generally individual. Shell shock required expert medical testimony to guide the state in dealing with a mass problem occurring in the heart of state operations. Psychiatrists were called on to develop universalizing frames or explanations for a phenomenon that presented itself in uniquely contingent ways. Psychiatric power needed to recognize and define the *type* of life of the individual (the *bios*, or politically qualified life, rather than the *zoe*, or mere state of being alive, according to Aristotle's classification), so that the state could make the decision of life or death, or the decision between inclusion or exclusion within the state's protection, which marks it as sovereign. The parliamentary investigation into shell shock is the medico-legal case *par excellence*, in which the state must bring in a massive medical and psychological apparatus to justify the fundamental aspect of its claims to sovereignty: its right to decide on what is or is not politically qualified life.[45]

---

44   Michel Foucault, *Abnormal: Lectures at the College de France, 1974-1975 Abnormal: Lectures at the College de France, 1974-1975*, trans. Graham Burchell. (New York: Picador, 1999), 18.

45   Indeed, the Aristotelian distinction between *bios* and *zoe*, the basis of modern biopolitical discourse, relates directly to the physiological/psychological distinction that creates this crisis of sovereignty. Roberto Esposito explains the problem succinctly in dealing with modern cases of biological or mental indeterminacy confounding state power: "What appears undecidable in terms of the law is the relation between biological reality and the juridical person, that is, between life and a form of life" (*Bios: Biopolitics and Philosophy*, trans. Timothy Campbell [Minneapolis: University of Minnesota Press, 2008], 3).

In *Madness and Civilization* (1961) and his later Collège de France lectures, Foucault traced these connections between madness and the foundations of juridical state power. He argues that Western thought conceives of the criminal as the natural, pre-Hobbesian "man of the forest," one who puts individual interests ahead of the social pact.[46] The shell shock victim, unlike the wounded soldier, is by definition outside the social contract. The constantly deferred or receding *objective* demarcation between reason and unreason parallels the exceptional space between the sovereign and bare life that Giorgio Agamben reads as constitutive of power.[47] Thus, the state, not the subject, determines the quality of any given human life. In general, damaged subjectivity matters little, if at all. Individual cases of crime may compel expert testimony, but an indeterminable psycho-criminal epidemic during the largest conflict in England's history, and at a point at which state security was threatened more than it had been in at least a century, constituted a genuine threat to sovereignty.

The historical, medical, legal, and military necessity of categorizing, controlling, and containing shell shock became more and more clear as the war progressed, and became a topic of much speculation and introspection in the reflective interwar years, as well as a primary concern of British writers who addressed the personal and cultural aftereffects of the war. British literature of shell shock tends to wonder what it is, or if it is a thing at all. There is much at stake, and the dismissal of the whole concept as a hoax could return British views of masculinity to the Edwardian *status quo*. The problem, however, is too pervasive for such a superficially tidy ending.

---

46 Foucault, *Abnormal*, 94.

47 Giorgio Agamben, *Homo Sacer: Sovereign Power and Bare Life*, trans. Daniel Heller-Roazen, (Stanford: Stanford University Press, 1998).

Anticipating Shell Shock in America: "A Standard of Absolute Normality"

One reason that shell shock has not been a major focus of American modernist studies is that it seems to appear so much less frequently in the American war experience. As W. H. R. Rivers, noted, mental breakdown in the conditions of the war was nearly inevitable, given enough time, and the American active duty in the war lasted only about an eighth of the time of the British fighting. Furthermore, if less obviously, by the time the American soldiers arrived, the war had become much more active. While most of the British conscripts of August 1914 were encouraged to envision the war as a grand adventure, full of action, the experience was often passive, characterized by long bouts of inactivity combined with a ceaseless anxiety.[48] As Rivers also noted, exposure to danger with no possibility of acting was one of the main causes of breakdown, and one of the most distressing qualities of the war of attrition was the inability to act.

With the entry of the U.S., the long war of attrition gave way to movement. While three years of fighting had begun to wear the edges off the purposes of the war espoused in 1914, the American cause was new, and the propaganda fresh. Americans, having observed the war for so long, and having benefited economically by supplying materiel to the belligerent nations while trying to avoid involvement, could feel their purpose more optimistically, particularly in the face of what felt like the unprovoked danger of Germany's submarine attacks.[49] Although

---

48   Paul Fussell, *The Great War and Modern Memory* (Oxford: Oxford University Press, 1975).

49   After the German U-Boat sinking of the British passenger ship *Lusitania* in 1915, which killed 128 U.S. citizens, and the subsequent sinking of the *Arabic*, which killed two U.S. citizens, Germany agreed to curtail its submarine campaign. However, Germany was secretly amassing a much larger fleet of U-Boats, and would resume its campaign in early 1917 providing the final catalyst for Woodrow Wilson's April 2, 1917 request to congress for a declaration of war against Germany. Robert Zieger, *America's Great War: World War I and the American Experience* (Rowan & Littlefield: Lanham, 2000), 22.

Woodrow Wilson had won re-election in 1916 under the slogan "He Kept Us Out of the War," when Wilson did ask congress to declare war on Germany, the majority of the nation was supportive, thanks in no small part to the enormous and pervasive propaganda campaign orchestrated by a new organization called the Committee for Public Information which was run by George Creel, a journalist who had been an active supporter of Wilson's.[50]

Certainly, Americans suffered mental and emotional trauma during the Great War, and many returned from their experience disillusioned, but the mental health of demobilized soldiers was not immediately recognized as precarious or compromised, as it was in Europe. Shell shock had been mysterious to the British as it was emerging. Military and civilian doctors and psychiatrists were busy, during the first several years of the war, determining whether or not it was an actual condition, and then, in the later years of the war and after, trying to figure out what kind of a condition it was and how it could be treated. Throughout the interwar period there were ongoing arguments in Great Britain about whether the condition was physical or mental. The U.S. Army, on the other hand, knew of the existence of shell shock and had been researching it before the U.S. entered the war. Shell shock had gotten popular attention in the U.S., as reports of "strange new diseases apparently having their origin in the stress and special horrors of modern warfare" came across the Atlantic.[51] The U.S. was unique among the major belligerent nations of the war in being forewarned about those strange new diseases, and, though Americans were initially as skeptical about shell shock as most Britons were, they were much better prepared to face it.

---

50 Zieger, 79.

51 The Medical Department of the United State Army in the World War: Volume X: Neuropsychiatry (Washington: U.S. Government Printing Office, 1929), 1.

Another factor to consider is that relatively few acclaimed American authors served in the war. Ernest Hemingway, John Dos Passos, and E. E. Cummings were ambulance drivers. William Faulkner claimed to have served with the British Royal Flying Corps, even fabricating a limp and telling various stories about having crashed his airplane. In reality, though he was accepted into a training program, he did not complete the training and most likely never flew an airplane.[52] The list of canonical British authors who served in the war, however, is extensive, and even many who felt themselves too old for combat (Ford Madox Ford enlisted at the age of forty) served directly in the government's propaganda campaign.[53] In England, news of the war was omnipresent, and the fighting just across the English Channel was audible in London. Authors such as Virginia Woolf, H.G. Wells, Rudyard Kipling, and Rebecca West, among many others, recorded the inescapable war culture of the home front.

Despite the greater geographical and cultural distance, shell shock did have a strong impact on American literature of the Great War and the interwar period, and the later literature that reflects on that time. Though it is rarely as central an issue to American authors as it was for the British, shell shock is a quietly but surprisingly potent factor in many canonical American novels. Its treatment and its significations in American literature, however, are qualitatively quite different than in British Literature, as the essays in this volume demonstrate. Although there is and can be no

---

52   Daniel J. Singal. *William Faulkner: The Making of a Modernist* (Chapel Hill: U of North Carolina Press, 1997), 45.

53   The propaganda campaign was organized by C.F.G. Masterman. Mark Wollaeger names, among those who attended the first Wellington House Meeting "William Archer, J.M. Barrie, Arnold Bennett, Robert Bridges, G.K. Chesterton, Arthur Conan Doyle, John Galsworthy, Anthony Hope Hawkins, Thomas Hardy, George Trevelyan, H.G. Wells, and Israel Zangwill." Additionally, "Rudyard Kipling and Arthur Quiller Couch could not attend, but sent messages offering their services. With the exception of Hardy, all those in attendance chose to help, and many others, including Ford Madox Ford and Joseph Conrad, joined the campaign later" (*Modernism, Media, and Propaganda: British Narrative from 1900 to 1945* [Princeton: Princeton University Press, 2006], 14).

universally applicable rule about how these two nations processed the trauma of shell shock through literature, comparative analysis does reveal that U.S. literature about shell shock often imbues the condition and its sufferers with mysticism and otherworldly insight, while British literature is often more concerned with its concrete manifestations.

Much less research has been done into shell shock in American literature for the understandable reason that there was not nearly as much of a social, political, or scientific engagement with psychological war trauma in the United States during and after World War I. The condition did not pose a theoretical problem to the sovereignty of the United States Government, and it could not be looked to as a metaphor for social and cultural unraveling during an interwar period that was, for the U.S., a time of optimism, economic prosperity, and increasing global influence, despite the disillusionment of the Treaty of Versailles and the immediate postwar Influenza epidemic.

In Great Britain and across Europe, the war had been foreseen as a dim possibility for years before hostilities broke out, and though American citizens had watched the war unfold, knowing their nation might get involved more than economically in the conflict for several years, the U.S. entry into the war came about fairly suddenly and demanded rapid mobilization. Unlike the British and European young men who eagerly enlisted in early August of 1914, Americans, having lived in the shadow of the war, faced involvement from the start more as a duty than an adventure, and enthusiasm was whipped up *ex nihilo* by George Creel's propaganda machine (epitomized in the ubiquitous war anthem "Over There," composed by George M. Cohan) and a thorough censorship of any thoughts or views that might question American involvement in the war.

As a matter of efficiency and professional interest the U.S. Army Medical Department investigated shell shock before, during, and after the war. In 1929, the department published a massive fourteen volume report on the medical effects and conditions of the war, with Volume IX entitled and focusing exclusively on *Neuropsychiatry*. This is an invaluable resource for understanding the ideological and official anticipation and reception of shell shock in the U.S., but it remains somewhat aloof from the quotidian culture of the U.S. Unlike the Parliamentary investigation into shell shock, its British counterpart published in 1922, its findings would have been of little public interest, and not reported widely in the press. However, this report provides the clearest official response to shell shock and helps to clarify why shell shock became, in much U.S. literature, a mysterious, even mystical condition, instilled with otherworldly qualities and insights.

Compiled over the decade immediately following the war, the volume on *Neuropsychiatry* isn't nearly as concerned with figuring out what exactly happened during the war that resulted in so much trauma, or even in the question of whether that trauma was legitimate or faked, or physical or psychological. It is a much more pragmatically-minded investigation that sets out to make use of the "unparalleled opportunity" to study mental illness that shell shock presented, although it does show a concern for the well-being of the soldiers that is similar to that which motivated Lord Southborough to propose the Parliamentary investigation in the U.K.. The American report's authors are aware that they are working in the clarity of hindsight, with enough distance to observe the major trends that the war prompted, internationally, in the treatment of mental illness. The goal of the entire report was to maximize military efficiency in future warfare through detailed examination of how the military had dealt with the medical crises of the Great War. The committee points out almost immediately that they saw a "uniformly high standard which characterized provisions for the diagnosis and treatment of physical disorders in the base hospitals visited, in contrast with the meager provisions for the care of the mentally ill."[54]

---

54   The Medical Department of the United State Army in the World War: Volume X: Neuropsychiatry, 1.

In the British evolution of the understanding of shell shock, dramatized by the oppositional treatments provided by Yealland and Rivers, there is a movement away from the punitive and paternalistic and towards a more humane and psychological understanding of the condition and its best treatment. As the American Military prepared to deal with cases of mental breakdown, there was also, initially, a strongly punitive and derogatory attitude toward the treatment of mental patients. The committee describes this evolution in terms of the rhetoric and terminology surrounding the treatment facilities:

> The first plans drawn by the War Department for a building for nervous and mental patients were labeled "Isolation-insane." Later, wards in which these patients were cared for were officially designated as "Psychiatric wards." The transition from one to the other was more than a mere change in names. "Isolation-insane" was all the term implies in misunderstanding and professional discouragement and indifference. "Psychiatric ward," on the other hand, approximated, at least, and in some places largely attained, what the term implies in hospitalization—understanding and professional hope and activity.[55]

The buildings themselves were also transformed. The committee describes the "Isolation-insane" buildings as having been almost totally carceral in appearance, and essentially functioning as prisons attached to base hospitals. In contrast, "Psychiatric wards" were "open, bright, airy wards, in some hospitals, without bars or mesh of any kind."

The committee goes on to describe a concerted attempt by the military medical establishment to recognize, and to convince the rest of the military, that these new diseases brought about by the new forms of fighting were

---

55 Ibid., 40.

mental, rather than physical, but no less legitimate than physical wounds, and needing a certain type of care. The degree of success in creating psychiatric wards in base hospitals often "depend[ed] on the standards of the local officer himself, and his ability to convince his commanding officer that hospitals and not jails were being built. For a lieutenant or captain new to military service to convince a commanding officer of the "isolation-insane" school was no small task."[56]

As these examples of the U.S. military's preparation demonstrate, the U.S. took steps to obviate the problem of shell shock from the very start. One of the biggest differences between the British and American militaries was the extent to which pre-emptive measures could be taken to avoid enlisting soldiers with pre-existing mental conditions. While the British Army, by the spring of 1917, was, like other European forces, taking almost any soldiers it could get, the American Army was more discriminating for pragmatic reasons. The committee's report emphasizes repeatedly, throughout this section on neuropsychiatry, the absolute necessity of screening and rejecting men likely to develop war neuroses, and it reveals the fine lines that had to be established in considering a prospective soldier's mental health. The main point emphasized is the need to keep psychologically unfit men from service. While most men whose "personalities" rendered them unfit for military service were eventually found out, "it was not until after a considerable period of training during which they received pay, maintenance, and equipment, wasted the time of those endeavoring to instruct them, interfered with the training of their brighter or better-adjusted comrades, and occupied hospital beds which were often urgently needed for others." These men would go on to be an even greater economic burden to the state because, although many of them "rendered practically no service to the country" and their period in the army was deemed a waste of resources, they could go on to draw

---
56   Ibid., 41.

compensation from the government, and in 1927 nearly half of the patients receiving aid from the United States Veteran's Bureau were "ex-service men with neuropsychiatric disabilities."[57]

From the point of view of the U.S. Army Medical department, as these concerns demonstrate, shell shock is located at an ambiguous nexus of medical, military, legal, psychological, and economic concerns and practices. No precedent existed for tackling this issue, and even the training or the ability to recognize the problem varied enormously within the Army. While specialists could see the necessity of rigorous screening to avoid the problems shell shock would present, most soldiers probably had an attitude very similar to their British counterparts, i.e., if there was no evident physical problem, then a soldier's capacity to perform his responsibilities was merely a matter of "pulling himself together," or "getting the right idea." Not surprisingly, many army doctors and officers objected to what they saw as the unnecessary burden of psychological screening. The report explains that "[d]ivision surgeons complained that specialists interfered with the prompt getting in order of their camps, which was true, and line officers were not hard to find who maintained that if the specialists did not stop eliminating the unfit, there would be no army left."[58]

The U.S. Army, unlike that of Great Britain, was dealing with shell shock as a potential, even an expected, epidemic. The apparatus of the military had to become more intimately acquainted with its recruits, in more personally invasive ways, than during any past conflict, and it did so in unsurprisingly bureaucratic ways. The parliamentary report on shell shock was partially correct in its assertion that the condition arose in men who were ill-equipped to handle the demands of military life and particularly combat, but in the British Army, as W. H. R. Rivers's work demonstrates, and the intensity and

---

57   Ibid., 57.

58   Ibid., 58.

volume of afflicted officers as well as privates shows, virtually everybody could be pushed to the limits of his capacity and suffer breakdown; when and how this breakdown would occur was a matter of personal experience. As a result of the intense screening, however, the American Army no doubt rejected most of the soldiers who were already showing signs of neuroses or who would plainly not be beneficial to the army. The idea that shell shock was a fraudulent form of malingering persisted in the American Army, but the intense stigma that would attach to anybody's rejection from the army (or other branches of service, such as the nursing corps) makes the idea that malingering was commonplace untenable. A discharge on psychological grounds was universally seen as intensely shameful, probably more so than in the U.K., where the extremity of the war's violence was more directly understood (although that is not to say that malingering did not exist in other forms in the U.S. Army: it was noted, for example, that a case study of soldiers who were being treated for the aftereffects of cerebrospinal meningitis "showed rather sudden improvement within a few days of the signing of the armistice").[59]

Culturally, it is hard to imagine the kind of examinations performed on American recruits at all levels being done in the British Army. The degree of screening and the kinds of questions asked would have seemed invasive, even implicitly accusatory, in a country known for its refusal, as Ford Madox Ford has put it, to discuss "things."[60] Similarly, it is hard to imagine many

59 Ibid., 124.
60 In his ethnographic trilogy *England and the English*, Ford analyzes what he sees as the distinctly English, and certainly harmful, repression of emotions, which he attributes to the fact that "the Englishman feels very deeply and reasons very little" (311). Because of this surfeit of emotion over reason, any discussion of "things" is strictly forbidden among "good people." Ford recounts an incident from his youth in which he had gone rowing with a young female acquaintance of his and "began to talk to the fair, large, somnolent girl of some problem or other—I think of poor umbrella tassel menders or sweated industries that at that time interested me a great deal." The girl is unresponsive, and the next day Ford is drawn aside by her mother to be told that he's a "'good boy,'" but he mustn't discuss "'things'" with her daughter. Ford claims to have been bewildered, although in the subsequent years he has "learned what 'things' are; they include, in fact, religious topics, questions of the relations of the sexes, the conditions of poverty-stricken districts—every subject from which one can digress into

American recruits, with little or no experience of the army and coming from a vast array of ethnic and socioeconomic backgrounds, seeing these questions as more than ordinary bureaucracy.

This intense scrutiny into the mental faculties of recruits was further complicated by the ethnic and racial diversity of the pool from which the U.S. army recruited. The British Military certainly had to unify soldiers from the constituent members of the U.K., and propaganda was devised specifically to represent Irish, Scottish, Welsh, and English soldiers as distinct but united for a common cause. British colonial powers, like African Americans, were segregated into their own regiments. White American regiments included Americans from diverse ethnic, racial, and geographical backgrounds, but, as Robert Zieger points out, attitudes toward the war had differed greatly throughout America's diverse population, and many American citizens had roots in the belligerent nations of both the Allied and the Central powers.[61] True to the racial pseudoscience of its day, the Army Medical Department provides a thorough breakdown of the sorts of mental afflictions and predispositions common among specific races and ethnicities, and unsurprisingly attributes specific traits of character or personality to race.

The intrusion into the minds of the soldiers by specialists sent to screen them may have been regarded as superfluous by the established doctors, but the report points out that "It may seem strange, but it is nevertheless true, that the line officers appreciated the value of neuropsychiatric examinations much more readily than did the medical officers."[62] Considering the ongoing debate in Great Britain about whether or not shell shock was a physical or mental disorder, this is hardly surprising. As the report continues to demonstrate, line officers were always concerned with the exact issues the

---

anything moving." (*England and the English,* ed. Sara Haslam [Manchester,: Carcanet, 2003], 312).

61   Zieger, *America's Great War*, 15.

62   Neuropsychiatry, 73.

neuropsychiatrists were there to investigate: the competence and ability of the soldiers to adjust to military life.

On August 1, 1917, the Surgeon General issued a circular which explained what the neuropsychiatric examiners would be looking for when they arrived at army bases. After explaining the necessity of these screenings, the letter explains that all officers should be on the lookout for signs of abnormality in recruits:

> A soldier is too important a unit for such variations from a standard of absolute normality not to be looked into before the recruit who represents them is accepted for service. To aid the neurologist and psychiatrist in these ways the camp surgeon shall direct all medical officers, dental surgeons, instructors, hospital sergeants, and other who come in close contact with recruits to refer to him (the camp surgeon) all recruits who persistently show any of the following characteristics: Irritability, seclusiveness, sulkiness, depression, shyness, timidity, overboistrousness, suspicion, sleeplessness, dullness, stupidity, personal uncleanliness, resentfulness to discipline, inability to be disciplined, sleepwalking, nocturnal incontinence of urine, and any of the various characteristics which gain for him who displays them the name of "boob," "crank," "goat," "queer stick" and the like.[63]

Given the extensiveness and pervasiveness of this screening, it is clear that, while the European Armies were not prepared in any way for shell shock, the American Army went to great lengths to obviate the problem. The necessity of all soldiers to conform to this "standard of absolute normality," though, could easily have led to the reverse problem of that faced in Europe by this point in the war, the problem of generally competent men being rejected for minor idiosyncrasies.

---

63 Ibid., 67.

As a result of the anticipation of shell shock, the problem *seemed* far smaller, after the armistice, than anybody had expected. The Medical Department report congratulates itself, somewhat, on the relatively low numbers of U.S. Soldiers who returned from the war with neuroses or other problems. Concomitant with the armistice, the report claims, "war neuroses had ceased to exist as a problem, [...] cases from the American Expeditionary Force dwindled, and those under treatment in this country made rapid recoveries."[64]

This optimistic outlook would prove to be unfounded. Rather than dwindling away, cases of shell shock in the U.S. were no doubt ignored, especially in an atmosphere that was eager to forget the war and to reap its immediate economic rewards in the short term. In the longer term, many of the returned veterans' suffering only increased under the harsh conditions of the Great Depression, when sympathy for any hardship was spread very thin throughout the general population.[65]

During the years between the wars and even after World War II, shell shock remained a mysterious and unnerving modern psychological phenomenon, and provided an analytic framework for both American and British authors to explore the psychological impacts of modernity. Although the immediate trauma of this war has passed out of existence with its last survivors in recent years, the mystery of shell shock remains, as does our obligation to engage and understand war trauma of both the past and present.

---

64   Ibid., 45.

65   Dodman, 6. Also of note, E.Y. Harburg and Jay Gorney's Depression era anthem "Brother, Can You Spare a Dime" is significantly told from the point of view of a struggling veteran.

Austin Riede is an associate professor specializing in British modernism at the University of North Georgia. He has published articles on Ford Madox Ford's novels *The Good Soldier* and *Parade's End,* Vera Brittain's WWI memoir *Testament of Youth*, the elegiac wartime poetry of W.B. Yeats, Lewis Grassic Gibbon's novel *Sunset Song*, and David Jones's epic WWI poem *In Parenthesis.* He teaches British Literature II, Modern and Contemporary British Literature, Victorian Literature, Science Fiction, Horror, Literature and Film, and Composition. He is currently working on representations of conscientious objection, labor, and the body in Great War literature.

"STRANGE HELLS"

Shell Shock, Trauma, and Transatlantic Poetry of the First World War

Argha Banerjee

Abstract

It was psychologist Charles Myers (1873-1946) who gave shell shock a place in medical discourse by publishing his article in the *Lancet* in February 1915. The crucial significance of shell shock is central to a proper understanding of poetry of the First World War. War poetry perhaps provides the deepest form of understanding of the intricacies that plagued the shell-shocked mind of a combatant. Poetry, given the plethora of published volumes during the years of the hostilities, served as a significant catalyst to noted writers, soldiers and civilians alike. The interrelationship between mental trauma, poetry, and the unprecedented violence unleashed by the first modern technological conflict is evidently reflected in the transatlantic poetry of the war. Negotiations of shell shock in verse, as this essay explores, underline the deep sense of horror and vulnerability that characterize most responses. Close perusals of some poems reveal the predominant ominous specter of disenchantment that pervade these poetic negotiations, struggling to tackle an unparalleled emotional crisis. Through a fairly broad survey of both British and American male poets who directly experienced and participated in the conflict as either combatants, ambulance drivers, or volunteers, this chapter tries to trace the transatlantic kinship of spirit among various poets hailing from both sides of the Atlantic.

"Writing poetry is, in psychoanalytic terms, a sublimatory activity, a re-channeling of basic drives so as to make them socially acceptable and potentially useful." [1]

Patrick Campbell

COMPOSED just prior to his confinement in the City of London Mental Hospital at Dartford, Ivor Gurney's "Strange Hells" (1922) explores the scars ailing the troubled mind of a combatant exposed to the horrors of trench warfare during the First World War. During the summer of 1922, Gurney had delusions that his life was being controlled by electrical impulses radiating from the wireless radio. In a delirious fit he threatened to commit suicide, going so far as calling the police department and demanding a revolver. Diagnosed as suffering from "Deferred Shell Shock," his mental trauma originated in his traumatic experiences of the war. Four years earlier (during the spring of 1918), when he was recuperating in Britain following his experiences—which included being gassed—in the Passchendaele offensive, Gurney had experienced a severe psychological crisis, threatening suicide and claiming to be in conversation with Beethoven.

---

1 Patrick Campbell, *Siegfried Sassoon: A Study of the War Poetry* (London, Jefferson, North Carolina: McFarland &Company, Inc., Publishers, 1999), 157.

"Strange Hells" is a journey into the "hell" of a soldier's mind following his exposure to the unprecedented violence of the war. As Adam Thorpe observes, Gurney's poem is both a "private rumination" and a "public address:"[2] "There are strange hells within the minds war made / Not so often, not so humiliatingly afraid / As one would have expected— the racket and fear guns made."[3] His lyric moves on to contrast the camaraderie of the soldiers at the front with the inadequate reception of combatants in post-war Britain. Given Gurney's innate musical flair (he won a scholarship to the Royal College of Music in London in 1911 and stayed there till his participation in the war in 1915), sound and music play a key role in several of his poems including "Strange Hells". The poem displays the triumph of the collective combative strength of the soldiers (symbolized through music) against the ongoing shellfire. The solidarity of the soldiers in the poem is reinforced by the collective humming of a war-born tune: *"Apres la guerre finie."* The mêlée that ensues between the harmonious solidarity (inspired by the war-born refrain) and the hostile anarchic forces of bombardment is further enhanced by Gurney's effective violent language ("bombardment," "black shout," "eighteen pounders hammering," etc.). As Daniel Hipp observes, "Gurney represents the power of the song by describing the voices as weapons: 'combined black shout/ Of fury,' 'diaphragms fixed beyond all dreads,' and 'tin and stretched wire tinkle.'"[4] "Strange Hells" records an aesthete's struggle through a dark world of horror and mental torment, where redemption seems to lie in camaraderie, human cohesion, and the pursuit of art. Gurney reinforces

---

2 Adam Thorpe, "Strange Hells", Saturday 10th November 2007, https://www.theguardian.com/books/2007/nov/10/featuresreviews.guardianreview4.

3 Ivor Gurney, *Collected Poems*. Ed. P.J. Kavanagh (Oxford: Oxford University Press, 1982).

4 Daniel Hipp, *The Poetry of Shell Shock: Wartime Trauma and Healing in Wilfred Owen, Ivor Gurney and Siegfried Sassoon* (Jefferson, North Carolina and London: McFarland &Company, Inc., Publishers, 2005), 144.

the trauma of his experience of the war by using the word "hell[s]" four times in the brief span of the sonnet.

Gurney's exploration of the "hells" of the mind recurs in varied forms in several of his other poems, including "Pain," "First Time In," "Of Grandcourt," "The Silent One," and "To His Love" among several others. The hellish nature of trench warfare reappears as a subject not only in Gurney's verse but in the war verse composed by other combatant poets as well. "I have suffered seventh hell,"[5] wrote Wilfred Owen to his mother; while Sassoon's "Memorial Tablet (Great War)" asserts: "I died in hell— (They called it Passchendaele)."[6] In "Break of Day" Sassoon describes hell as a place "Where men are crushed like clods, and crawl / to find some crater for their wretchedness,"[7] while Robert Graves in "The Leveller" recalls the death of a soldier ("Senseless and limp like slaughtered sheep")[8] by a shell near Martinpuich, during a "night of hell." In his post war poem "Hugh Selwyn Mauberley" Ezra Pound speaks of veterans who "walked eye-deep in hell,"[9] suggesting the lingering sense of waste, squalor, and deprivation.

The "hell" that recurs in war verse, is a perennial source of torment with which the shell shocked combatants continually struggled for the rest of their lives. It was the psychologist Charles Myers (1873-1946) who gave shell shock a place in medical discourse by publishing his article in the *Lancet* in February 1915. As Tracey Loughran points out, "[t]he centrality of shell shock in imaginings of the First World War is, therefore, highly important because of the place of this conflict in the modern (particularly

---

5   Wilfred Owen, *Collected Letters*, eds Harold Owen and John Bell (London: Oxford University Press, 1967), 427-28.

6   Siegfried Sassoon, *War Poems of Siegfried Sassoon* (New York, Mineola: Dover Publications Inc., 2004), 101.

7   Ibid., 70.

8   Robert Graves, *Complete Poems*, vol. 1, eds. Beryl Graves, Dunstan Ward (London: Carcanet Press, 1999), 110.

9   Ezra Pound, *Collected Shorter Poems* (London: Faber & Faber, 1968), 208.

British) cultural landscape."[10] War poetry perhaps provides the deepest form of understanding of the intricacies that plagued the shell-shocked mind of a soldier. The relationship between mental trauma, poetry, and the unprecedented violence unleashed by the first modern technological war is reflected in the transatlantic poetry of the war.

On the occasion of the centennial remembrance of the Great War, Anthony Richards (Head of documents for the Imperial War Museum, London) rightly pointed out: "No conflict has ever been so closely linked with the poetry and literature of its age than the First World War."[11] In this context, however, it is essential to remember that poetry served as a significant catalyst to writers hailing from both sides of the Atlantic, several of them rushing to print with their works. This creative outburst is clearly evidenced by the thousands of poems written and published during the conflict by British and American poets. Catherine Reilly's crucial work *English Poetry of the First World War: A Bibliography* (1978) lists 2,225 published poets during the war years. In Britain, shortly after the declaration of hostilities, newspapers like *The Times* and *Daily Mail* were inundated with poetic contributions. In June 1915, the *Daily Mail* amusingly whinged about the literary epidemic that had suddenly led to "A Serious Outbreak of Poets." It unambiguously stated that more poetry had "found its way into print in the last eleven months than in the eleven preceding years."[12] Besides prolific compositions from the civilians, the surfeit of poetic contributions even from the combatants created problems for newspapers like *The Wiper Times* and the *Westminster Gazette*. The former, a humorous

---

10 Tracy Loughran, "Shell Shock, Trauma, and the First World War: The Making of a Diagnosis and Its Histories," *Journal of the History of Medicine and Allied Sciences*, vol. 67, no.1, January 2012, 97.

11 Anthony Richards, "How First World War poetry painted a truer picture," 28 February 2014. www.telegraph.co.uk/history/world-war-one/inside-first-world-war/part-seven/10667204/first-world-war-poetry-sassoon.html.

12 Twells Brex, "A Serious Outbreak of Poets," The Daily Mail, June 23, 1915. 11.

journal published by and for the soldiers at the Western Front, referred to the poetic fad as "an insidious disease" that had contributed to "a hurricane of poetry."[13] Through a fairly broad survey of both American and British poets who experienced the war as either combatants, ambulance drivers, or volunteers, this chapter traces the transatlantic kinship of spirit among various poets from both U.S. and the U.K., acknowledging the hollowness and futility that pervaded the great crisis of human civilisation that unfolded on the threshold of the twentieth century.

The U.S. was actively involved in the war rather briefly, not entering until April 1917. However, even prior to its intervention in the Great War, the U.S. had indirectly felt the impact of the ongoing conflict. In 1915, it had incurred civilian losses in the infamous sinking of the *Lusitania* by a German U boat. Writing to his mother from France on this particular incident, the American poet Alan Seeger wondered: "Why in the name of all dignity does not the American government act or shut up, for the *Gazette de Cologne* explicitly states that all indignant protestations will be received with absolute coldness?"[14] In the poem "The White Ships and the Red," Joyce Kilmer expressed his indignation at the loss of innocent lives: "My wrong cries out for vengeance, / The blow that sent me here / Was aimed in Hell. My dying scream / Has reached Jehovah's ear. / Not all the seven oceans / Shall wash away that stain / Upon a brow that wears a crown / I am the brand of Cain."[15] Kilmer's poetic reaction and the outrage of other writers raised a question about America's neutral stance towards the ongoing hostilities. Percy MacKaye's sonnet entitled "American Neutrality" captured

---

13   Anonymous, "Notice," *The Wiper Times or Salient News*, vol. 2, No 4 (March 20, 1916), unpaginated.

14   Alan Seeger, Letters and Diary, May 10, 1915; as cited in Chris Dickon, *A Rendezvous with Death: Alan Seeger in Poetry, at War* (Wickford: New Street Communications, 2017), 139-40.

15   Mark W. Van Wienen, ed. *Rendezvous with Death: American Poems of the Great War* (Urbana & Chicago: University of Illinois Press, 2002), 97.

the mood of the hour asserting: " . . . —Being American, / Our souls cannot keep neutral and keep true."[16] The civilian losses suffered due to sinking of the Lusitania, coupled with other marine fatalities and the mounting reports of German brutalities in Belgium, ultimately incited the U.S. military intervention on behalf of the Allies. The geographical distance did not hinder the urgency of American intervention, though as John Matthews argues, during the initial years of the First World War, the conflict remained more of a virtual reality for most U.S. citizens.[17]

In spite of its late involvement and physical distance, however, as in Britain, poetry served as a key catalyst in America's engagement with the war. The appeal of the genre was both intellectual and emotional, and this is clearly evinced in the deluge of poetry publications. Approximately eighty anthologies of war poetry were published in the U.S. between 1914 and 1920. Different periodicals carried poems, and hundreds of war poems were published by the *New York Times* alone during those years. As Timothy D. Rives observes in "The Work of Soldier Poetry in Kansas, 1917-1919:"

> When the United States entered the war in April 1917, the poetry factory remained in production, the muse in high gear. Filling a weekly column called the "Poet's Corner", *Stars and Stripes* newspaper printed more than 100,000 lines of soldier verse in less than two years. "All of (the American Expeditionary Force) read poetry", a staff writer said, and "most of them wrote it."'[18]

---

16   Percy MacKaye, *Poems and Plays* vol. 1 (New York: Macmillan, 1916), 30.

17   John T. Matthews, "American writing of the Great War," in *The Cambridge Companion to the Literature of the First World War*, ed. Vincent Sherry (Cambridge: Cambridge University Press, 2005). 217.

18   Timothy D. Rives, "The Work of Soldier Poetry in Kansas, 1917-1919," *New Directions in Folklore*, Issue 7 (Special Issue Military Folklore), 2003. https://scholarworks.iu.edu/journals/index.php/ndif/article/download/19890/25960.

Mental Cases: Shell Shock, Trauma, and British Poetry

In Britain, negotiations of war trauma through poetry is unsurprising, especially for a society with such high literacy levels and a population exposed to a school curriculum that thrived on the patriotic verse of Rudyard Kipling, Alfred Austin, and Henry Newbolt during the late Victorian and Edwardian periods. For the more literary minded, as George Walter points out, "the emergence of the Imagist and Georgian movements in the years immediately prior to the outbreak of war offered more contemporary and more stimulating models of poetic expression."[19] The literary tradition, however, in the context of American war poetry was slightly different. As Paul Fussell observes in his chapter "Oh, What a Literary War" in *The Great War and Modern Memory*: "It was not so in America, which had always done very well without a consciousness of a national literary canon."[20] According to Fussell, "in the absence of a line of important 'philosophic' poets running back to the fourteenth century, in a vacuum devoid of a Chaucer, a Spenser, a Shakespeare, a Milton, a Keats . . . American writing about the war tends to be spare and one-dimensional."[21] Fussell's criticism about the "one-dimensional" aspect of American poetic responses to the Great War is, however, subject to scrutiny, as the First World War opened the gates for great modernist experimentations in English verse by American writers like Ezra Pound, T. S. Eliot, Hilda Doolittle and E. E. Cummings, among others.

Owen was not a solitary exception to this cult of verse during the war. The obsession with poetry is evident in an adage that gained currency

---

19 George Walter, Introduction, *The Penguin Book of First World War Poetry* ed. George Walter (London: Penguin 2006) xii.

20 Paul Fussell, *The Great War and Modern Memory* (Oxford: Oxford University Press, 1975, reprinted 2000), 158.

21 Ibid.

during the later years of the conflict: "Went to war with Rupert Brooke, came home with Siegfried Sassoon."²² The two poets serve as emblems of oppositional poetic reactions to the war that resonate through the larger body of war verse composed on both sides of the Atlantic. Even the relatively restricted body of American Great War poetry combines this dual element of romantic zest and fervour on the one hand and the bitter disillusionment and horror of protracted conflict on the other. Like Rupert Brooke, the lure of the romantic vision of martial sacrifice is deeply ingrained in the verse of Alan Seeger (who unlike Brooke was also exposed to the harsh reality of the war); while quite akin to the poetic reactions of British soldier poets, the later poetry of the American combatants and ambulance drivers (like Ernest Hemingway, Hervey Allen, Joyce Kilmer, and others), was more rooted in the bitter realities of shell shock and trench warfare.

Following his enlistment in October 1915, Wilfred Owen experienced trench warfare, initially from January to May 2017, and later from 1 September 1918 until his demise during the final week of the war. His first stint exposed him to the "physical and psychological reality of suffering," which was absolutely "central to his experience" of the Great War.²³ According to Fussell, "what he encountered at the front was worse than even a poet's imagination could have conceived."²⁴ Besides the actual conditions of trench warfare, various other circumstances exacerbated Owen's trauma. Even Sassoon expressed surprise after learning about the actual horrors that Owen had undergone: "I discovered that Wilfred had endured worse things than I had realised from the little he told me."²⁵ As Daniel Hipp points out, "the primary cause of Owen's trauma can be established as having been a single

---

22 As cited in Claire M Tylee, *The Great War and Women's Consciousness* (London: Macmillan, 1990), 79.
23 Hipp, 46.
24 Fussell, 289.
25 Siegfried Sassoon, *Siegfried's Journey* (New York: Viking, 1945), 90-91.

vivid and horrifying experience—the days spent in the dugout, in which he played the role of passive observer."[26] During the night of 13/14 March 1917, Owen fell down a fifteen foot hole (maybe a well), hitting the back of his head and being trapped there for over a day. The sheer jolt of the sudden descent resulted in concussion, following his hospitalisation for the next couple of weeks, where he recuperated reading the poems of Elizabeth Barrett Browning and corresponding with his family members. Writing to his mother, he narrated his traumatic experience:

> I am in a hospital bed, (for the first time in life.) After falling into that hole (which I believe was a shell-hole in a floor, laying open a deep cellar) I felt nothing more than a headache, for 3 days . . . for I felt too weak to wrestle with the mud, and sneaked along the top, snapping my fingers at a clumsy sniper. When I got back I developed a high fever, vomited strenuously, and long, and was seized with muscular pains.[27]

More than a month later, the trauma on the battlefield took its toll on Owen's psychological health, manifesting itself in stammering and general disorientation. In late April, he survived a shell blast, but remained in a "badly shelled forward position for days looking at the scattered pieces of a fellow officer's body."[28] On the 1st of May 1917, his commanding officer, Lieutenant Colonel Luxmoore, observed him behaving strangely. Subsequently, when Owen reported to the Battalion Medical Officer, the latter found him to be unstable and timorous, with a muddled memory. Under shell shock he was not in a condition to participate in further military action. Writing to his mother on 2 May, from the 13th Casualty Clearing Station, Owen aptly summed up his situation:

---

26   Hipp, 52.
27   Jon Stallworthy, *Wilfred Owen* (London: Oxford University Press and Chatto Windus, 1974), 171.
28   Fussell, 289.

> Here again! The Doctor suddenly was moved to forbid me to go into action next time the Battalion go . . . I did not go sick or anything, but he is nervous about my nerves, and sent me down yesterday—labelled Neurasthenia. I still of course suffer from the headaches traceable to my concussion.[29]

Being diagnosed as unfit for military service for six months, he was sent to the Craiglockhart Hydropathic Establishment, outside Edinburgh (in the village of Slateford, Scotland), for special observation and treatment under Dr Arthur Brock, who preferred the "occupation cure" to rehabilitate his patients. In the present day psychiatric parlance, as Paul Norgate surmises, Owen's symptoms were Indicative of a deep rooted anxiety disorder with the archetypal symptoms of being "tense, withdrawn, depressed, suffering from nightmares, afflicted with a slight stammer."[30] In this context, it is important to remember that, as Susanne Christine Puissant observes, diagnoses of neurasthenia often considered it "a flight from reality, indicating a general weakness of character resulting in a lack of self-control and a childish or womanly attitude towards the dangers of daily life."[31] Puissant draws attention to the fact that such an attitude among the contemporary population "might even have increased the symptom, as fear was suppressed rather than acknowledged, until it finally became overwhelming."[32] In Owen's case, we find evidence of such pressure on his mind in Robert Graves's observation, when meeting Owen while paying a visit to Siegfried Sassoon at the Craiglockhart: "It preyed on his mind that

---

29   Jon Stallworthy, *Wilfred Owen*.(London: Oxford University Press and ChattoWindus, 1974), 184.

30   Paul Norgate, "Shell Shock and Poetry: Wilfred Owen at Craiglockhart Hospital", *English* 36 (1987): 1-35.

31   Puissant, 135.

32   Ibid., 135.

he had been unjustly accused of cowardice by his commanding officer."[33] Owen's poem "The Dead Beat" which was composed in August 1917 during his stay at the hospital alludes to the contemptuous disparaging reactions of the life savers: "We sent him down at last, out of the way. / Unwounded; —stout lad, too, before that strafe. / Malingering? Stretcher-bearers winked, 'Not half!' / Next day I heard the Doc's well-whiskied laugh: / 'That scum you sent last night soon died. Hooray!'"[34] According to Kenneth Simcox, "the dreadful irony is that he who is dead beat through no fault of his own should be in conflict, not with the enemy he's been sent to fight, but with those who belong on his own side."[35]

Dr. Arthur Brock, under whose supervision Owen recovered, believed that shell shock was not purely a wartime phenomenon but rather an "acute manifestation of a chronic condition,"[36] which could be warded off by improving the patient's immediate environment. As Hipp points out: "according to Brock, in fact, the person could not be healed unless he was able to see the value of improving the community at large."[37] As a part of the healing process or ergotherapy, Owen became a member of the "Field Club" at Craiglockhart, a society that researched and delivered lectures on the natural environment around Slateford. As part of this palliative exercise, Owen gave a lecture entitled "Do Plants Think?" on 30 July 1917. The lecture which reveals Owen's deep bonding with plant life, is also crucial in our understanding of Owen's attitude towards nature, and his attempt ". . . to demonstrate by a number of instances, that Plants have all the elements of

---

33 Fussell, 289.

34 Wilfred Owen, *The Collected Poems of Wilfred Owen* ed., C.Day Lewis and with a Memoir by Edmund Blunden (New York: New Directions Publishing Corporation, 1965), 72.

35 Kenneth Simcox, http://www.wilfredowen.org.uk/poetry/deadbeat.

36 Thomas E F Webb, "Dottyville—C.W. Hospital and shell-shock treatment in First World War," *Journal of the Royal Society of Medicine*, 2006 July, 99 (7) 342-46.

37 Hipp, 57.

perception, and if not consciousness, at least *senscience*. . . ."[38] Owen's poetic reflection on nature, as evinced from the subject of this lecture, renders a moral dimension to it, underlining his deep sense of guilt in the act of participation in the war—an obvious cause of environmental upheaval. On the one hand, he is apprehensive of nature's backlash (being a participant in the act of environmental desecration through war), on the other, he is deeply aware of the symbiotic bonding between human beings and nature.

In "Exposure," Owen directly correlates his guilt-ridden war experience with nature. He portrays the latter as a hostile force, aggravating the soldiers' anxious existence in the squalid trenches during the bitter winter months. Even the conventional notion of optimism associated with the "dawn" is inverted in the poem, as it is depicted as a harbinger of "poignant misery."[39] The "dawn . . . in the east" is personified as assembling or "massing . . . her melancholy army" to inflict further casualties on humankind.[40] It is the same anxiety, coupled with a deep fear of loss of faith in the benevolence of nature, that leads to Owen's ironic depiction of the "sun" in "Futility."[41] The eternal source of life is portrayed as an impotent agent in the poem, failing to infuse life in the dead soldier. The apprehension of being abandoned by benign nature lies at the heart of poems like "Asleep" and "Spring Offensive." While the former portrays the paralytic sinking of a soldier in the lap of an indifferent nature, "Spring Offensive" depicts the sudden horrific transformation of therapeutic nature to an ominous anarchic hell of death and destruction.

Owen's time at Craiglockhart from June to October 1917 was crucial for his poetic career. Besides his historic rendezvous with Siegfried Sassoon,

---

38   Jon Stallworthy, *Wilfred Owen: Chatterton Lecture on an English Poet* (British Academy, vol. lvi, London: Oxford University Press, 1970), 22-23.

39   Owen, 48-49.

40   Ibid., 48.

41   Ibid., 58.

he also went on to edit the hospital magazine *The Hydra*, which served as a healing exercise. Owen's meeting and his friendship with Sassoon, which has been explored in considerable detail, extended to a constructive influence on his writing. At Craiglockhart, he started experimenting with his pararhyme and wrote "My Shy Hand," "The Next War," "Anthem for Doomed Youth," "Greater Love," "Six o'clock in Princes Street," "Song of Songs," "S.I.W," "The Dead Beat," "Disabled," "Dulce Et Decorum Est," "Inspection," "The Sentry," and others. Most of these poems were later revised at Scarborough, or gradually evolved through subsequent amendments.

"S.I.W." (self-inflicted wound) explores the threefold psychological pressure that combatants endured: the horror of the war, military convention, and duty towards family and the patriarchal state: "One dawn, our wire patrol / Carried him. This time, Death had not missed. / We could do nothing but wipe his bleeding cough."[42] "S.I.W" is reminiscent of Sassoon's "The Hero," in which the central protagonist is "blown to small bits."[43] However, it is the false consolation rendered to family members (in both these poems) that reveals the underlying vicious cycle that not only deceived young combatants but also beguiled the civilians at home. In Owen's poem "Tim" is erroneously believed to have "died smiling"[44] while in Sassoon's verse, the false solace is rendered in the form of heroic status being granted to the victim.

Sassoon's "Suicide in the Trenches" uses a similar simple ballad stanza, three tetrameter quatrains, to portray the traumatic impact of the ongoing hostilities. The "simple soldier boy" in the poem is described as being particularly young and vulnerable, and ultimately forced to "put a bullet through his brain."[45] Instead of portraying the conditions of the trenches,

---

42 Ibid., 74.
43 Sassoon, 28.
44 Owen, 75.
45 Sassoon, 64.

the poem explores the psychological impact of prolonged exposure to violence. In the first stanza, the young combatant is unaffected by darkness prior to his enlistment in the war. The experience in the "winter trenches"[46] (second stanza) reverses his youthful exuberance of the spring. Sassoon's "Lamentations" and "The Effect" also portray the metamorphosis of innocent cheerfulness to squalor and despondency, and even suicidal despair.

Initially titled "The Deranged" Owen's "Mental Cases" explores a similarly anguished state of mind. Along with "Dulce et Decorum Est" and "The Sentry," the poem reveals how young soldiers are gradually transformed into senile wrecks. "Mental Cases" is a revolutionary poem in the sense that (like Gurney's "Strange Hells") besides being a personal testimony of trauma, it also serves as a plea for scarred minds in need of empathy and palliative care. Owen aims at shocking his reader by describing the ghastly psychosomatic manifestations of the shell-shocked soldiers. The gruesome imagery of the poem builds on Owen's reading of Dante, as in successive images, he portrays the horrors and mental sufferings of the soldiers in an allusive manner: "purgatorial shadows" (2), "multitudinous murders" (12), "blood-black" (21), "human squander" (17), "walk hell" (9), etc.[47] The poet acknowledges his own share of guilt which is further intensified through his use of blood imagery: "treading blood from lungs" (14), "carnage incomparable" (17), "blood smear" (21), and "a wound that bleeds afresh" (22).[48]

Owen started writing "The Sentry" at Craiglockhart while receiving treatment during the autumn of 1917 and finished it in France a few weeks before his death. Based on a specific incident at the front, Owen described the circumstances of its inspiration in a 16 January 1917 letter to his mother:

---

46 Sassoon, 64.

47 Owen, 69.

48 Ibid., 69.

My dug-out held 25 men tightly packed. Water filled it to a depth of 1 or 2 feet, leaving say 4 feet of air. One entrance had been blown in and blocked. So far, the other remained. The Germans knew we were staying there and decided we shouldn't. Those fifty hours were the agony of my happy life. Every ten minutes on Sunday afternoon seemed an hour. I nearly broke down and let myself drown in the water that was now slowly rising over my knees . . .

In the Platoon on my left the sentries over the dug-out were blown to nothing. One of these poor fellows was my first servant whom I rejected. If I had kept him he would have lived, for servants don't do Sentry Duty. I kept my own sentries halfway down the stairs during the more terrific bombardment. In spite of this one lad was blown down and, I am afraid, blinded. This was my only casualty.[49]

As the poet seeks refuge in a water-logged dugout, the sentry, keeping vigilance above, is blown down the stairs in a flood of muck, being blinded in the process. Though the poet sends for the stretcher and briefly tries to calm him down, he is soon forced to forget him, preoccupied with other commitments in the dugout. Though the blinded casualty is forcibly cast into oblivion, in the chaos of the battle, the hapless victim recurs to torment the poet in his dreams. The sentry's blasted eyes and agitated outcry haunt the poet. Owen's deep sense of guilt ("my first servant whom I rejected")[50] perhaps exacerbated his plight. Owen's letters around this time repeatedly mention recurrent nightmares: "having bellicose dreams of late," and "disastrous dreams."[51] These dreams continued even after his release from Craiglockhart. In a letter dated 24 June 1918 from Scarborough, he writes:

---

49 Owen, *Collected Letters*, 427-28.
50 Ibid., 427-28.
51 Ibid., 486, 490.

"War dreams have begun again; but that is because of the flapping of the canvas all night in the high winds; or else the hideous faces of the Advancing Revolver Targets I fired at last week."[52]

Haunting nightmares served as a recurrent theme for other war poets too. Ivor Gurney's "Ballad of the Three Spectres" uses "three jeering fleering spectres" who mock a duty-bound soldier on the battlefield. The apparitions foretell three different fates for the poet. While the first predicts injury and subsequent recuperation back home, the second foretells death in the freezing mud. The final apparition curses the soldier to live until the last hours of the war only to endure interminable agony afterwards. The sardonic visions of the spectres range from the comforting "Blighty" (8) through the inevitability of decease "on Picardy" (12) to the "hour of agony" (16).[53] Similar to Owen and Gurney, Robert Graves, in his poem "Haunted," recounts waking visions of fellow combatants who died on the Somme: "I met you suddenly down the street / Strangers assume your platform faces, / You grin at me from daylight places, / Dead, long dead, I'm ashamed to greet / Dead men down the morning street."[54] In fact such was the agonising torment of the horror-stricken, shell-shocked soldier that nightfall was acutely dreaded—even in the apparent security of Craiglockhart. As Sassoon describes in *Sherston's Progress*:

> In the daytime, sitting in a sunny room, a man could discuss his psycho-neurotic symptoms with his doctor, who could diagnose phobias and conflicts and formulate them into scientific terminology. Significant dreams could be noted down, and Rivers could try to remove repressions. But by night each man was back in his doomed

---

52   Ibid., 560.

53   Ivor Gurney, "Ballad of the Three Spectres" in *The Wordsworth Book of First World War Poetry* ed. Marcus Clapham, (Hertforshire: Wordsworth Editions Limited, 1995), 30.

54   https://www.poemhunter.com/poem/haunted-56/.

sector of horror stricken Front line, where the panic and stampede of some ghastly experience was re-enacted among the livid faces of the dead. No doctor could save him then, when he became the lonely victim of his dream disasters and delusions.[55]

Owen's poem "Greater Love" is also a product of his creative period at Craiglockhart. The poem is Owen's personal response to the war with the combatant being identified with Christ in the fourth stanza, carrying the cross for redemption of humankind. The blood-stained stones of the dead British soldiers in the poem outshine the redness of the combatants' lips. In negotiation of trauma in this poem, Owen uses a series of macabre images. The first of these images insists that the eyes that have been blinded are more alluring than others; it is followed by the horrid image of "limbs knife-skewed"(8)[56] and the heart that had been shot through. The intense creative period at Craiglockhart that produced "Greater Love" and "Anthem for Doomed Youth" also witnessed a fervent denunciation of the jingoistic verse in vogue in his famous "Dulce et Decorum Est," a poem that was further revised in 1918. As Santanu Das observes, in this poem Owen

> sets the war-ravaged body and mind against the abstract rhetoric of honour and sacrifice. In the process, he plays three separate experiences—a night march, a gas attack and traumatic neurosis—along an almost single vertical bodily axis as he traces the very pulse of pain as it moves from exposed feet in the first stanza to exposed nerves in the final one.[57]

---

55 Siegfried Sassoon, *Sherston's Progress* (London: Faber &Faber, 1936), 54.

56 Wilfred Owen, *The Collected Poems* of Wilfred Owen, 41.

57 Santanu Das, "'Dulce et Decorum Est', a close reading", https://www.bl.uk/20th-century-literature/articles/a-close-reading-of-dulce-et-decorum-est.

The poem reveals a nightmarish guilt in the poet's inability to help the soldier choking on poison gas. The trauma recurs in his dreams, as the victim keeps on "guttering, choking and drowning" in recurrent nightmares. Das observes: "Mustard gas corrodes the body from within. In Owen's depiction, the testimony of the gas attack moves accordingly from visual impressions to guttural processes, from sounds produced between the body and the world—fumbling, stumbling, flound'ring, drowning—to sounds within the body: guttering, choking, writhing, gargling."[58]

Sassoon's "Survivors" also provides a scathing portrayal of the symptoms of shell shock, as soldiers speak in an incoherent manner throughout the poem. The poetic narrative alludes to Sassoon's own nightmares that haunted him subsequent to his hallucinating corpses lying on the road, inviting the poet to join them. The poem literally catalogues the "shock and strain" of the "broken and mad" world of the war-ridden combatants, with the obvious tell-tale signs of shell-shock: "stammering, disconnected talk," "old, scared faces," "haunted nights" of "ghosts of friends who died" and "dreams that drip with murder."[59] Sarah Cole points out: "In his landscape of defiance, Sassoon's shell-shocked relics present an especially outraging spectacle: a community whose frustration can only be expressed outwardly in angry looks, or, more tragically, in the inwardly directed violence of nightmare, even suicide."[60]

Though extremely enthusiastic at the start of the war, Sassoon grew disillusioned with his experience, going on to make his historic statement in July 1917: "I have seen and endured the sufferings of the troops and I can no longer be a party to prolong these sufferings for ends which I believe to be evil and unjust. I am not protesting against the conduct of the war,

---

58 Das, "'Dulce et Decorum Est.'"

59 Sassoon, 83.

60 Sarah Cole, "Siegfried Sassoon" in T*he Cambridge Companion to the Poetry of the First World War* ed., Santanu Das (Cambridge: Cambridge University Press, 2013), 98.

but against the political errors and insincerities for which the fighting men are being sacrificed."[61] The course of treatment Sassoon received at Rivers's hands, in contrast to Brock, mainly consisted of hour-long sessions of analysis in his office. This allowed Sassoon to explore and interact with others at Craiglockhart including visitors from London like Lady Morrell and Robbie Ross. Writing to Lady Morrell on 30 July 1917, Sassoon describes his psychotherapist: "My doctor is a sensible man who doesn't say anything silly. His name is Rivers, a notable Cambridge psychologist. But his arguments don't make any impression on me. He doesn't pretend that my nerves are wrong, but regards my attitude as abnormal. I do not know how long he will go on trying to persuade me to modify my views."[62] In his fictionalised autobiography *The Complete Memoirs of George Sherston*, Sassoon described his observations of shell shock and its effects on soldiers:

> How many a brief bombardment had its long-delayed after effects in the minds of these survivors, many of whom had looked at their companions and laughed while inferno did its best to destroy them. Not then was their evil hour, but now; now, in the sweating suffocation of nightmare, in paralysis of limbs, in the stammering of dislocated speech. Worst of all in the disintegration of those qualities through which they had been so gallant and selfless and uncomplaining—this, in the finer types of men, was the unspeakable tragedy of shell-shock . . . In the name of civilisation these soldiers had been martyred, and it remains for civilisation to prove that their martyrdom wasn't a dirty swindle.[63]

---

61 Siegfried Sassoon, Appendix B, *Cambridge Poets of the Great War: An Anthology* ed., Michael Copp (Madison, Teaneck: Fairleigh Dickinson University Press; London: Associated University Press, 2001), 251.

62 Siegfried Sassoon, *Siegfried Sassoon's Diaries: 1915-1918*, ed. Rupert Hart-Davis, (London: Faber and Faber, 1983), 183-84.

63 Siegfried Sassoon, *Complete Memoirs of George Sherston* (London: Faber & Faber Ltd, 1949), 557.

A Rendezvous with Death: American Verse and Negotiations with Trauma / Shell Shock

In transatlantic poetry the common experiences of pain, irritation and struggle inspired verse, which though occasionally amusing, underlines the perennial stress and enduring capacity of the soldiers at the front. An American soldier amusingly referring to the human "body" as a "busy cootie mart" in his poem, asserts that the parasite does not discriminate between any nationality: "He dotes on Yank and French / And the English in the trench. . . ."[64] At a more literary level, the British poet Isaac Rosenberg wonderfully explores the excruciating annoyance of lice and flea in the trenches in his poems "Louse Hunting" and "The Immortals." In the latter, Rosenberg directly sketches his plight with humour: "I used to think the Devil hid / In women's smiles and wine's carouse. / I called him Satan, Beelzebub. / But now I call him, dirty louse."[65] As Neil Corcoran observes, in Rosenberg's verse:

> . . . we gain access to such things as the distressed insomnia of being conveyed to war "Grotesque" and "queerly huddled" in "The Troop Ship"; the unendurable irritation of being lousy and flea-riddled, outstandingly defined in "Louse Hunting" (Rosenberg at least once slept naked in the rain rather than endure his lousy clothing any longer); and the queasy repugnance and self-disgust of being a stretcher-bearer or a member of a burying party in "Dead Man's Dump". That poem makes its raw report ("A man's brain's splattered on / A stretcher-bearer's face") even as it discovers an enduring conceit for being shot to death.[66]

---

64   Anonymous as cited in George Brown, *An American Soldier in World War I* ed., David L.Snead (Lincoln & London: University of Nebraska Press, 2006), 51.

65   Isaac Rosenberg, *The Selected Poems of Isaac Rosenberg* ed. Jean M Wilson (London: Cecil Woolf, 2003) 47.

66   Neil Corcoran, "Isaac Rosenberg" in *The Cambridge Companion to the Poetry of the First World War.* 113.

Akin to British soldier poets like Isaac Rosenberg, Edward Thomas, or Wilfred Owen, the American combatant poet Joyce Kilmer was also killed in the Great War. Having enlisted for the New York National Guard, he was deployed to France with the 69th Infantry Regiment in 1917 and was killed by a sniper's bullet at the Second Battle of the Marne in 1918, aged 31. Most of Kilmer's poems were published in his third and final volume *Main Street and Other Poems* (1917). This volume contained World War I poems such as "The White Ships and the Red" (inspired by Kilmer's outrage over the sinking of the "Lusitania"), "Rouge Bouquet" and "Prayer of a Soldier in France." Each of these poems balances an acknowledgment of the pain and trauma with a deep conviction that a war fought valiantly and nobly for a cause can bring about redemption. These themes recur in his final poem "The Peacemaker" which he wrote in France just prior to his death in July 1918. This Petrarchan sonnet uses irony and paradox to contend that by acquiescing himself to suffering in the war, the combatant redeems himself, much in the model of the crucified Christ, paving the way for life and resurrection out of death. The ironies in the octave of the sonnet— especially the lines "That Pain may cease, he yields his flesh to pain/ To banish war, he must a warrior be."—are resolved in the sestet, especially through an assonant decree on liberty:

What Matters death, if Freedom be not dead?
No flags are fair, if Freedom's flag be furled.
Who fights for freedom, goes with joyful tread
To meet the fires of Hell against him hurled,
And had for Captain Hun whose thorn-wreathed head
Smiles from the Cross upon a conquered world.[67]

---

67 Joyce Kilmer, *Poems, Essays and Letters*, edited with a memoir by Robert Cortes Holliday (New York: George H Doran Co 1917), 108.

In his poem "Prayer of a Soldier in France" written in 1918, Kilmer, like Owen, echoes Keats's "Ode to a Nightingale:" "My shoulders ache beneath my pack / (Lie easier, Cross, upon His back). / I march with feet that burn and smart / (Tread, Holy Feet, upon my heart)."[68] The reconciliation, as in the earlier poem, is achieved again through the identification with Christ. Religious consolation here serves as a means of negotiating with the horrors of the war:

> My rifle hand is stiff and numb
> (From Thy pierced palm red rivers come).
> Lord, Thou didst suffer more for me
> Than all the hosts of land and sea.
> So let me render back again
> This millionth of Thy gift. Amen.[69]

The most notable of Kilmer's poems is perhaps "Rouge Bouquet" which elegized the deaths of traumatized combatants of his regiment in American trench positions in the Rouge Bouquet forest, northeast of the French village of Baccarat. During the course of the war, it was a relatively quiet sector of the Front, but the first battalion was struck by a German heavy artillery bombardment on the afternoon of 7 March 1918 that resulted in heavy casualties:

> In a wood they call the Rouge Bouquet
> There is a new-made grave to-day,
> Built by never a spade nor pick
> Yet covered with earth ten metres thick.

---

68   Ibid., 109.

69   Ibid., 109.

> There lie many fighting men,
> Dead in their youthful prime,
> Never to laugh nor love again
> Nor taste the Summertime.[70]

These lines seem to resonate with the loss of youth portrayed in Owen's poems. However, unlike Owen, during his tenure as a soldier, Kilmer sought more challenging assignments involving hazardous duties on the Front. Writing to his wife from France he remarked "I am having a delightful time out here—absolutely beautiful country and very nice people."[71]

Kilmer's poetry offers an interesting contrast to the other American combatant poet of the Great War, Alan Seeger. Subsequent to graduating from Harvard in 1912, Seeger left for Mexico and Europe before settling down in Paris as a poet, joining the French Foreign Legion in 1915. His correspondence with his parents and occasional articles in journals reveal an intense sense of belonging and commitment towards France as a nation. Justifying his participation in the war, Alan Seeger spoke for many in his article in *The New Republic* in 1915:

> I have talked with so many of the young volunteers here. Their case is little known, even by the French, yet altogether interesting and appealing . . . Paris—mystic, maternal, personified, to whom they owed the happiest moments of their lives—Paris was in peril. Were they not under a moral obligation, no less binding than their comrades were bound legally, to put their breasts between her and destruction? Without renouncing their nationality they had yet chosen, to make their homes here beyond any other city in the world. Did not the benefits and the

---

70 Ibid., 105.

71 Ibid., 167.

blessings they had received point them a duty that heart and conscience could not deny?[72]

Seeger was killed in action on 4 July 1916, at the village of Belloy-en-Santerre while encouraging his fellow soldiers in a successful retaliatory offensive after being struck several times by machine gun fire. During his two years of service Seeger composed a set of soldier's sonnets, a number of longer lyrics, and two public poems, one prodding and persuading Americans to join the Great War, the other memorializing the sacrifice of the war dead. Most of his manuscripts were collected by his friends and published posthumously in 1916. However, the traditional diction of the poems and their uncritical approval of the war led to the relegation and marginalization of his work in the post-war literary landscape. As Fussell observes: "The best known American poem of the war, Alan Seeger's 'I Have a Rendezvous with Death' operates without allusion, without the social instinct to invite a number of canonical poems into its vicinity for comparison or ironic contrast." Comparing Seeger's poem with some of his British counterparts, like Blunden's "Vlamertinghe: Passing the Chateau, July, 1917," Herbert Read's "The Happy Warrior," and Wilfred Owen's "Exposure," Fussell dismisses Seeger's poem as "unresonant" and "inadequate for irony."[73] Yet any discussion of American poetry of the First World War must acknowledge "I have a Rendezvous with Death." Seeger negotiated with his trauma by exploring a romanticized notion of the violent war. The poem's flowing lyricism resonates with the romantic zeal of sacrifice for the larger freedom of humanity, much in tune with the passion and zest of the pro-war sonnets composed by Rupert Brooke. Ironically, like Brooke, Seeger too voiced his deep desire to end his life gloriously at an early age:

---

72   Alan Seeger, "As a Soldier Thinks of War," *The New Republic*, May 22, 1915. 66.

73   Fussell, 158.

> God knows 'twere better to be deep
> Pillowed in silk and scented down,
> Where love throbs out in blissful sleep,
> Pulse nigh to pulse, and breath to breath,
> Where hushed awakenings are dear.
> But I've a rendezvous with Death
> At midnight in some flaming town,
> When Spring trips north again this year,
> And I to my pledged word am true,
> I shall not fail that rendezvous.[74]

The entire poem juxtaposes the lure of life with the romanticized notion of death and duty. There is a deeper sense of transcendence in the poet's silent transit to the "dark land." The season of spring appears with its "rustling shade," "apple blossoms," "meadow flowers," perhaps in an implied contrast with the larger threat of obliteration of the trenches. The idyllic and occasional sublime allusions to human love tend to underline what the reader has to relinquish for the call of duty and sacrifice. In sharp contrast to Rupert Brooke's war sonnets, this romantic notion of the war, in most of Seeger's poems is fused with a deep sense of fatality and irrevocable destiny.

Despite his idealized notion of war, some of Seeger's poems recognize the trauma and futility of the conflict. In "The Hosts" the speaker's concern for nature leads to transcendence. The "fair horizons full of light" in the poem, indicate a liberating sublimity: "With bayonets and flags unfurled, / They scaled the summits of the world/ And fade on the farthest golden height/ In fair horizons full of light."[75] In "The Aisne (1914-15)" the images of nature are dark and sombre, indicating the hostility of nature: "Winter

---

74   Alan Seeger, *Poems*, Introduced by William Archer (New York: Charles Scribner's Sons, 1917), 144.

75   Ibid., 138.

came down to us. The low clouds, torn / In the dark branches of the river pines, / Blurred the white rockets that from dusk till morn / Traced the wide curve of the close-grappling lines."[76] Seeger's evocation of nature in this poem is quite similar to that of Wilfred Owen's "Exposure" or "Spring Offensive," where nature does not offer traditional nostalgic succour. On the contrary, it functions as a hostile deceptive force, closely aligned with the forces of violence unleashed by the war.

Besides the soldier poets, several British and American writers volunteered in the war as ambulance drivers or participated in other miscellaneous allied activities in close proximity to the Front. The war also witnessed casualties among the ambulance drivers. For transatlantic writers such as John Dos Passos, Malcolm Cowley, Sidney Howard, Julian Green, John Masefield, Russell Davenport, and Somerset Maugham, enlisting as an ambulance driver sometimes served as a substitute for being unable to join the army.

At eighteen years old, Ernest Hemingway volunteered to serve in Italy as an ambulance driver with the American Red Cross, having failed to qualify for the U.S. army. In July 1918 while running a mobile canteen for the combatants, Hemingway was wounded by Austrian mortar fire near the village of Fossalta, on the Piave river. "Then there was a flash, as when a blast-furnace door is swung open, and a roar that started white and went red . . . I tried to breathe, but my breath would not come,"[77] he recalled. Despite his injuries Hemingway carried a wounded Italian soldier to safety and was injured again by machine gun fire. The mortar round blew off his kneecap and forced him to wear a rubber support for the rest of his life. According to Hemingway's biographer Michael Reynolds, the month-long experience at

---

76   Seeger, 131.

77   Earnest Hemingway, *Hemingway on War* (New York: Scribner 2003) xxi.

the front made him learn "all he would ever need to know about war."[78] He asserts that "one did not need years in the trenches to know fear, to dream residual nightmares, to remember always one's brief test of nerve, to smell again the sweet odour of one's own blood."[79] For his bravery Hemingway received the Silver Medal of Valor, the Croce di Guerra from the Italian government—one of the first Americans to be so honoured. Commenting on this experience years later in *Men at War,* Hemingway wrote: "When you got to war as a boy you have a great illusion of immortality. Other people get killed; not you. It can happen to other people; but not to you . . . Then when you are badly wounded the first time you lose that illusion and you know it can happen to you."[80]

Though Hemingway famously captures the temper of post-war enervation in works like *In Our Time* and *The Sun Also Rises,* his experimentations in verse (inspired by personal experiences of the conflict) paved the way for a new means of negotiating with war time trauma. In poems such as "Captives," "Champs d' Honneur," "D'Annunzio," and "Shock Troops," he captured his first-hand observations. "Captives" echoes the state of physical and mental exhaustion of the soldiers almost echoing "Dulce Et Decorum Est:" "Some came in chains / Unrepentant but tired. / Too tired but to stumble / Thinking and hating were finished. / Thinking and fighting were finished. / Cures this a long campaign, / Making death easy."[81] In "Champs d' Honneur," the soldiers "smother in a ditch" as they choke to death and sink into annihilation. In this poem, Hemingway responds to Alan Seeger's allusion to "that rare chance of

---

78 Michael Reynolds, *Hemingway: The Paris Years* (New York, London: W.W. Norton & Company, 1989; paperback, 1999), 56.

79 Reynolds, 56.

80 Ernest Hemingway, *Introduction to Men at War* (Based on a play by William Kozlenko), (Berkley: Crown Publishers, 1942), 7.

81 Ernest Hemingway, *The Collected Poems of Ernest Hemingway* (New York: Haskell House Publishers Ltd, 1970), 20. www.worldwar1/.com/heritage/hemingway.htm.

dying well" in the following lines: "Soldiers never do die well; / Crosses mark the places— / Wooden crosses where they fell, / Stuck above their faces."[82] Hemingway further echoes Owen in the lines: "Soldiers pitch and cough and twitch— / All the world roars red and black; / Soldiers smother in a ditch, / Choking through the whole attack."[83] Hemingway uses tough unromantic language to convey his message, and even the crosses are not placed but are merely "stuck." Perhaps Hemingway's most vivid description of shell shock is in "Killed Piave - July 8, 1918," in which the war returns to haunt the witness:

> Desire and
> All the sweet pulsing aches
> And gentle hurtings
> That were you,
> Are gone into the sullen dark.
> Now in the night you come unsmiling
> To lie with me
> A dull, cold, rigid bayonet
> On my hot-swollen, throbbing soul.[84]

In "All armies are the same . . . ,"[85] Hemingway reflects upon the dissipated state of the shell-shocked combatants: "Old soldiers all have tired eyes / All soldiers hear the same old lies / Dead bodies have always drawn flies."[86] Corresponding with his family members from Milan, while recuperating from the trench mortar wounds, Hemingway gives a candid expression to his experience of "hell" during the First World War:

---

82 Hemingway, Collected Poems . . . , 21.
83 Ibid.
84 https://www.poemhunter.com/poem/killed-paive-july-8-1918/ .
85 https://allpoetry.com/-All-armies-are-the-same.
86 Ibid.

You know they say there isn't anything funny about this war and there isn't. I wouldn't say it was hell, because that's been a bit overworked since Gen. Sherman's time, but there have been about 8 times when I would have welcomed Hell. Just on the chance that it couldn't come up to the phase of war I was experiencing. For example. In the trenches during an attack when a shell makes a direct hit in a group where you are standing. Shells aren't bad except direct hits. You must take chances on the fragments of the bursts. But when there is a direct hit your pals get spattered all over you. Spattered is literal. During the six days I was up in the Front line trenches, only 50 yds from the Austrians, I got the rep. of having a charmed life. The rep of having one doesn't mean much but having one does! I hope I have one. That knocking sound is my knuckles striking the wooden bed tray.

Hemingway's portrayal of "hell" reminds the reader of Gurney's "Strange Hells," a poem that initiates this critical discussion on transatlantic verse and shell shock. Negotiations of shell shock in verse, as explored in this essay, underline the deep sense of trauma and vulnerability that characterize most responses in verse. A looming spectre of disenchantment seems to unite the myriad voices of verse from both sides of the Atlantic. More significantly, this large body of verse chronicles the larger emotional crisis at the threshold of the twentieth century, as poets struggled to negotiate, explore, and articulate the psychological devastation and horror unleashed by the first instance of modern technological warfare. This psychological desolation even left its mark in the post-war cynicism and disillusionment which continued to pervade most verse composed in the decades immediately following the war.

BIBLIOGRAPHY

Bertholf, Robert J. "'The salty taste of glory': Some American Poetry of World War I." *Gravesiana: The Journal of the Robert Graves Society*, vol. IV, no. 1, 2014, https://download/the-salty-taste-of-glory-some-american-poetry-of-world-war-i-robert-j-bertholf.

Brown, George. *An American Soldier in World War I*, edited by David L. Snead, University of Nebraska Press, 2006.

Campbell, Patrick. *Siegfried Sassoon: A Study of the War Poetry*. McFarland & Company Inc Publishers, 1999.

Cole, Sarah. "Siegfried Sassoon." *The Cambridge Companion to the Poetry of the First World War*, edited by Santanu Das, Cambridge University Press, 2013, pp. 94-104

Corcoran, Neil. "Isaac Rosenberg." *The Cambridge Companion to the Poetry of the First World War,* edited by Santanu Das, Cambridge University Press, 2013, pp. 105-116.

Das, Santanu. "'Dulce Et Decorum Est', a close reading." *The British Library*, 23 June 2017, https://www.bl.uk/20th-century-literature/articles/a-close-reading-of-dulce-etdecorum-est.

---. *The Cambridge Companion to the Poetry of the First World War.* Cambridge University Press, 2013.

Dayton, Tim. "'Sammy's right there, shoulder deep in the mess!' American Literature & the First World War." *Against the Current,* vol. 31, no. 2, May/June 2016, p. 32.

Fussell, Paul. *The Great War and Modern Memory.* Oxford University Press, 1975, rpt. 2000.

Graves, Robert. *Complete Poems,* vol. 1, edited by Beryl Graves, Dunstan Ward, Carcanet Press, 1999, https://www.poemhunter.com/poem/haunted-56/, Accessed July 20, 1918.

Gurney, Ivor. *Collected Poems.* Edited by P.J. Kavanagh. Oxford University Press, 1982.

---. "Ballad of the Three Spectres." *The Wordsworth Book of First World War Poetry,* edited by Marcus Clapham, Hertforshire, Wordsworth Editions Limited, 1995.

Hemingway, Ernest. *Hemingway on War.* Scribner, 2003.

---. Introduction to *Men at War.* Crown Publishers, 1942.

---. *The Collected Poems of Ernest Hemingway.* Haskell House Publishers Ltd, 1970, www.worldwar1.com/heritage/hemingway.htm.

---. *Selected Letters 1917-1961.* Edited by Carlos Baker, Scribner Classics, 1981.

---. https://www.poemhunter.com/poem/killed-paive-july-8-1918/. Accessed July 20, 2018. https://allpoetry.com/-All-armies-are-the-same. Accessed June 19, 2018.

Hipp, Daniel. *The Poetry of Shell Shock: Wartime Trauma and Healing in Wilfred Owen, Ivor Gurney and Siegfried Sassoon.* McFarland & Company Inc. Publishers, 2005.

Hughes, Langston. *The Collected Works of Langston Hughes.* vol. 1, edited with an introduction by Arnold Rampersad, University of Missouri Press, 2001.

---. "The Colored Soldier." *The Collected Poems of Langston Hughes,* edited by Arnold Rampersad, Vintage, 1995.

Kilmer, Joyce. *Poems, Essays and Letters*. Edited with a memoir by Robert Cortes Holliday, George H. Doran Co., 1917.

Loughran, Tracy. "Shell Shock, Trauma, and the First World War: The Making of a Diagnosis and Its Histories." *Journal of the History of Medicine and Allied Sciences*, vol. 67, no. 1, January 2012, https://doi.org/10.1093/jhmas/jrq052, pp. 94-119.

MacKaye, Percy. *Poems and Plays*. vol. 1, Macmillan, 1916.

Matthews, John. "American Writing of the Great War." *The Cambridge Companion to the Literature of the First World War*, edited by Vincent Sherry, Cambridge University Press, 2005, pp. 217-244.

Monroe, Harriet. "Will Art Happen?" *Poetry*, vol. 10, no. 4, 1917.

---. "War Poetry Again." *Poetry*. Vol.12, no.5, 1918.

Myers, Charles. "A Contribution to the Study of Shell Shock." *The Lancet*, vol. 185, no. 4772, 13 Feb 1915, pp. 316-330.

Norgate, Paul. "Shell Shock and Poetry: Wilfred Owen at Craiglockhart Hospital." *English*, vol. 36, 1987, pp. 1-35.

"Notice." *The Wiper Times* or *Salient News*, vol. 2, no. 4, 20 March 1916.

Owen, Wilfred. *The Collected Poems of Wilfred Owen*. Edited by C. Day Lewis and with a Memoir by Edmund Blunden, New Directions Publishing Corporation, 1965.

Owen, Wilfred. *Collected Letters*. Edited by Harold Owen and John Bell, Oxford University Press, 1967.

Owen, Wilfred. *Wilfred Owen: Selected Letters*. Edited by John Bell, Oxford University Press, 1985.

Pound, Ezra. *Collected Shorter Poems*. Faber & Faber, 1968.

Puissant, Susanne Christine. *Irony and the Poetry of the First World War.* Palgrave Macmillan, 2009.

Reynolds, Michael. *Hemingway: The Paris Years.* W.W. Norton & Company, 1999.

Richards, Anthony. "How First World War poetry painted a truer picture." *The Telegraph,* 28 February 2014, www.telegraph.co.uk/history/world-war-one/inside-first-world-war/part-seven/10667204/first-world-war-poetry-sassoon.html.

Rives, Timothy D. "The Work of Soldier Poetry in Kansas, 1917-1919." *New Directions in Folklore,* no. 7 (Special Issue Military Folklore), 2003, https://scholarworks.iu.edu/journals/index.php/ndif/article download/19890/25960.

Rosenberg, Isaac. *The Selected Poems of Isaac Rosenberg.* Edited by Jean M Wilson, London, Cecil Woolf, 2003.

Sandburg, Carl. "Grass." *Poetry Foundation,* https://www.poetryfoundation.org/poems/45034/grass56d2245e2201c.

---. *The Complete Poems of Carl Sandburg.* Harcourt, Inc. 1970.

Sassoon, Siegfried. *Siegfried's Journey.* Viking, 1945.

---. *Sherston's Progress.* Faber & Faber, 1936.

---. Appendix B, *Cambridge Poets of the Great War: An Anthology.* Edited by Michael Copp Madison, Teaneck, Fairleigh Dickinson University Press; London, Associated University Press, 2001.

---. *Siegfried Sassoon's Diaries: 1915-1918.* Edited by Rupert Hart-Davis, Faber & Faber, 1983.

---. *Complete Memoirs of George Sherston.* Faber & Faber, 1949.

---. *War Poems of Siegfried Sassoon.* Dover Publications Inc., 2004.

Seeger, Alan. "As a Soldier Thinks of War," *The New Republic*, May 22, 1915.

---. *Letters and Diary*, 10 May 1915. *A Rendezvous with Death: Alan Seeger in Poetry, at War*, Chris Dickon, Wickford, New Street Communications, 2017.

---. *Poems.* Introduced by William Archer, Charles Scribner's Sons, 1917.

Simcox, Kenneth. http://www.wilfredowen.org.uk/poetry/deadbeat.

Stallworthy, Jon. *Wilfred Owen.* Oxford University Press and Chatto Windus, 1974.

---. *Wilfred Owen: Chatterton Lecture on an English Poet.* British Academy, vol. lvi, Oxford University Press, 1970.

Thorpe, Adam. "Strange Hells." *The Guardian*, 10 November 2007, https://www.theguardian.com/books/2007/nov/10/featuresreviews.guardianreview4.

Twells, Brex. "A Serious Outbreak of Poets," *The Daily Mail*, 23 June 1915.

Tylee, Claire M. *The Great War and Women's Consciousness.* Macmillan, 1990.

Walter, George. Introduction to *The Penguin Book of First World War Poetry.* Edited by George Walter. Penguin, 2006.

Webb, Thomas E. F. "Dottyville—C.W. Hospital and shell-shock treatment in First World War." *Journal of the Royal Society of Medicine*, vol. 99 no. 7, July 2006, pp. 342-346.

Wienen, Mark W Van. ed. *Rendezvous with Death: American Poems of the Great War.* University of Illinois Press, 2002.

Wyeth, John Allan. *This Man's Army: A War in Fifty-odd Sonnets.* University of South Carolina, 2008.

Dr. Argha Kumar Banerjee is currently the Dean of Arts, St. Xavier's College (Autonomous), under Calcutta University. He was a Commonwealth Research Scholar at the Department of English, Sussex University, U.K. where he wrote his doctoral dissertation on poetry of the First World War. Recipient of the Charles Wallace Fellowship to the U.K., his published books include *Female Voices in Keats's Poetry* (2002), *Poetry of the First World War: A Critical Evaluation* (2011), and *Women's Poetry and the First World War* (2014).

"FLESH AND BLOOD IS WEAK AND FRAIL, SUSCEPTIBLE TO NERVOUS SHOCK"

T. S. Eliot, Shell Shock, and the First World War

Qiang Huang

Abstract

As has been explored in Wyatt Bonikowski's *Shell Shock and the Modernist Imagination: the Death Drive in Post-World War I British Fiction* (2013), the phenomenon of shell shock, as well as shell-shocked soldiers, has been aestheticized in some modernist fictions, such as Ford Madox Ford's *Parade's End* (1924-1928), Rebecca West's *The Return of the Soldier* (1918), and Virginia Woolf's *Mrs. Dalloway* (1925). However, the topic of shell shock is seldom associated with Eliot's writings during the Great War in the previous studies. Thus, drawing upon Eliot's biography during the Great War, my study explores both the ways in which the phenomenon of shell shock becomes a literary theme in Eliot's wartime writings and how Eliot responds to the War in his poems. In doing so, I would like to suggest in this chapter that the Great War exerts a perceptible impact on both Eliot's life and his writings, while the War becomes a literary theme in his contemporary poems, challenging the existing point of view that Eliot wartime poetry was silent about the war.

AS Wyatt Bonikowski has demonstrated, the phenomenon of shell shock has been aestheticized in many modernist novels, such as Ford Madox Ford's *Parade's End* tetralogy (1924-1928), Rebecca West's *The Return of the Soldier* (1918), and Virginia Woolf's *Mrs. Dalloway* (1925). However, the topic of shell shock is seldom associated with T. S. Eliot's writings during the Great War. Through readings of a number of newly-published materials on Eliot's life and writings during the Great War, this study will explore the ways in which Eliot was involved in the War, and then contextualise Eliot's wartime writings in the contemporary period in an attempt to challenge the existing point of view that Eliot's wartime poetry was "silent about the war."[1] Rather, I ultimately suggest that Eliot, consciously or otherwise, responded to the War in his poetry by taking the phenomena of gas shells and shell shock as literary themes.

When the Great War broke out in the summer of 1914, Eliot was attending a summer school in Marburg, Germany. After the summer school was cancelled, Eliot, as a foreign national, left Germany. On 21 August 1914, he arrived in London, "from which almost all its young men were withdrawn, and only the sick and unfit, the elderly, the women, the workers, and a few pacifist intellectuals—outcasts—remained."[2] After his arrival, Eliot

---

1   Hilda D. Spear, *Remembering, We Forget: A Background Study to the Poetry of the First World War* (London: Davis-Poynter, 1979), 41.

2   Lyndall Gordon, *T. S. Eliot: An Imperfect Life* (London: Vintage, 1998), 136.

often talked about the War in letters to his family and friends, and started to observe the War "from the estranged angle of a non-participant."[3] However, it did not take a long time for the War to leave "a very deep impression" on Eliot, who realized that "some of the towns" where he had visited had become battlefields, while some of his friends "must be fighting each other."[4] With the feeling that the once-familiar world had been transformed by the War into a different space, Eliot found it difficult to either "write interestingly about the war" or "adopt a wholly partisan attitude, or even to rejoice or despair wholeheartedly."[5] He felt unable to find an appropriate expression to describe the ongoing War. This inability to write about the War was a common phenomenon among writers at the time. John Gould Fletcher, for example, observed in December 1916 that no poet was ready to respond honestly to wartime feeling and experience due to the domestic partisan patriotic fervor.[6] On the other hand, the British government carried out a series of policies of strict censorship during the Great War.[7] As a result, it is difficult for Eliot, a non-combatant, to know many details of what was truly happening at the Front then, though he must have known "the gloom, the privation, and the deadness of London in those war years."[8] Being stuck in a country at war, Eliot felt that "the War suffocate[d]" him, while he did not "know [his] own plans for the future."[9] In wartime England, Eliot felt uncertain about his future, since everything became impossible to predict in the midst of war.

---

3   Ibid.

4   Valerie Eliot, ed., *The Letters of T. S. Eliot, vol. 1, 1898 – 1922* (London: Faber and Faber, 1988), 62.

5   Ibid.

6   John G. Fletcher, "On Subject-Matter and War Poetry," *Egoist* 3, no. 12 (1916), 188.

7   Peter Buitenhuis, *The Great War of Words: British, American, and Canadian Propaganda and Fiction, 1914-1933* (Vancouver: University of British Columbia Press, 1987), xvi. Randall Stevenson, *Literature and the Great War, 1914-1918* (Oxford: Oxford University Press, 2013), 24.

8   Gordon, *T. S. Eliot: An Imperfect Life*, 136.

9   Valerie Eliot, ed., *The Letters of T. S. Eliot, vol. 1, 1898 – 1922*, 95.

Eliot's downcast feeling towards the War arguably came through in one of his wartime writings, "The Hippopotamus" (1917). The poem was finished in 1917, and was first read to the public at a poetry reading at Sybil Colefax's house on 12 December 1917.[10] The poem has been widely considered as both Eliot's early poetic exploration of religious themes in terms of its biblical references, and a satirical poem questioning the moral principles of modern religion because of its juxtaposition of the gross mammalian body of a physical hippopotamus and the spiritual Church. According to Grover Smith, "the hippopotamus" represents "the weakness of the natural man, lukewarm in religious zeal but more acceptable to God than a disingenuous episcopacy," while the Church is the advocate of "the hypocritically austere."[11] However, the poem could also be related to the Great War, if it is understood in the contemporary context. In the first stanza, the speaker observes a "broad-backed hippopotamus," which "[r]ests on his belly in the mud" (2).[12] Later, the speaker makes it clear that the hippopotamus ascends from "the damp savannas" (26).[13] Although "savannas" had a potential eastern African or South American resonance, their damp landscapes and the lack of trees, I argue, evoke the famous, and infamous, "No Man's Land," and the trenches themselves, which were often inundated with mud. Due to the weather condition in winter, this area was often in a muddy and miry condition, which is similar to the condition of the place where the hippopotamus is resting in the poem. It could also be argued that the image of the marshy landscape alludes to Eliot's recollection of his deceased friend, Jean Verdenal. Verdenal was killed in the

---

10 Thomas S. Eliot, *The Poems of T. S. Eliot*, vol. 1, ed. Christopher Ricks and Jim McCue (London: Faber and Faber, 2015), 521.

11 Grover Smith, *T. S. Eliot's Poetry and Plays: A Study in Sources and Meaning* (Chicago: University of Chicago Press, 1956), 39-40.

12 Thomas S. Eliot, *The Complete Poems and Plays of T. S. Eliot* (London: Faber and Faber Limited, 1969), 49.

13 Ibid., 50.

Gallipoli Campaign on 2 May 1915 "while tending a wounded soldier on the battlefield."[14] Eliot mentioned Verdenal's death in a letter to Conrad Aiken on 10 January 1916.[15] Later, Verdenal's death became an important source to understand the opening lines of *The Waste Land* (1922).

> April is the cruellest month, breeding
> Lilacs out of the dead land, mixing
> Memory and desire, stirring
> Dull roots with spring rain. (1-4)[16]

This passage alludes to the General Prologue of Geoffrey Chaucer's *The Canterbury Tales*, but Eliot made it clear in April 1934 that his

> own retrospective is touched by a sentimental sunset, the memory of a friend coming across the Luxembourg Gardens in the late afternoon, waving a branch of lilac, a friend who was later (so far as I could find out) to be mixed with the mud of Gallipoli.[17]

Although Eliot did not specify the name of his friend, the description of his friend's death in Gallipoli shows that the unnamed friend was very likely Jean Verdenal.

In "The Hippopotamus," the second allusion to the battlefield scene is in the second stanza, in which the speaker makes a comparison between the fragile "[f]lesh and blood" and the solid foundation of the Church.[18]

---

14 Gordon, *T. S. Eliot: An Imperfect Life*, 137.
15 Valerie Eliot, ed., *The Letters of T. S. Eliot, vol. 1, 1898 – 1922*, 137.
16 Eliot, *The Complete Poems and Plays of T. S. Eliot*, 61.
17 Thomas S. Eliot, *The Criterion, 1922-1939, vol. XIII, October 1933 – July 1934* (London: Faber and Faber, 1967), 452.
18 Eliot, *The Complete Poems and Plays of T. S. Eliot*, 49.

> Flesh and blood is weak and frail,
> Susceptible to nervous shock;
> While the True Church can never fail
> For it is based upon a rock. (5-8)[19]

In the first half of this passage, the speaker points out the fragility of the "[f]lesh and blood." Their weakness is not only closely related with their corporeal body, but also signalled by their mental susceptibility to "nervous shock," a phenomenon shared by many soldiers who fought in the Great War. On the one hand, war exerts a destructive impact on soldier's corporeal bodies. It is likely that Eliot was aware that the soldiers were suffering physical hardships on the front line, and Eliot's limited knowledge of the frontline battlefield probably came from those who returned from the front, particularly his brother-in-law, Maurice Haigh-Wood.[20] Maurice graduated from Sandhurst Military Academy, and was commissioned as a second lieutenant in the 2nd Battalion, Manchester Regiment, Lincolnshire, on 11 May 1915. After Maurice was sent to France with his troop, he wrote several letters to the Eliots, describing the battlefield scenes. On 18 November 1915, Eliot told his mother about Maurice's front-line experiences:

> It seems very strange that a boy of nineteen should have such experiences—often twelve hours alone in his 'dug-out' in the trenches, and at night, when he cannot sleep, occupying himself by shooting rats with a revolver. What he tells about rats and vermin is incredible—Northern France is swarming, and the rats are as big as cats.[21]

---

19   Ibid.

20   According to Brian Bond, the leading national newspapers did not regularly publish casualty lists until the later stages of the war due to censorship. *The Unquiet Western Front: Britain's Role in Literature and History* (Cambridge: Cambridge University Press, 2002), 24.

21   Valerie Eliot, ed., *The Letters of T. S. Eliot, vol. 1, 1898 – 1922*, 132.

In September 1916, Maurice described the gory scenes on the Western Front in a letter to Eliot. On 17 June 1917, Eliot forwarded an extract of that letter to the editor of *The Nation*, who published it a week later. According to Maurice,

> [p]erhaps you are tempted to give them a picture of a leprous earth, scattered with the swollen and blackening corpses of hundreds of young men. The appalling stench of rotting carrion mingled with the sickening smell of exploded lyddite and ammonal. Mud like porridge, trenches like shallow and sloping cracks in the porridge—porridge that stinks in the sun. Swarms of flies and bluebottles clustering on pits of offal. Wounded men lying in the shell holes among the decaying corpses: helpless under the scorching sun and bitter nights, under repeated shelling. Men with bowels dropping out, lungs shot away, with blinded, smashed faces, or limbs blown into space. Men screaming and gibbering. Wounded men hanging in agony on the barbed wire, until a friendly spout of liquid fire shrivels them up like a fly in a candle.[22]

It is clear that Maurice's words gave Eliot a vivid description of the fragility of soldiers' bodies, and enabled the young American poet to know the cruelty of war and war's traumatic effect on human bodies. Besides, Eliot's knowledge of the tough frontline battlefield is explicitly shown in *The Waste Land*. As David Chinitz points out, the gruesome scene of "I think we are in rat's alley / Where the dead men lost their bones" (115-6) recalls the "reeks of the trenches and of the "No Man's Land" between them, where rats nightly devoured the corpses of the slain.[23]

22　Thomas, S. Eliot, Jewel Spears Brooker, and Ronald Schuchard, *The Complete Prose of T. S. Eliot: The Critical Edition: Apprentice Years, 1905 – 1918* (Baltimore: The Johns Hopkins UP, 2014), 547-8.

23　David E. Chinitz, "T. S. Eliot: *The Waste Land*," In *A Companion of Modernist Literature and Culture*, ed. David Bradshaw and Kevin J. H. Dettmar (Oxford: Blackwell Publishing Ltd., 2006), 326.

On the other hand, war also inflicts a torture on soldier's mental health. During the War, a great number of soldiers were affected by the "repeated shelling" on the Western Front.[24] Many of them suffered from shell shock, a common psychological illness caused by prolonged exposure to active warfare. According to Ben Shephard, by December 1914 a large number of British soldiers "were being evacuated from the British Expeditionary Force in Europe with 'nervous and mental shock,'" and "[s]ome 7-10% of all officers and 3-4% of all ranks [. . .] were being sent home suffering from nervous or mental breakdown."[25] In "The Hippopotamus," the image of "nervous shock," I suggest, might also exemplify Eliot's imagination of the Western Front, and allude to his reflections on war's impact on soldiers' physicality and mentality.

In "The Hippopotamus," Eliot's imagination of the front is primarily associated with his intention of satirising the modern Church, as he writes, "While the True Church can never fail/For it is based upon a rock" (7-8).[26] In this passage, the image of a church on a rock is a biblical reference, which is an affirmation of the stability of the Church. However, it also alludes to an innuendo about the modern Church when it is juxtaposed with the previous description of the fragility of the human body and mind. During the War, when human bodies were mutilated by the weapons of destruction, and when their minds were traumatized by the fear of bombardment, the Church seemed to be unaffected and continued to "gather in its dividends" (12), refreshed by "fruits of pomegranate and peach [. . .] from over sea" (15-6).[27] The image of "dividends," and the

---

24   Thomas, S. Eliot, Jewel Spears Brooker, and Ronald Schuchard. *The Complete Prose of T. S. Eliot: The Critical Edition: Apprentice Years, 1905 – 1918*, 548.

25   Ben Shephard, *A War of Nerves: Soldiers and Psychiatrists in the Twentieth Century* (Cambridge, Massachusetts: Harvard University Press, 2001), 21.

26   Eliot, *The Complete Poems and Plays of T. S. Eliot*, 49.

27   Ibid.

meter and rhyme scheme, have a source in Thomas Hood's comments on the charge of two shillings to see Poets' Corner at Westminster Abbey: "The profitable Abbey is / A sacred change for stony stock, / Not that a speculation 'tis— / The profit's founded on a rock."[28] For the speaker, the pecuniary motives have to some degree degraded the Church from a sacred institution to a corrupted organization. Besides, the juxtaposition between the Church and the image of "pomegranate" again subtly implies a satirical attitude toward the Church, as the image of "pomegranate," possibly a word-play, reminds readers of the explosive grenade, which was widely used in the Great War. The etymology of the word "grenade" is derived from the Old French word, "pomegranate," in that the shape of a grenade resembles that of a pomegranate. The Mills bomb, the first modern fragmentation grenade, was used by British front-line troops during the War. According to Brian Murdoch, the image of the grenade was also written in some English poems of functional hostility, published by trench magazine and used on all fronts.[29] If the image of "pomegranate" symbolizes a destructive weapon, its juxtaposition with the Church seems to do suggest that it is impossible for the Church to restore its strength or vigour by refreshing itself with "pomegranate." In "The Hippopotamus," another example that satirises the modern Church is the image of "quiring angels" (27).[30] In the poem, "quiring angels" are around the "Hippopotamus," singing "[t]he praise of God, in loud hosannas" (28).[31] Superficially, this passage presents a harmonious scene of a group of angels surrounding the "hippopotamus," praising God. However, Eliot chose the word "quiring" instead of the word "choiring." His choice of words creates a foreground effect, and the first

---

28   Francis J. Child, *The British Poets, vol. 4*. (London: Forgotten Books, 2013), 289.

29   Brian Murdoch, *Fighting Songs and Warring Words: Popular Lyrics of Two World Wars* (London: Routledge, 1990), 32.

30   Eliot, *The Complete Poems and Plays of T. S. Eliot*, 50.

31   Ibid.

two letters of the word "quiring" remind readers of the image of "quacks" in one of Eliot's earlier poems, "A Fable for Feasters" (1905). It seems to suggest that the angels around the "hippopotamus" are like the "monks" in "A Fable for Feasters," who are "the quacks" (2), since they are "quiring" instead of "choiring."[32]

In the final stanza, the speaker's satire on the modern Church comes to an end with a description of the environment around the Church: While the True Church remains below / Wrapt in the old miasmal mist." (35-6). "[T]he True Church" is surrounded by the harmful vaporous exhalation, which suggests a corruptive influence from the external. By locating the Church in a "miasmal" atmosphere, Eliot reaffirmed his satire on the Church in this poem. However, I suggest that the image of "miasmal mist" in this passage could be considered an allusion to the poisonous gas when the context of the Great War is taken into account. During the War, all of the major belligerents used lethal gases, such as chlorine and phosgene, as an effective weapon in their military actions, often on a large scale. The use of poisonous gases caused a large number of casualties on the battlefield, while it also became a literary theme in some contemporary writings, such as Wilfred Owen's "Dulce et Decorum est" (1917).

In retrospect, Eliot knew of the use of poisonous sulphuric gases, as he mentioned gas, or the major chemical components of poisonous gas, in one of his post-World War I prose works: "Tradition and the Individual Talent" (1919). In the essay, Eliot emphasizes that originality in literature is compatible with a poet's learning from literary tradition and literary predecessors in that "the whole of the literature of Europe [. . .] has a simultaneous existence and composes a simultaneous order."[33] In order to indicate the role of a poet in the process of writing, he used a metaphor of catalyst, writing that "[w]hen the two gases previously mentioned [oxygen

---

32 Ibid., 587.

33 Thomas, S. Eliot, Jewel Spears Brooker, and Ronald Schuchard, *The Complete Prose of T. S. Eliot: The Critical Edition: Apprentice Years, 1905 – 1918*, 106.

and sulphur dioxide] are mixed in the presence of a filament of platinum, they form sulphurous acid."[34] It is clear that Eliot's analogy is not correct in that there is an error with the product of the chemical reaction.[35] However, the chemicals in this analogy, particularly "sulphur dioxide" and "sulphurous acid," have close connections with the production of poisonous sulphurous gases in the Great War. Sulphur is an important component in Mustard gas, also known as sulphur mustard, which was first used by the German army against British and Canadian soldiers near Ypres in 1917. Besides, before mustard gas was deployed in the war, "sulphur dioxide" had already been used by the Germans in the Second Battle of Ypres against the 1st Canadian Division on 24 April 1915.

It is possible for Eliot to become familiar with such chemicals as "sulphur dioxide" and "sulphurous acid" during the War, because British newspapers at the time often published reports on the use of poisonous gas during the War, while the rumour that the Germans planned to use mustard gas bombs to attack Britain even caused a panic in British society. On 26 April 1915, *The Times* reported German's use of "asphyxiating gases in his attacks upon the Allies," and explained the "nature of the asphyxiating gas."[36] On 30 April 1915, *The Times* published another report "The Poisonous Gas Zone," in which it condemned Germany for its violation of international law, and listed the types of gases, including "chlorine, vapour of formol, nitrous vapours, and sulphurous anhydride, and a gas not yet determined."[37] In the following three years, the news regarding military sulphurous gases were often mentioned in *The Times*.[38] On 10 September 1917, *The Times*

---

34 Ibid., 109.

35 Valerie Eliot and John Haffenden, eds., *The Letters of T. S. Eliot, vol. 3, 1926 – 1927* (London: Faber and Faber, 2012), 212-3.

36 "The Attack North Of Ypres," *Times*, April 26, 1915.

37 "The Poisonous Gas Zone," *Times*, April 30, 1915.

38 "Another Summit Captured," *Times*, June 28, 1915. "Another Defeat In Verdun Zone," *Times*,

published "Mustard Gas," which was an official statement of the Secretary and War office. The statement aimed to quash the rumor that the ordinary gas mask did not "give complete protection against this gas," and to ensure civilians that they would be able to protect themselves with gas masks when mustard gas bombs were dropped in England.[39] All of those newspaper reports not only enabled those living in Great Britain to know about the poisonous gas, but also reflect the pervasive anxieties about a potential gas attack in England. Thus, I speculate that Eliot might gain knowledge of the lethal gas, though limited, through wartime newspaper reports. If that is the case, when he was writing "the True Church" is "wrapt in the old miasmal mist," Eliot suggested not only his intention of satirising the degradation of the modern Church, but also the idea that the degradation of the Church was closely related to the ongoing war.

Furthermore, two of his following poems of 1918 also suggest an imagination of the Front. In "Sweeney among the Nightingales," when the image of "Apeneck Sweeney" is contextualized in the Great War, the description of the protagonist with a simian look arguably recalls the appearance of a soldier wearing a gas mask. As has been mentioned, all the major belligerents carried out gas attacks during the First World War, and the gas attacks resulted in heavy casualties among both the Allies and the Central Powers. As a countermeasure to gas attacks, a variety of gas masks were employed on the front line during the War. At the same time, gas mask imagery was often shown in newspapers, such as *The Times*, so that the general public on the Home Front was familiar with the image of a gas mask.[40] When a soldier is wearing a gas mask, his face is hidden from both his enemies and his companions, and "the changing appearance

---

March 21, 1916.

39   "Mustard Gas," *Times*, September 10, 1917.

40   "Gas Bombs," *Times*, March 26, 1915.

of soldiers seemed to confirm a hardening inhumanity at the time."[41] The bizarre and somewhat bestial masks suggest the danger posed by the war, since soldiers have to "degrade" themselves into animalistic creatures so as to survive the frequent poison gas attacks. During the War, human beings have been degraded to what Julia Kristeva calls the *abject*, epitomized by the animalistic image of Sweeney in this poem. Neither man nor matter, neither wholly human nor bestial, Sweeney becomes a powerful example of the *abject*, and "confronts us [. . .] with those fragile states where man strays on the territories of animal."[42] This phenomenon has been noted by many poets of the First World War. Siegfried Sassoon observed that gas masks turned his companions into "grotesque goggle-faced creatures."[43] Likewise, Edmund Blunden considers that the introduction of gas masks symbolised "the change that was coming over the war, the induration from a personal crusade into a vast machine of violence."[44] In "Sweeney Among the Nightingales," Sweeney's posture resembles the sub-human creature with a mask, and its juxtaposition with the image of "arms" implicitly suggests a connection between him and a soldier.

Likewise, it could be argued that an imagination of the battlefield was suggested in Eliot's other "Sweeney" poem, "Sweeney Erect" (1919). The poem was published in *Art and Letter* in the summer of 1919, but it was considered to be finished between 1917 and 1918.[45] Despite being a wartime poem, the major theme of "Sweeney Erect" is not war, and it has been widely considered as Eliot's reflection on modern human sexuality. In the poem, Sweeney's sexuality does not generate any meaning. This to some

---

41   Stevenson, *Literature and the Great War, 1914-1918*, 213.

42   Julia Kristeva, *Power of Horror: An Essay on Abjection*, trans. Leon S. Roudiez (New York: Columbia University Press, 1982), 12.

43   Siegfried Sassoon, *The Complete Memoirs of George Sherston* (London: Faber and Faber, 1949), 257.

44   Edmund Blunden, *Undertones of War* (Harmondsworth: Penguin, 1986), 53.

45   Thomas S. Eliot, *The Poems of T. S. Eliot, Vol. 1*, 497.

extent prefigures Eliot's two later poems, *The Waste Land* and "Gerontion," which display that one primary characteristic of what Eliot saw as the problem of modernity is mechanized intercourse without any meaning and of course without reproduction. "Sweeney Erect" starts with the speaker's depiction of a majestic picture of a mythic shore, which suggests the poem's connection with classical Hellenistic culture. However, the image of "the insurgent gales" (6) in the second stanza also is considered by Vincent Sherry as an allusion to the contemporary Irish insurrection.[46] According to Sherry, the image of "the insurgent gales" invites readers to associate it with "the insurgent Gaels," and argues that the juxtaposition of the protagonist Sweeney and his rising from the sheets in steam again suggests a connection with the Easter Rising in 1916.[47] Drawing upon Sherry's association between this poem and Irish politics, I would like to further suggest that the poem might have a more complex, though subtle, connection with the theme of war. On the one hand, "Sweeney Erect" retains the image of apeneck Sweeney which appears in "Sweeney Among the Nightingales."[48] In the third stanza of "Sweeney Erect," "Morning stirs the feet and hands / (Nausicaa and Polypheme). / Gesture of orang-outang / Rises from the sheets in steam. (9-12)[49] In the morning, "the feet and hands" are stirred, while the anti-hero protagonist Sweeney "[r]ises from the sheets in steam" with the gesture of an orang-outang. In this passage, the description of his simian posture suggests a connection between the image of orang-outang-like Sweeney and the image of apeneck Sweeeny in "Sweeney Among the Nightingales." Although the image of Sweeney could have a different symbolic meaning in "Sweeney Erect," it still suggests a possibility that

---

46 Eliot, *The Complete Poems and Plays of T. S. Eliot*, 42.

47 Vincent Sherry, *Modernism and the Reinvention of Decadence* (New York: Cambridge University Press, 2015), 255.

48 Eliot, *The Complete Poems and Plays of T. S. Eliot*, 56.

49 Ibid., 42.

we could arrive at an understanding of the image of "Sweeney Erect" by taking its symbolic meaning in "Sweeney Among the Nightingales" into consideration. As has been explored above, the image of apeneck Sweeney is evocative of the appearance of a soldier wearing a gas mask. Although Sweeney's facial appearance does not look like an ape any more in "Sweeney Erect," his simian posture implies that those two figures might be the same person, or at least belong to a group of persons with similar characteristics. In this sense, the image of orang-outang-like Sweeney could also be deemed as both a pre-human ape and a kind of post-human machine, or rather, an allusion to the image of soldiers, which is fundamentally troglodytic and debased against the backdrop of the War.

On the other hand, the connection between "Sweeney Erect" and the theme of war could be suggested by the image of "steam." Like the "miasmal mist" in "The Hippopotamus," the image of "steam" could be understood as a literary representation of poisonous gas, if the poem is contextualized in its history. I believe that *The Times*'s reports on the Gas Attacks at Hulluch of April 1916 showcase a way in which the third stanza of "Sweeney Erect" could be read as an imagination of a gas attack on the Front. However, by offering the Gas Attacks at Hulluch as an example, I do not mean that this specific historical event is the source of the third stanza of "Sweeney Erect." Instead, what I would like to suggest is that it is possible to relate what Eliot wrote in his poem with what actually happened during the War, and, after taking some specific historical events into consideration, we perhaps could have a nuanced understanding of the subtle, complex, and implicit relationship between Eliot's poetry and the theme of war.

The Gas Attacks at Hulluch were two German cloud gas attacks on British troops, 27-29 April 1916, during the Easter Rising. Just before dawn on 27 April, the 16th Division, an Irish division, was subjected to a cloud gas attack near Hulluch, and suffered greatly. According to Christopher Duffy, the 16th Division had lost 3,491 out of a total of 10,845 men by the end of May 1916 on the Loos sector, including heavy casualties from bombardment and a heavy chlorine and phosgene Gas attack at Hulluch in April.[50] *The Times* reported this battle in its article "Gallantry Of Irish Division" on 29 April 1916, in which it quoted a telegraphic dispatch received from General Headquarters in France: "[e]arly this morning the enemy tried to enter our trenches at two points north of Roclincourt, after exploding five mines, followed by artillery and trench-mortar bombardment. The enemy was successfully repulsed."[51] Two days later the Germans began another gas attack but the wind turned and blew the gas back over the German lines, causing a large number of German casualties. According to James Edward Edmonds, the 16th Division lost 442 men on 27 April, and the total British casualties between 27 April and 29 April were 1,980, of whom 1,260 were gas casualties, 338 being killed.[52] Later, Major William Hoey Kearney Redmond issued an appeal of reinforcement, published as "Deeds Of An Irish Division" in *The Times* on 17 October 1916, in which he praised the heroic endeavor of the 16th Irish Division and gave a more detailed report of the gas attacks on April 27 and 29:

> The division withstood on April 27 and 29 two very severe attacks, in which the enemy used poison gas in its most concentrated form. On the latter of these two occasions the division suffered heavy casualties, but Providence was on our side for, the wind suddenly changing, the gas blew back over the German trenches where the Bavarians had

---

50 Christopher Duffy, *Through German Eyes: The British and the Somme 1916* (London: Phoenix, 2007), 101.

51 "Gallantry of Irish Division," *Times*, April 29, 1916.

52 The casualties include those of the 15th Division, which is a Scottish infantry division. James E. Edmonds, *Military Operations: France and Belgium, 1916: Sir Douglas Haig's Command to the 1st July: Battle of the Somme* (Nashville, TN: Battery Press, 1993), 195-6.

already massed for attack. Taken by surprise, they left their front line and ran back across the open under the heavy and well-directed fire of our artillery.[53]

As has been mentioned, the first gas attack took place before dawn (at around 6 am) on 27 April, when many soldiers were still sleeping. Presumably, when the German gas mines were exploded and the following artillery bombardment started, the Irish soldiers were woken up with a start, and the whole trench was very likely to be in a chaos. Eliot's description of the bedroom scene in the morning—"[m]orning stirs the feet and hands"— echoes, to some degree, the chaotic trench scene on 27 April 1916. This line is immediately followed by a pair of abrupt parentheses, in which there are two Odyssean characters—"Nausicaa and Polypheme." The former helps the shipwrecked Odysseus, while the latter alludes to the Cyclops Polyphemus, whose only eye was blinded by Odysseus. In "Sweeney Erect," the appearance of these two Odyssean characters alludes to Sweeney's connection with classical Hellenistic tradition. On the other hand, they might allude to the Irish soldiers' physical reaction to poison gas, since Nausicaa and Polypheme are evocative of "nausea" and "blindness," which remind us of vomit and sore eyes, two common symptoms of mustard gas poisoning. When the poison gas, such as the chlorine and phosgene, was blown by the wind to the Irish trench, the Irish soldiers were poisoned. However, nausea and sore eyes are physical pains that can only be felt by those soldiers themselves. They are not as visible as their stirred "feet and hands," and that is perhaps why "Nausicaa and Polypheme" are placed in parentheses, which indicates the unspeakable physical agony. In the speaker's imagination, the Irish soldiers again are degraded into animalistic creatures, since all of them, no matter whether they are poisoned or not, look like orang-outangs. For those who are

---

53   William H. K. Redmond, "Deeds of an Irish Division," *Times*, October 17, 1916

quick enough to put on their gas masks, their appearances are transformed into dehumanized creatures, which have been mentioned in the previous sections. For those who have been poisoned, they lost the control of their own bodies and act like frenzied apes—in a "gesture of orang-outang"—due to the physical agony. Because of the war, their bodies are reduced to a bestial status, which has been prefigured by "the snarled and yelping seas" (4) in the first stanza.[54] For many Irish soldiers of the 16th Division, the morning of 27 April is indubitably a nightmare, since "Aeolus," the God of the winds, blew the poison gas to their trenches, and woke them up "in steam." The poisonous "steam" and the physical reactions of the Irish soldiers in the Gas Attacks at Hulluch are suggested in Eliot's "Sweeney Erect," which again shows his interest in the war and his contemplation of the human physicality in the context of the First World War.

In conclusion, Eliot observed the War from the perspective of a non-combatant as a resident in wartime London, and he responded to the War in his wartime writings by taking the phenomena of gas shells and shell shock as literary themes. By doing so, Eliot reflected on the fragility of human physicality and mentality in the War, highlighting the War's disastrous impact on both the human body and mind. Contextualizing Eliot's wartime writings allows his readers to rethink the relationship between Eliot's wartime poetic works and his post-World War I poems, such as *The Waste Land* and "Gerontion," in which a connection with the topic of war is more clearly shown.

---

54   Eliot, *The Complete Poems and Plays of T. S. Eliot*, 42.

Bibliography

Bond, Brian. *The Unquiet Western Front: Britain's Role in Literature and History*. Cambridge University Press, 2002.

Bonikowski, Wyatt. *Shell Shock and the Modernist Imagination: the Death Drive in Post-World War I British Fiction*. Farnham, Ashgate, 2013.

Blunden, Edmund. *Undertones of War*. Penguin, 1986.

Buitenhuis, Peter. *The Great War of Words: British, American, and Canadian Propaganda and Fiction, 1914-1933*. University of British Columbia Press, 1987.

Child, Francis J. *The British Poets, Vol. 4*. London, Forgotten Books, 2013.

Chinitz, David E. "T. S. Eliot: *The Waste Land*." *A Companion of Modernist Literature and Culture*, edited by David Bradshaw and Kevin J. H. Dettmar, Oxford, Blackwell Publishing Ltd., 2006, pp.324-32.

Duffy, Christopher. *Through German Eyes: The British and the Somme 1916*. London, Phoenix, 2007.

Edmonds, James E. *Military Operations: France and Belgium, 1916: Sir Douglas Haig's Command to the 1st July: Battle of the Somme*. Battery Press, 1993.

Eliot, Thomas S. *The Complete Poems and Plays of T. S. Eliot*. Faber and Faber Limited, 1969.

---. *The Criterion, 1922-1939*. vol. XIII, October 1933 – July 1934, Faber and Faber, 1967.

---. *The Poems of T. S. Eliot*. vol. 1, edited by Christopher Ricks and Jim McCue, Faber and Faber, 2015.

Eliot, Thomas S., Jewel Spears Brooker, and Ronald Schuchard. *The Complete*

Prose of T. S. Eliot: The Critical Edition: Apprentice Years, 1905 – 1918. The Johns Hopkins UP, 2014.

Eliot, Valerie, ed. *The Letters of T. S. Eliot, Vol. 1, 1898 – 1922.* Faber and Faber, 1988.

Eliot, Valerie, and John Haffenden, eds. *The Letters of T. S. Eliot, Vol. 3, 1926 – 1927*, Faber and Faber, 2012.

Fletcher, John G. "On Subject-Matter and War Poetry," *Egoist* 3, no. 12, 1916, pp. 188-9.

Gordon, Lyndall. *T. S. Eliot: An Imperfect Life.* Vintage, 1998.

Kristeva, Julia. *Power of Horror: An Essay on Abjection.* Translated by Leon S. Roudiez, Columbia University Press, 1982.

Murdoch, Brian. *Fighting Songs and Warring Words: Popular Lyrics of Two World Wars.* Routledge, 1990.

Redmond, William H. K. "Deeds Of An Irish Division." *Times, 17* October 1916.

Sassoon, Siegfried. *The Complete Memoirs of George Sherston.* Faber and Faber, 1949.

Shephard, Ben. *A War of Nerves: Soldiers and Psychiatrists in the Twentieth Century.* Harvard University Press, 2001.

Sherry, Vincent. *Modernism and the Reinvention of Decadence.* Cambridge University Press, 2015.

Smith, Grover, Jr. *T. S. Eliot's Poetry and Plays: A Study in Sources and Meaning.* University of Chicago Press, 1956.

Spear, Hilda D. *Remembering, We Forget: A Background Study to the Poetry of the First World War.* Davis-Poynter, 1979.

Stevenson, Randall. *Literature and the Great War, 1914-1918*. Oxford University Press, 2013.

Times. "Another Defeat In Verdun Zone." 21 March 1916.

Times. "Another Summit Captured." 28 June 1915.

Times. "Gallantry Of Irish Division." 29 April 1916.

Times. "Gas Bombs." 26 May 1915.

Times. "Mustard Gas." 10 September 1917.

Times. "The Attack North Of Ypres." 26 April 1915.

Times, "The Poisonous Gas Zone." 30 April 1915.

Dr. Qiang Huang is lecturer in English at the School of English and International Studies, Beijing Foreign Studies University.

4

"IT STILL HAUNTS ME"

Trauma and Shell Shock in the Writings of the Nurses of the First World War

Samraghni Bonnerjee

Abstract

With the introduction of conscription in 1916, more British men left to fight at the Front, and British women were entrusted entirely with the industry of care. In the course of performing these functions, they were exposed to horribly-mutilated male bodies, were themselves often victims of shelling, and were witnesses to soldiers suffering from acute neurasthenia and shell shock.

In this chapter, I will consider what effect this exposure and witnessing have on the minds of the nurses themselves, and I will turn to their diaries and memoirs to read how they struggle and seek to understand and represent their experiences in their writings. I will also uncover symptoms of war neurosis and shell shock, which had been relegated only to front-line warfare, and as afflictions unique only to men. Using Kristeva's theories of abjection, Freud's notion of the uncanny, and Lacan's seminars on anxiety, the texts I will be reading are Vera Brittain's *Testament of Youth*, Helen Zenna

Smith's *Not So Quiet...*, Mary Borden's *The Forbidden Zone*, Ellen N. La Motte's *The Backwash of War*, and Lyn Macdonald's collection of interviews of British and American nurses of the First World War in the late seventies, *The Roses of No Man's Land*.

Mental illness, trauma, and shell shock among the nurses of the First World War are under-researched areas in literature and the history of medicine, and this chapter will therefore reveal what Margaret Higonnet has called "an alternate history of First World War traumas."

"'The strain all along,'" I repeated dully, "'is very great . . . very great.'" What exactly did those words describe? The enemy within shelling distance—refugee Sisters crowding in with nerves all awry—bright moonlight, and aeroplanes carrying machine-guns—ambulance trains jolting noisily into the siding, all day, all night—gassed men on stretchers, clawing the air—dying men, reeking with mud and foul green-stained bandages, shrieking and writhing in a grotesque travesty of manhood—dead men with fixed, empty eyes and shiny, yellow faces. . . . Yes, perhaps the strain all along *had* been very great. . . .[1]

ALMOST the whole canon of First World War poetry has been written by shell-shocked men who experienced combat. The frightening image of the shell-shocked soldier cowering in fear, stuttering, unable to hold a cup of tea without being overcome by tremors has endured in the minds of later generations reading about combat in the First World War. Indeed, just like the gendered nature of the War itself, with its dichotomy between

---

[1] Vera Brittain, *Testament of Youth*, (London: Penguin Books, 2005), 423.

the masculine War Front and the feminine Home Front, war trauma has also been irrevocably gendered.[2] In her influential book *The Female Malady*, Elaine Showalter writes,

> The efficacy of the term "shell shock" lay in its power to provide a masculine-sounding substitute for the effeminate associations of "hysteria" and to disguise the troubling parallels between male war neurosis and the female nervous disorders epidemic before the war.[3]

The suffering of war trauma and shell shock were owned entirely by male combatants, while the rhetoric of the treatment was also careful to distinguish this condition from the distinctly female hysteria.[4] However, as subsequent research on First World War neuroses has shown, war neuroses were not the prerogative of only the male combatant.[5] Female nurses

---

2   Indeed, Sandra Gilbert and Susan Gubar offer a powerful counterpoint to this argument in their book *No Man's Land*, where they claim a sense of female autonomy in women's First World War work-experience. However, critics such as Jane Marcus and Sharon Ouditt problematize this view by urging to look at "alternative feminist" histories and "ambiguous subject" identities. See: Sandra M. Gilbert and Susan Gubar, *No Man's Land: The Place of the Woman Writer in the Twentieth Century, Volume 3: Letters from the Front* (New Haven, CT: Yale University Press, 1996); Sharon Ouditt, *Fighting Forces, Writing Women: Identity and Ideology in the First World War* (London: Routledge, 1994); Jane Marcus, "Corpus/Corps/Corpse: Writing the Body in/at War," Afterword to Helen Z. Smith's *Not So Quiet...* (New York: Feminist Press, 1988).

3   Elaine Showalter, *The Female Malady: Women, Madness and English Culture, 1830—1980* (London: Virago Press, 1987), 172.

4   See ibid.

5   Trudi Tate writes a chapter on "Civilian war neuroses" in her book *Modernism, History and the First World War* (Manchester: Manchester University Press, 1998), 10—40. This is also an important point to pause and think about the work on Post Traumatic Stress Disorder (PTSD), brought to notice especially after combats in the late 20th and 21st centuries, and the gendering in its treatment. While PTSD treatment also began as programmes to treat male combat veterans, subsequent measures were introduced for the treatment among female veterans, and their different needs were recogniZed. PTSD now extends beyond combat to include cases of sexual assault. See: Quyen Q. Tiet, Yani E. Leyva, Kathy Blau, Jessica A. Turchil, Craig S. Rosen, "Military Sexual Assault, gender, and PTSD Treatment Outcomes of U.S. Veterans," *Journal of Traumatic Stress*, 28 (2), April 2015, 92—101.

working in Casualty Clearing Stations (CCSs) and hospital tents close to the Front, were not only witnesses to the severe physical wounding and mental traumas of soldiers, but were themselves regularly subjected to enemy shelling. As Vera Brittain writes in the lines I have quoted above, these nurses worked under extreme mental strain, especially during the "big push," with their "nerves all awry," and had their own lives constantly under threat. Nurses had experience of and treated extreme mutilation, disfigurement, and wounding hitherto unseen in combat; their stations were bombed, many nurses lost their lives; risking life and safety, many of them fled CCSs.[6] They did show symptoms similar to the neurasthenia suffered by the soldiers, and did have breakdowns, both physical and mental. This chapter will uncover these alternate testimonies and memoirs of suffering, reclaiming some of the ownership of wartime trauma and shell shock from its distinctly masculine domain, thus uncovering what Margaret Higonnet has aptly called "an alternate history of World War I traumas."[7] However, I will not simply look for shell shock symptoms or signs of traumas in their writings. As Higonnet has written, the similarities between the techniques of fragmented Modernist writings and those of testimony and trauma writings may jeopardize the question of "authenticity" of experience.[8] I will also unfold what Jay Winter has called the "metaphor" and "metaphysical" nature of shell shock, uncovering the variety of threats faced by nurses, leading on to parallels in mental suffering between male soldiers and female nurses, thus curbing the gender dichotomy of war trauma.[9] Suffering is

---

6 While an exact number of nurses who lost their lives during the First World War is not available, some estimates reveal that roughly 236 nurses were killed during the war. Source: http://www.redcross.org.uk/~/media/BritishRedCross/Documents/Who%20we%20are/History%20and%20archives/VAD%20casualties%20during%20the%20First%20World%20War.pdf. Accessed on July 20, 2017.

7 Margaret Higonnet, "Authenticity and Art in Trauma Narratives of World War I" in *Modernism/Modernity*, 9 (1), 92.

8 Ibid.

9 Jay Winter, "Shell-shock and the Cultural History of the Great War," *Journal of Contemporary*

subjective, and manifests itself physically and mentally in a variety of ways. The diversity of trauma and suffering, and its (un)conscious representation among certain women will be the focus of this chapter.

However, at the outset, it is important to provide some contextualization about the use of (medical) terminology in this chapter. Although the term "shell shock" has been in popular use since the First World War, Charles Myers, the consultant psychologist to the British Expeditionary Forces, who had been the first to use the term officially in a *Lancet* article in 1915, later pointed out its shortcomings: "A shell, then, may play no part whatever in the causation of 'shell shock': excessive emotion, e.g. sudden horror or fear, indeed any 'psychical trauma' or 'inadjustable experience' is sufficient."[10] The literal meaning of the term "shell shock" suggests an association with trench warfare and direct exposure to shell blasts, thus relegating it only to male combatants, who could have had such an exposure. It is this lack of breadth in the effects of "shell shock" to non-combatant women which I will redress in this chapter, by reading not only the diagnoses of shell shock but also the gamut of symptoms associated with war neuroses, in the writings of nurses. In "Beyond the Pleasure Principle," Sigmund Freud clarified that,

> Such external excitations as are strong enough to break through the barrier against stimuli we call traumatic. In my opinion the concept of trauma involves such a relationship to an otherwise efficacious barrier. An occurrence such as an external trauma will undoubtedly provoke a very extensive disturbance in the workings of the energy of the organism, and will set in motion every kind of protective measure. [. . .] The terrible

---

History, 35, 1 (2000), 7—11.

10   C. S. Myers, "A Contribution to the Study of Shell Shock: Being an Account of Three Cases of Loss of Memory, Vision, Smell, and Taste, Admitted into the Duchess of Westminister's War Hospital, Le Touquet," *Lancet*, 13 February, 1915.

war that is just over has been responsible for an immense number of such maladies. . . .[11]

W. H. R. Rivers would build upon the Freudian "protective measure" for his theory on war repression. In this chapter, I will read the nurses' experiences against the contemporary medical diagnostic writing and theories, specifically that of Rivers and William Turner, neurologist to the Home Forces. Important work on trauma theory has been developed since the 1960s, especially during the treatment of Holocaust survivors; and I will adapt the theories of Cathy Caruth, Dori Laub, and Shoshana Felman as an overarching framework to read the traumatic narratives in the writings of the nurses. I will finally refer to Julia Kristeva's theories of abjection in reading certain accounts. Kristeva's theory is especially important here because of how her work centers on "women [who] are marginalised in relation to the symbolic, and thus estranged from linguistic agency."[12] Ultimately, Kristeva's theory of "primal repression" is an important point to consider, when looking at accounts of witnessing severe wounds in Front hospitals, because it ties in with the debate on war repression as a whole:

> We are no longer within the sphere of the unconscious but at the limit of primal repression that, nevertheless, has discovered an intrinsically corporeal and already signifying brand, symptom, and sign: repugnance, disgust, abjection.[13]

The texts I will be reading are Vera Brittain's *Testament of Youth*, Mary Borden's *The Forbidden Zone*, Enid Bagnold's *A Diary without Dates,* and

---

11   Sigmund Freud, *Beyond the Pleasure Principle* (London: The International Psychoanalytic Library, 1922), 34, 8.

12   Jane Garrity, *Step-daughters of England: British Women Modernists and the National Imaginary* (New York: Manchester University Press, 2003), 250.

13   Julia Kristeva, *Powers of Horror: An Essay on Abjection* (New York: Columbia University Press, 1982), 11.

Lyn Macdonald's collection of interviews of British and American nurses of the First World War in the late seventies, *The Roses of No Man's Land*.

"I Shall Never be the Same Person Again"

In October 1915, after spending just over a month at the military hospital in Camberwell, Vera Brittain writes in a letter to her lover Roland Leighton,

> Personally after seeing some of the dreadful things I have to see here, I feel I shall never be the same person again, and wonder if, when the War does end, I shall have forgotten how to laugh. The other day I did involuntarily laugh at something and it felt quite strange.[14]

She notes that witnessing the atrocities of the War reduces individual consciousness until one is left feeling empty. Over the next few months, she too, like most of the other nurses, would perfect the art of working "without emotion."[15]

> I had not yet realised—as I was later to realise through my own mental surrender—that only a process of complete adaptation, blotting out tastes and talents and even memories, made life sufferable for someone face to face with war at its worst.[16]

---

14   Brittain, *Testament of Youth*, 215.

15   Ibid., 216. A number of critics have commented on Brittain's war-work as a means of her mourning the deaths of her lover, brother, and friends. See: Victoria Stewart, *Women's Autobiography: War and Trauma* (New York: Palgrave Macmillan, 2003); Richard Badenhausen, "Mourning through Memoir: Trauma, Testimony, and Community in Vera Brittain's *Testament of Youth*," *Twentieth Century Literature* 49, no. 4 (2003): 421–48; Austin Riede, "Vera Brittain's testaments of Labor, Work, and Action," *Iowa Journal of Cultural Studies* 12/13 (Spring & Fall 2010): 79–95.

16   Ibid., 217.

Despite not being in combat, the nurses were at war, too. Brittain uses the military metaphor of "surrender" to demonstrate how completely these women had to give up all feelings and emotions, and even memories of a happier past, to be able to live through war. The blotting out of memories is also a traumatic after-effect of war; the obliteration is complete—the physical body is wrecked, emotions are killed:

> But the War kills other things besides physical life, and I sometimes feel that little by little the Individuality of You is being as surely buried as the bodies are of those who lie beneath the trenches of Flanders and France.[17]

It is through the metaphor of the burial of one's individuality that Brittain connects the bodies and minds of the nurses with those of the soldiers who had been physically buried in the trenches. By an interesting turn of phrase, the "Individuality of You," Brittain (like Irene Rathbone just before her in *We That Were Young*) conveys the systematic demise of hope, aspirations, and subjectivity, of the generation that fought in the First World War. The imagery of burial also acts as a metaphor for the repression of war experience, as elaborated by W. H. R. Rivers, as I will discuss shortly.

In his 1915 essay "Thoughts on the Times of War and Death," Freud refers to the altered attitude towards death which disillusionment with the First World War had brought upon people. At the same time, this inability to feel emotions any more was a prime sign of being shell-shocked. Grief is unquantifiable, and the death of a loved one is certainly a traumatic event, yet the nurses had to go on caring for more wounded men after they lost their loved ones in combat. When Roland Leighton died, Vera Brittain believed that a part of her had died with him: "The last three months have been dark,

---

17 Ibid., 218.

confused, nightmare-like—I can barely remember what has happened in them, any more than one can properly remember a terrible illness after it is over."[18] Her grief is strikingly physical, manifesting itself through lack of sleep and fatigue.

> As I was conspicuously not sleeping and must have appeared the ghost of the excited girl who went on leave—indeed, I felt as though I had gone down to death with Roland and been disinterred as someone else—the Matron sent for me and offered to put me, with Betty, back on duty.[19]

Her symptoms here match with contemporary diagnosis of war neuroses. In the Bradshaw Lecture on Neuroses and Psychoses of War, delivered before the Royal College of Physicians of London on November 7, 1918, William Aldren Turner listed the symptoms of clinical war neuroses, explaining that in one type, patients present a "dazed and confused appearance" and commonly fall "victim of an anxiety condition in which intense headache, battle dreams, insomnia, vertigo, lack of mental concentration, and fatigue are prominent symptoms."[20] Vera Brittain's sleeplessness, fatigue, and mental confusion match with Turner's diagnosis. Once back on duty, Brittain's psychological misery is in tandem with the physical suffering of a wounded soldier, and her lack of feeling here, which she is slowly beginning to master, is noteworthy: "To complete my nervous misery, a paralytic patient required constant uninviting ministrations, and drove me half crazy with the animal noises which he emitted at intervals throughout the night."[21]

---

18 Ibid., 263.

19 Ibid., 245.

20 William Aldren Turner, "The Bradshaw Lecture on Neuroses and Psychoses of War" in *The Lancet*, November 9, 1918.

21 Ibid., 246.

In addition to experiencing regular shelling of their hospitals, nurses crossing the Channel to serve on the continent were in constant danger of having their hospital ships torpedoed and then drowning in the sea. Brittain writes of a "young, cheerful" Sister she had met on their voyage to Mudros, who was later on the hospital ship *Brittanic*, which was torpedoed.[22] When Brittain went to meet her in Floriana Hospital in Valletta, she found the Sister "completely changed" from the experience—"nervous, distressed and all the time on the verge of crying."[23] She could, nevertheless, succinctly describe the sinking of the *Britannic*: the explosion occurred during breakfast, blowing up an orderly together with the bottom staircase he was standing on; the nurses were asked to quickly snatch any valuables they could get and assemble on the deck, from which they were lowered onto the boats; as they sat on their boats, they saw the propeller of the *Brittanic* cut another boat "in half and fling its mutilated victims into the air."[24] In this scene, in addition to the horror of having their ship attacked in the middle of the sea, it was the witnessing of their neighboring boat, full of people they knew and worked with, being destroyed, that is especially chilling.

Although Freud mentions "self-reproach" as early as 1896, the clinical concept of survivor's guilt emerges in the 1960s, only during the treatment of Holocaust survivors.[25] Dr. Dori Laub, in *Testimony: The Crisis of Witnessing in Literature, Psychoanalysis, and History*, writes about three distinct levels of witnessing separate from each other, in relation to the Holocaust experience: "the level of being a witness to oneself within the experience; the level of being a witness to the testimonies of others; and the level of being a witness

---

22   Brittain, *Testament of Youth*, 312.

23   Ibid.

24   Ibid., 313.

25   John J. Hartman, "Anna Freud and the Holocaust: Mourning and survival guilt" in *The International Journal of Psychoanalysis*, 95 (6), December 2014.

to the process of witnessing itself."[26] There is an uncanny resemblance between the need of the survivors and witnesses of the Holocaust to tell their story and the First World War nurses attempting to take stock of their situation by writing (or narrating) their testimonies. Talking about the *Brittanic* disaster that this Sister witnessed and experienced "seemed to bring her relief."[27] This fits in neatly with the argument W. H. R. Rivers made in his post-war paper "The Repression of War Experience," in which he argued that "The cessation of repression was followed by the disappearance of the most distressing symptoms, and great improvement in the general health."[28] The cessation of repression with the recounting of the traumatic event, however, leads to what Laub calls the "ceaseless struggle" of the process of testimony.[29]

Vera Brittain, who listens to the Sister's testimony and reports it in her diary ("I meditated as I listened"), comes to be "a participant and co-owner of the traumatic event;" through witnessing the Sister's trauma resulting from the sinking of the ship, Brittain comes to partially experience trauma herself.[30] She had herself sailed on the *Brittanic* to reach Malta about a month before the ship's fatal final voyage: "'We are in danger!' I kept saying as I lay awake in the dark that night."[31] Her dread did not leave her after she reached Malta,

> My letters from Malta are full of wrecks and drowning; the sinking of ships provided much the same drama for us as a great battle for the

---

26   Shoshana Felman and Dori Laub, M.D. *Testimony: The Crises of witnessing in Literature, Psychoanalysis, and History* (New York: Routledge, 1992), 75.
27   Brittain, *Testament of Youth*, 312.
28   W. H. R. Rivers, "The Repression of War Experience," *Lancet* February 2, 1918.
29   Felman and Laub, *Testimony*, 75.
30   Brittain, *Testament of Youth*, 313; Felman and Laub, *Testimony*, 57.
31   Brittain, *Testament of Youth*, 296.

hospitals of England and France. The *Arabia* was torpedoed a month after I landed, and constant rumours of submarine damage or alleged threats of bombardment by Austrian vessels kept our excitement up to fever pitch.[32]

Brittain remembers that the news of the sinking of the *Britannic* "galvanised the island like an electric shock."[33] With news of more sinking of ships, the shock transformed into a long-lasting, "disintegrating" fear.

Six months afterwards, writing to my mother about the torpedoing of the *Asturias* with two of our most popular Malta V.A.D.s on board, I tried to describe the disintegrating fear which left me with a sick reluctance to undertake long voyages that ignominiously persists to this day.[34]

Felman and Laub write that the listener to the trauma is so impacted by the relation of the victim to the trauma, that they feel "the bewilderment, injury, confusion, dread and conflicts" of the trauma victim.[35] Vera Brittain, the listener to the Sister's traumatic experience, already addresses each of these emotions because she has almost been the victim herself. In her case, the line between the victim and the listener gets blurred, not only because she is so intimately related to the victim(s) and their sufferings, but also because she is suffering with them. Felman and Laub's insistence that the listener is "also a separate human being and will experience hazards and struggles of his own, while carrying out his function as a witness to the trauma witness" assumes special poignancy in the case of Brittain,[36]

---

32   Ibid., 311.
33   Ibid., 312.
34   Ibid., 297.
35   Felman and Laub, *Testimony*, 57.
36   Ibid

Each new wreck was followed by an influx of half-drowned patients suffering from shock; having lost everything but the clothes they had arrived in, they bought up half the garments in Valletta. [. . .] As the clothing stores in Valletta were now temporarily depleted, we supplied the refugees with our own pyjamas and undergarments and hot-water bottles until they could return to England and re-equip.[37]

Listening to the Sister's testimony of survival makes Brittain an active listener; however, having sailed in the same ship which was later torpedoed makes her a survivor, too. Her "hazards and struggles" assume special significance because of this blurring of identities and her involvement with the caring for the survivors.

It is important to note that the etymological roots of the word "trauma" in both Greek and German reveal that trauma originally meant physical wound or damage. Christine Hallett explains that the work of the nurses of the First World War was manifested by a process of "containing trauma"—of creating "safe boundaries within which healing could take place."[38] Any rupture in that containment made appearance in the form of a physical wound—the "trauma."[39] The First World War was unprecedented in its use of new weapons of warfare as well as chemical weapons, which inflicted hitherto unseen wounds and mutilation on the body. Reflecting on the first operation he observed during the war, the Australian artist Daryl Lindsay wrote, "How was I going to translate what looked like a mess of flesh and blood into a diagram that a student could understand?"[40] Nevertheless,

37 Brittain, *Testament of Youth*, 312.

38 Christine Hallett, *Containing Trauma: Nursing Work in the First World War* (Manchester: Manchester University Press, 2009), 16.

39 For a detailed analysis of physical wounding and the containment of trauma, see "Containing Physical Trauma on the Western Front" in Christine Hallett's *Containing Trauma*, 27–83.

40 Sir Daryl Lindsay, "The Sir Richard Stawell Oration," *The Medical Journal of Australia* 1, no. 3 (1958), 62. Quoted in Suzannah Biernoff, "Flesh Poems: Henry Tonks and the Art of Surgery," *Visual*

like Lindsay himself, the nurses not only looked upon and treated, but also ultimately translated the mess of flesh and blood into words in their private writings. In addition to looking at grotesque wounds and mutilation, with the strictest injunction against looking away—"'Always look a man straight in the face,' one Sister instructed her staff. 'Remember he's watching your face to see how you're going to react.'"—the nurses faced other hazards.[41] Vera Brittain writes of "possibilities hitherto unrealised": of being chased "up and down the hut by a stark naked six-foot-four New Zealander in the fighting stage of delirium," and when the latter was finally strapped to his bed by two male orderlies, Brittain writes of sitting by her table "with a beating heart, listening to his fury exploding in a torrent of such expressive language as had not yet assailed my innocent years even in two and a half years of Army life."[42] It is the additional fear of the possibility of being attacked by a wounded soldier, in addition to the daily threats of Front hospital life, manifested by the "beating heart," that adds to the reasons for neuroses in the nurses.

"My Sword of Damocles, the Ever-Brooding Panic"

The writings of nurses reveal the intense hard work and exertion that they underwent every day. The only entry Enid Bagnold can write in her diary at the end of her first day comprises five words, ellipses, and an exclamation mark:

My feet ache, ache, ache . . . ![43]

Culture in Britain, 11 (1), March 2010.
41   Lyn Macdonald, *The Roses of No Man's Land*, (London: Papermac, 1984), 149.
42   Brittain, *Testament of Youth*, 394.
43   Ibid., 15.

Yet, these brief words and the careful punctuation speak volumes about the tireless service that these women gave over the duration of the War. What they lacked in experience, they made up with physical hard work. Bagnold's writing is so palpable, that reading about their chores fills our bodies with exhaustion and aches.

> Aches and pains. . . .
> Pains and aches. . . .
> I don't know how to get home up the long hill. . . .[44]

There runs the—by now—common theme of hunger, along with the reassurance that with time and practice, one gets used to starvation, the long hours, and the exertion.

> The new V.A.D. doesn't talk much at present, being shy, but tonight I can believe she will write in her diary as I wrote in mine: "My feet ache, ache, ache. . . ." Add to that that she is hungry because she hasn't yet learnt how to break the long stretches with hurried gnawing behind a door, [. . .] that her hands and feet grow cold and her body turns to warm milk, that she longs so to sit on a bed that she can almost visualise the depression her body would make on its counterpane, and I get a glimpse of the passage of time and of the effect of custom.[45]

Fatigue features predominantly in Turner's lecture on War neuroses and psychoses. Fatigue and nervous exhaustion are the prominent symptoms of clinical types of war neuroses; along with psycho-genetic factors, physical causes such as fatigue were considered to be a cause for shell shock and

---

44 Enid Bagnold, *A Diary Without Dates* Oxford, (Benediction Classics, 2014), 45.

45 Ibid., 66.

war neuroses.[46] On writing about the extreme fatigue and exhaustion that V.A.D.s were subjected to, Vera Brittain uses the violent imagery of "tired girls not yet *broken in* to a life of hardship."[47] It perhaps required the violence of breaking a body to let the young women's bodies get accustomed to the fatigue and exhaustion. Unsurprisingly, all that exertion eventually led to sickness. Brittain was too preoccupied to notice a mild epidemic of German measles among the nursing staff of several London fever hospitals, and on finding her arms "speckled with red from wrist to elbow," she reported sick and was sent to a fever hospital in south-west London.[48] With her characteristic brevity, Enid Bagnold refers to a similar experience, by writing only one word: "Measles. . . ."[49] On her first foreign service, Vera Brittain, along with most of her fellow-nurses on board the ship *Galeka* to Malta, fell violently sick. A "feverish discomfort" that first emanated from headaches and acute diarrhea, quickly metamorphosed into a mysterious disease of "shivering fits and a stiffening of the limbs." (Un)Fortunately, it was only as a patient in one of the hospitals that these nurses found "a few days of rest for an aching body and of release from introspective torment for a tired mind."[50]

In his essay "The Repression of War Experience," W. H. R. Rivers writes that repression tends to be harmful when it "fails to adapt the individual to his environment," especially during times of special stress, such as wartime.[51] He explains this through the example of the newly- and hastily-trained army recruit.

---

46   Turner, "The Bradshaw Lecture."
47   Brittain, *Testament of Youth*, 208. Emphasis mine.
48   Ibid., 265.
49   Bagnold, *A Diary*, 45.
50   Brittain, *Testament of Youth*, 265.
51   Rivers, "The Repression of War Experience," 2.

The training of a soldier is designed to adapt him to act calmly and methodically in the presence of events naturally calculated to arouse disturbing emotions. His training should be such that the energy arising out of these emotions is partly damped by familiarity, partly diverted into other channels. The most important feature of the present war in its relation to the production of neurosis is that the training in repression normally spread over years has had to be carried out in short spaces of time, while those thus incompletely trained have had to face strains such as have never previously been known in the history of mankind. Small wonder that the failures of adaptation should have been so numerous and so severe.[52]

While this is true in case of soldiers (especially Officers—the class with the highest number of patients suffering from war neuroses), it is as true for V.A.D.s, who were similarly positioned in class as the Officers (and hence different from trained nurses), who were untrained in the intricacies of military medical nursing until the outbreak of the War, an event which led to the demand of a large and continuous supply of carers.[53] While their physical bodies needed considerable time to be broken in to a life of supreme exertion, their minds too needed adequate time to adapt to a heightened state of continued danger and urgency. With the duration of the War, there grew a routinization in the work and stress of the daily machinations of a wartime military hospital:

> my letters home tell the same story of perpetual convoys, of haemorrhages, of delirium, of gas-gangrene cases doomed from the start

---

52 Ibid.

53 For an analysis of hysteria and neuroses among officers see "Male Hysteria: W. H. R. Rivers and the Lessons of Shell Shock" in Showalter, *The Female Malady*, 167–94.

who watched our movements with staring, fear-darkened eyes, afraid to ask the questions whose answers would confirm that which they already knew.[54]

And what effects do these perpetual convoys have on the nurse? Mary Borden, running the Hôpital Chirurgical Mobile No. 1 near Rousbrugge in Flanders, writes how used to the cannonade she is, which is her "lullaby," lulling her to sleep every night,

> If it stopped I could not sleep. I would wake with a start. The thin wooden walls of my cubicle tremble and the windows rattle a little. That, too, is natural. It is the whispering of the grass and the scent of the new-mown hay that makes me nervous.[55]

The sounds of war get adapted into the sounds of everyday life, until the sounds of the everyday act as an intrusion and affect the nurse. Borden demonstrates how deep the effect of the War has been on the body and mind of the nurse: the rattle of the windows regularly pairs with the rattle of her nerves. Borden also informs that the nurse, who works with drugs all day, administering them to the soldiers, is herself "drowsy and drugged with heavy narcotics, with ether and iodoform and other strong odours," prompting us to think about the very real threat of substance dependence amongst the carers.[56] The strain of working under constant urgency and threat to life ultimately takes its toll on the body and mind of the nurse by making her immune to all feelings and emotions:

---

54 Ibid., 383.

55 Mary Borden, *The Forbidden Zone* (London: Hesperus Press, 2008), 39.

56 Ibid., 42.

She is no longer a woman. She is dead, just as I am—really dead, past resurrection. Her heart is dead. She killed it. She couldn't bear to feel it jumping in her side when Life, the sick animal, choked and rattled in her arms. Her ears are deaf; she deafened them. She could not bear to hear Life crying and mewing. She is blind so that she cannot see the torn parts of men she must handle. Blind, deaf, dead—she is strong, efficient, fit to consort with god and demons—a machine inhabited by the ghost of a woman—soulless, past redeeming, just as I am—just as I will be.[57]

The erasure of women is a trope that Mary Borden returns to continually in *The Forbidden Zone*. The mutilated bodies of the soldiers have become such a "defaced ideal," that Borden cries out "There are no men here. Why should I be a woman?" In a less than oblique reference to sexuality and the scopophilic drive, she reveals how haunted she is by what remains. "It is impossible to be a woman here" where men have lost their sexuality, where the signifiers of sex have been mutilated. As a result of the witnessing of that mutilation, the nurse is left numb—not only by the loss of her sexuality, but by the loss of all emotions, the death of her "heart." There is a sense of guilt and shame at play, with the realization that the able-bodied nurse is alive, while the wounded soldier she is tending to fights for his life. Her unconscious reaction is to shut down her body and her senses, to close her eyes from witnessing anymore mutilated bodies, to deafen her ears to escape the cries of pain, and to shut down her heart to emotions. The War has made her into an automaton, mechanically attending to her duty, while her soul is "past redeeming." Elaine Showalter, in tracing the figure of the literary shell-shocked soldier, writes of Woolf's Septimus Smith, that "Septimus's problem is that he feels too much for a man. His grief and introspection are emotions

---

57 Ibid., 43.

that are consigned to the feminine."⁵⁸ Ironically, it is the annihilation of the feminine emotion in the nurses that makes them more susceptible to war neuroses and trauma.

During her service in France, Brittain writes, "The roar of bombs dropping on Camiers soon after I arrived had awakened me to the petrifying realisation that there were no cellars in a camp."⁵⁹ Her petrification arises from never having experienced bombing before: the evening after she had departed for Malta, German zeppelins had dropped bombs on Purley, Streatham Hill, and Brixton, places through which she and her mother had passed before. She reminiscences later,

> how frightened I had been of air-raids when I first went to London, and reflecting that so close a conjunction of Zeppelins and submarines might entirely have annihilated that modicum of courage which, throughout the War, only just enabled me to keep my dignity in perilous situations.⁶⁰

Therefore her fear of being caught in the middle of a bombing raid in her hospital in Camiers is understandable, although it is the long-term effect of that fear, as she writes in retrospect, which is of interest while studying the effect of trauma on these women. During the great German offensive of March 1918, which was preceded by the bombing, the nurses were stretched to their limits by caring for the enormous numbers of wounded soldiers, as well as constantly facing threats to their lives. Nurses from the stations which were engulfed by the offensive, had to flee further down the line, and in many cases, they retreated for days, without sleep or food, without any

---

58   Showalter, *The Female Malady*.

59   Brittain, *Testament of Youth*, 408.

60   Ibid., 295.

belongings, and in constant threat to their safety. Several nurses died as a result of the bombing. Brittain vividly describes the state of her hospital tent during one such day,

> myself standing alone in a newly created circle of hell during the "emergency" of March 22nd, 1918, and gazing, half hypnotised, at the dishevelled beds, the stretchers on the floor, the scattered boots and piles of muddy khaki, the brown blankets turned back from smashed limbs bound to splints by filthy blood-stained bandages. Beneath each stinking wad of sodden wool and gauze an obscene horror waited for me—and all the equipment that I had for attacking it in this ex-medical ward was one pair of forceps standing in a potted-meat glass half full of methylated spirit.[61]

Her "sword of Damocles" is her persistent panic, yet she wasn't solitary in her demonstration of it—these nurses embarked on "the daily battle against time and death which was to continue, uninterrupted, for what seemed an eternity."[62] The manifestation of their trauma appears in the form of the "half hypnotised" stare, and being rooted to the spot in a "circle of hell," the site of "obscene horror," while death and destruction unfold around them. Several nurses did not survive the "crushing tension of those extreme days:"

> One young Sister, who had previously been shelled at a Casualty Clearing Station, lost her nerve and rushed screaming through the Mess; two others seized her and forcibly put her to bed, holding her down while the raid lasted to prevent her from causing a panic.[63]

---

61 Ibid., 410.
62 Ibid., 411.
63 Ibid., 417.

The parallel between the neurasthenic New Zealander running through the length of the hospital hut, and this Sister who had "lost her nerve" running through her mess is remarkable; both were held down and forcibly put to bed. The assault on the senses continued uninterrupted: sharp flashes of fire in the sky at night; "thudding crescendo," "ceaseless and deafening roar" caused by motor lorries and ammunition wagons on the move all day, and "thundering" trains with reinforcements, stretcher cases full with mutilated soldiers, suffering from wounds with congealed blood. The business of repairing them was a ceaseless process as one convoy followed another. There were physical manifestations of the stretching of unreliable nerves this emergency elicited. Groups of nurses with their teeth chattering out of sheer terror made their way to their huts when they were ordered to scatter, mirroring the familiar image of shivering soldiers in the trenches, with their teeth chattering in fear of the sniper's bullet. At the end Brittain writes,

> An uncontrollable emotion seized me—as such emotions often seized us in those days of insufficient sleep; my eyeballs pricked, my throat ached, and a mist swam over the confident Americans going to the front. The coming of relief made me realise all at once how long and how intolerable had been the tension, and with the knowledge that we were not, after all, defeated, I found myself beginning to cry.[64]

Being able to cry at last would have been cathartic. The "insufficient sleep" and fatigue that Brittain mentions, exactly match Turner's symptoms of war neuroses. Yet it is through the "uncontrollable emotion" of relief, tears, and the final release of the unbearable tension of the extreme mental strain that her neuroses find a physical manifestation.

---

64 Ibid., 421.

"It Still Haunts Me"

In *Powers of Horror*, Julia Kristeva refers to the "abject," and identifies it as "the jettisoned object, [which] is radically excluded and draws me toward the place where meaning collapses."[65] Such a reaction is primarily caused by witnessing a corpse; such a reaction is also elicited by looking at an open wound. Reading the nurses' accounts and placing them against Kristeva's theories of abjection helps one identify similar reactions as they struggled with the spectacle of wounded men's bodies. In her afterword to Helen Zenna Smith's *Not So Quiet . . .* Jane Marcus calls a section "Ears Only,"

> to mark the experience of war in Helen Zenna Smith's writing as a bombardment of the reader's ears in a text pock-marked with ellipses of silence and rushes of noisy belligerent words.[66]

While the daily work of the nurses in the Front was regularly interrupted by the sound of battle, bombs, bullets, and other belligerent noises, I would like to extend the different sensations experienced by these women from auditory and touch, to olfactory and sight. While trying to imagine what walking down a hospital ward would feel like at this time in history, one would often forget the smell. Yet the strong smell of disinfectants used to scrub the floor, mingled with the smell of the sterilizing solutions of instruments, the smell of dressing solutions used to dress wounds, and finally the smell of wounds, of gangrene, and of rotting flesh would assault the olfactory senses of the nurses.

With the formation of "Hypchlorous Acid ¼% Solution" by Doctors Carrel and Dakin, it was possible to treat early cases of gangrene. Nurses

---

65   Julia Kristeva, *Powers of Horror*, 2.

66   Jane Marcus's Afterword, in Helen Zenna Smith's *Not So Quiet . . .* (New York: The Feminist Press, 1989), 261.

would have to inject the solution into tubes connected to the wounds every three hours all day and through the night. If it wasn't too late, a limb could be saved from amputation, but although people still died from serious gangrenous wounds, the solution brought the numbers down. Nevertheless, the soldiers "hated it, it was so cold," and it was not especially popular with the nurses.[67] Looking back at the treatment using the Carrel and Dakin solution in the 1970s, VAD Hester Cotton remembers,

> I could never get the smell of that stuff out of my nose. I can still smell it even now, a sort of chlorate of lime smell, and of course the smell of the wounds themselves was terrible. If there was a case of gas gangrene in a ward you could smell it as you opened the door.[68]

Hester Cotton accurately describes the smell of the new solution—one of the many advances made in medical sciences entirely by necessity during the War years—and points out something that was perhaps true in most cases, and important to remember: "I could never get the smell of that stuff out of my nose. I can still smell it even now . . ." She further recalls her initial experience with a wounded man,

> It was very hard to do the dressings sometimes, because we weren't trained nurses and were only helping to hold things and pass them to Sister, but it was dreadful to look at them nevertheless. I only had to leave the ward once, and that was for the very first wound I saw. It was a man who'd had half his buttocks shot off, all the fleshy part, and never having seen a real wound before I was a bit taken aback. If the wound had been clean, it would have been red, because it was absolutely raw

---

67   Ibid., 91.

68   Ibid.

flesh. As it was, it was full of pus, absolutely suppurating with pus. You simply couldn't clean it up; you just had to keep on putting these wet things on until gradually it got cleaner and cleaner.[69]

For someone unaccustomed to seeing dreadful, open wounds, the first encounter with raw flesh and pus can come as a shock. The advice that was often dispensed was to "Put your head between your knees and you will be all right."[70] A new V.A.D. who came to Enid Bagnold's hospital turned away her face when she saw a patient's bloody arm. Bagnold wrote that she had done that, too, when she was new. The first dressing that Vera Brittain assisted, a "gangrenous leg wound, slimy and green and scarlet with the bone laid bare," turned her sick and faint for a moment.[71] She later remembered that experience with humiliation; the nurses simply got used to the suffering. As Kristeva writes, abjection "is not the white expanse or slack boredom of repression, not the translations and transformations of desire that wrench bodies, nights, and discourse; rather it is a brutish suffering..."[72] She complicates Rivers' concept of war repression as a means of treating war neuroses, by recognising the gamut of suffering always already present behind the veil of repression. The nurses did suffer, but there were rewards. Hester Cotton recalls, "He did get better, that man, but he had a terrible time. He had to be lying on his stomach and I remember when he was first able to inch round on to one side for the first time. That was a great day."[73]

Kristeva emphasizes the necessity to be aware of the link between the subject and the abject, especially because though the border between the two positions is imaginary, the abject does exist, in a liminal space, in the

---

69   Macdonald, *Roses*, 92.
70   Ibid.
71   Brittain, *Testament of Youth*, 211.
72   Julia Kristeva, *Powers of Horror*, 2.
73   Ibid.

unconscious mind. It manifests its presence by nausea, fear, and adrenalin. Nursing probationer, Drusilla (Maisie) Bowcott talked about her initial experience, before she got "hardened" to it.

> I was absolutely shaking at the knees as I approached the team at the bed where the dressing trolley stood. "Hold that stump," said Sister, and the poor chap must have felt dreadful because I gripped his leg well above the knee, and as the solution of Eusol and Peroxide was poured onto the stump the pus was pouring over my hands. Then I had two stumps, two Sisters, and I must have started to sway because I was carted out very ignominiously to the fire escape.[74]

It is noteworthy that the particular adverb "ignominiously" crops up quite regularly in the musings of the nurses. Feeling ignominious or being ashamed was a layered affect for these women. Being barred from actively serving their country like men could, at the hour of utmost need made them ashamed to have been born a woman. For V.A.D.s like Enid Bagnold, new to nursing and swiftly trained to meet an urgent demand, shame could be interspersed with the idea of being an impostor. Did they misconstrue their failure to provide immediate and complete relief to the soldiers' pain with their own failings in medical skill? Or did they misapprehend the failure of language to convey the depths of pain as their personal failure? Finally, as I have demonstrated earlier, were they shameful of their strong, able bodies in front of the quivering wreckages of the soldiers? "Ignominiously" carries refrains of all these layers of shame.

In some cases, hardening took time, and some nurses were haunted by the cases they treated or witnessed for years afterwards. Claire Elise Tisdall was a VAD ambulance nurse, who travelled with the ambulances,

---

74 Ibid., 92.

and took the wounded from the trains to the hospitals. The case that she encountered, that would haunt her for the next sixty years, took place at the Somme,

> The worst case I saw—and it still haunts me—was of a man being carried past us. It was at night, and in the dim light I thought that his face was covered with a black cloth. But as he came nearer, I was horrified to realise that the whole lower half of his face had been completely blown off and what had appeared to be a black cloth was a huge gaping hole. That was the only time that I nearly fainted on the platform, but fortunately I was able to pull myself together. It was the most frightful sight because he couldn't be covered up at all.[75]

Claire Tisdall's recollection and description of her "worst case" is very remarkable, as one can immediately draw parallels with Freud's theory of the "uncanny." There is an "uncanny" confusion between her *Phantasie* (imagination) and *Wirklichkeit* (reality)—the imagined black cloth vis-à-vis the hole in the soldier's face. In E. T. A. Hoffmann's story "The Sandman," Freud noted that the more striking instance of uncanniness was the idea of being robbed of one's eyes. In Claire Tisdall's narration, this idea of being robbed of sight acquires a double significance: first through the hindrance in the line of vision by what is assumed to be a black cloth; second, the negation of the existence of the black cloth, to reveal a gaping hole, an absence where the face should have been, and hence a hollowness, a vacuum in sight. On his seminars on anxiety delivered in 1962 and 1963, Jacques Lacan returned to Freud's notion of the uncanny, and lucidly explained the connection between absence and fantasy.

---

75   Ibid., 165.

there is profiled an image of ourselves that is simply reflected, already problematic, even fallacious; that it is at a place that is situated with respect to an image which is characterised by a lack, by the fact that what is called for there cannot appear there, that there is profoundly orientated and polarised the function of this image itself, that desire is there, not simply veiled, but essentially placed in relation to an absence, to a possibility of appearing determined by a presence which is elsewhere and determines it more closely, but, where it is, ungraspable by the subject, namely here, I indicated it, the o of the object, of the object which constitutes our question, of the object in the function that it fulfills in the phantasy at the place that something can appear.[76]

Yet Tisdall's "worst case" falls between Lacan's analysis of the uncanny and desire, and Kristeva's theory of the abject. If the soldier's missing face casts him out of the symbolic order, then Tisdall's reaction of horror at the sight is a prime example of abjection.

These moving accounts of nurses reveal how intricately their horrific experiences were directly responsible for neuroses, and dispel any notion of trauma by proxy for female non-combatants. In her influential work *Unclaimed Experience*, Cathy Caruth defines trauma as "the response to an unexpected or overwhelming violent event or events that are not fully grasped as they occur, but return later in repeated flashbacks, nightmares, and other repetitive phenomena."[77] This belatedness and repetition-compulsion certainly hold true for the nurses who spoke of their experiences to Lyn Macdonald in the 1970s. The other texts I read here also represent trauma in retrospect: Vera Brittain published *Testament of Youth* in 1933, fifteen years

---

76   https://www.valas.fr/IMG/pdf/THE-SEMINAR-OF-JACQUES-LACAN-X_l_angoisse.pdf Accessed on September 23, 2016.

77   Cathy Caruth, *Unclaimed Experience: Trauma, Narrative and History* (Baltimore: Johns Hopkins University Press, 2016), 94.

after the end of the War, and Mary Borden published *The Forbidden Zone* in 1929. Whether these women and others like them were wracked with undiagnosed neuroses in the intervening years is a matter of speculation; there were no adequate convalescent hospitals for nurses suffering from shell shock or war neuroses.[78] Brittain wrote of crippling "nervous fatigue" while in Oxford, in the immediate years after the War, ultimately hallucinating that she was beginning to "grow a beard, like a witch."[79] It is ironic that while PTSD is often seen as a failure of masculinity, its effects among women are ignored. These women experienced extreme physical and emotional strain and collapse over the course of the War. Their writings reflect the stress they experienced, from witnessing death and mutilation first hand, to being attacked, wounded, and being killed themselves. If shell shock was, as Showalter puts it, "the body language of masculine complaint, a disguised male protest, not only against the war, but against the concept of 'manliness' itself," then shell shock and trauma for the woman was a protest against the masculine industry of war, and the gender dichotomy between the War and Home fronts; lodged between the two, the nurses silently suffered in the metaphorical "No Man's Land."[80] Just like the shell-shocked men who struggled to fit in with civilian life after the War, these women too labored to return to the lives they had left behind. We can only fathom the enduring effects of trauma on these women by looking for covert signs in their lives several years after the War ended. In one instance, an octogenarian former nurse holding on to tea cups with shaking fingers, talks about scrubbing and cleaning hospital floors, unpacking supplies, making beds, beating and airing mattresses, setting up operating rooms, dressing wounds—there was

---

78   Denise J. Poynter, *"The Report on her Transfer was Shell Shock." A Study of the Psychological Disorders of Nurses and Female Voluntary Aid Detachments who Served Alongside the British and Allied Expeditionary Forces during the First World War 1914—1918*. Unpublished Thesis.

79   Brittain, *Testament of Youth*, 478, 484.

80   Showalter, *The Female Malady*, 172.

always dressing to do. Their trembling hands are remnants of the experiences their bodies lived through, the wounds they sustained. This is most clearly reflected in the words of one of Lyn MacDonald's interviewees:

> What comes through most strongly is their remarkable resilience, the casualness with which they refer to work in circumstances and situations which would appall [sic] most other people, the matter-of-fact way in which they refer to their "war wounds." "Oh dear, I'm sorry to be so clumsy. It's these stupid stiff fingers of mine." It was an apology I heard literally scores of times as a photograph slipped to the floor, or two drops of tea slopped into a saucer. The "stupid, stiff fingers" are mostly scarred where they were lanced to release the puss [sic] from a septic hand.[81]

---

81   Macdonald, *Roses*, 12.

Dr. Samraghni Bonnerjee is a literary and cultural historian of the First World War. She is a Research Associate in the AHRC-funded project "Literature, Psychoanalysis and the Death Penalty 1900—1950," at the University of Sheffield. Formerly, she was a Vice-Chancellor's Scholar at the University of Sheffield, where she read for a Ph.D. in English Literature. Her peer-reviewed journal articles have been published (or are forthcoming) in Australian Journal of Politics and History, Studies in Travel Writing, Women's History Review, and Endeavour; and her book chapters have been published in edited collections by Palgrave Macmillan. She is a Fellow of Higher Education Academy (FHEA).

TROPING SHELL SHOCK

The Anti-Sublime in American and British Women's Great War Narratives

Iro Filippaki

Abstract

American author and volunteer nurse Mary Borden's *The Forbidden Zone* (1929), British poet Edith Sitwell's *I Live Under a Black Sun* (1937), and British-Australian writer Evadne Price's *Not So Quiet: Stepdaughters of War* (1930) narrate Great War shell shock through dialogical descriptions that contest one of the most prevalent Great War tropes: the sublimity and unnarratability of war trauma. Borden's narrative was written as a creative testimony of her contribution in the war as a head nurse and consists of sketches and poems; Sitwell's novel is a political allegory that satirizes Jonathan Swift's life if it were set during the Great War; and Price's novel is a reworking of ambulance driver Winifred Youngs' Great War diaries. A comparison between these American and British narratives of the Great War reveals that Borden, Price, and Sitwell employ similar tropes to represent shell shock, namely the pastoral and the Bakhtinian carnivalesque. Not only does this tropological representation provide alternative views to the role of women in the Great War, both at the front and at home, but, importantly, pastoral and carnivalesque elements construct a picture of anti-sublimity. Quotidian, automatic, and repetitive elements cancel out the ineffability, immeasurability, and transcendence of traditional war representation, contributing to an understanding of shell shock in narrative terms, and to a measuring of trauma in terms of human scale.

A TALL woman in uniform that stands out in a crowd of soldiers and civilians: this is how Mary Borden's post-Great War novel *Sarah Gay* (1931) starts. As a young English "penniless daughter" who married rich,[1] and is a volunteer nurse for the French Red Cross during the Great War, Sarah Gay stands "taller than the women in black who stumbled after their men."[2] While Sarah Gay witnesses soldiers at the train station with "women clinging to them; wives, mothers, sisters and sweethearts,"[3] she seems unaffected by the public display of women's relationship to soldiers or their strong presence: "The English nurse paid no attention to the heavy stumbling crowd of men in faded blue."[4] Borden's novel descends into a dark construct where the fearless but shell-shocked English nurse becomes an infatuated paramour stigmatized by an unhealthy obsession with French Lieutenant John Gay. *Sarah Gay* may be more about an illicit love-story within Parisian salons of the inter-war period than about shell-shocked women of the Great War, but for the first few pages, Borden gives us a

---

1   Mary Borden, *Sarah Gay*, (London: Heinemann, 1931), 14.
2   Ibid., 4.
3   Ibid., 3.
4   Ibid., 4.

description of femininity 2.0 during the war. Clearly suffering from a form of shell shock, but working tirelessly for the cause and seeming "unaffected, apparently, by the smells of dirt, sweat, blood or gangrene,"[5] Borden's Sarah Gay stands in direct opposition to the medical representation of the rarely acknowledged shell-shocked British and American woman, who was defeminized and supposedly dangerous for society.[6]

In its medical representation, shell shock has been a metaphor for the unmanly man and the unwomanly woman.[7] If post-Great War theorization on shell shock has managed to connect tradition and modernity, Darwinism and posthumanism, and soldierly and civilian medical provision,[8] this theorization also showcased a problematic medical narrative that distinguished between traumatized or cowardly soldiers and assigned importance to trauma depending on whether the victim was literally under fire. Not only was Britain's medical community reluctant to attribute shell shock to women,[9] but the prevalent tendency was one of exclusion: the shell-shocked man was considered to be effeminate,[10] and popular belief reflected a reductive representation of women in military service as hysterical, "superfluous," or "malignant."[11] The gender problem, issues of transnationality,[12] and class

---

5   Ibid., 17.

6   Tiffany Joseph, "Non-Combatant's Shell-Shock: Trauma and Gender in F. Scott Fitzgerald's Tender Is the Night," *NWSA Journal* 15, No 3 (Fall 2003): 64- 81, accessed March 4, 2017, doi: 10.1353/nwsa.2004.0010.

7   Jay Winter, *The Cambridge History of the First World War: Volume 3, Civil Society*. (Cambridge: Cambridge UP, 2014).

8   Tracey Loughran, *Shell-Shock and Medical Culture in First World War Britain* (Cambridge: Cambridge UP, 2017).

9   Loughran, 2017.

10   Elaine Showalter, *The Female Malady: Women, Madness and English Culture, 1830-1980* (London: Virago, 1987).

11   Suzie Grogan, *Shell Shocked Britain: The First World War's Legacy for Britain's Mental Health* (Barnsley, South Yorkshire: Pen and Sword History, 2014) 79-81.

12   Winter, 2014.

and status parameters,[13] add to the complexity of narrating shell shock, as does the guilt complex: "if one had survived, one must have been less than those who died."[14] Kate McLoughlin notes that, because of its frequently undermined status, women's war writing oscillates nervously between graphic detail so that authenticity may be established, and declarations of inability to describe a war wherein women authors have not been "directly" implicated.[15] The latter is a more generic trope that, as is discussed further down, belongs to the tropology of sublimity and is extensively employed by men and women alike: as McLoughlin has established, "the most potent technique for conveying [the war's] magnitude" is claiming that the right words are not available: the trope of the adynaton.[16] This proves to be only partly true for women authors: the most wide-read war writing by women is one that narrates shell shock through the trope of the returning soldier as a mediator between the war and women; this is consistent with McLoughlin's claim, in that the returning soldier is a trope through which the author speaks about war without directly speaking about war. In the first pages of Rebecca West's *The Return of the Soldier*, for instance, one of the three female protagonists, Jenny, ponders her own situation in relation to Chris's return from the trenches:

> That day [spring's] beauty was an affront to me, because like most Englishwomen of my time I was wishing for the return of a soldier. Disregarding the national interest and everything except the keen

---

13   Joanna Bourke, *An Intimate History of Killing: Face to Face Killing in Twentieth Century Warfare* (London: Granta Books, 1999).

14   Samuel Hynes, *A War Imagined: The First World War and English Culture* (New York: Atheneum, 1991) 317.

15   Kate McLoughlin, *Authoring War: The Literary Representation of War from the Iliad to Iraq* (Cambridge: Cambridge UP, 2011) 2-3 and 33.

16   Kate McLoughlin, *The Cambridge Companion to War Writing* (Cambridge: Cambridge UP, 2009) 22.

prehensile gesture of our hearts towards him, I wanted to snatch my cousin Christopher from the wars.[17]

West depicts shell-shocked female characters, but their trauma is implied and not directly acknowledged; similarly, Christopher's amnesia and escape from the harsh realities of war into "a fantasy of love,"[18] emphasizes the idea that shell shock lies outside of the realm of logos and can only be accessed through a representation of absence rather than presence.

For McLoughlin, such "communication-by-implication" signifies the trope of the adynaton, whereby hyperbolic disclaimers about the war are made to show its immeasurability and immenseness, or clear signs of the devastating effects of war lead to an absent signifier.[19] [20] McLoughlin places the adynaton at the heart of the sublime tropology, prevalent in war writing since the Homeric times, representing an experience that "renders the despair of imaginative failure the precondition of joyful aesthetic judgement."[21] In the case of women's writing, however, the adynaton has shrouded the nuanced tropes used by women themselves to narrate their own shell shock and war trauma in general, and has led to the narration of trauma-by-proxy: women told stories of dealing with the shell-shocked as opposed to being shell-shocked, as West has done.[22] This tropological narration and its subsequent critical exploration is limiting for women's war writing, instances of which have been controversial if not outright subversive—

---

17   Rebecca West, *The Return of the Soldier* (Petersborough: Broadview Press, 2010) 48.

18   Wyatt Bonikowski, *Shell Shock and the Modernist Imagination: The Death Drive in Post-World War* (New York: Routledge, 2016) 159.

19   In *The Return of the Soldier*, for instance, Jenny experiences long bouts of staring into the void; recurring nightmares; and inability to control her thoughts, but none of these lead the author to claim that Jenny is also shell shocked. Instead, this narrative is released through Chris's character.

20   McLoughlin, *Companion*, 21-22.

21   Ibid., 21.

22   Bonikowski, 7.

although West's novel can be read as subversive, even this reading relies on Jenny's inability to express her own trauma. The question I wish to address in this chapter is the following: knowing the extent to which war and war trauma representation heavily relies on not finding the right words, what kind of narrative tropology is generated when authors avoid hyperbole and do claim to have the words to describe war?

American author and volunteer nurse Mary Borden's *The Forbidden Zone* (1929), British poet Edith Sitwell's *I Live Under a Black Sun* (1937), and British-Australian writer Evadne Price's *Not So Quiet: Stepdaughters of War* (1930) narrate Great War shell shock through quotidian descriptions. Perhaps the most important element that they share is that these narratives are dialogical: Borden's narrative was written as a creative testimony of her contribution in the war as a head nurse and consists of sketches and poems; Sitwell's novel is a political allegory that satirizes Jonathan Swift's life if it were set during the Great War; and Price's novel is a reworking of ambulance driver Winifred Youngs's Great War diaries. As a rule, American texts on the Great War are not as popular as British Great War texts, in part because they challenge "established cultural preferences and misconceptions about war literature;"[23] what I would like to argue here, however, is that there is a common tropological approach in both American and British women's war writing, most notably regarding the textual representation of shell shock and trauma more generally through anti-sublime tropes.

In the pages that follow, I compare the American and British narratives of the Great War, arguing that Borden, Price, and Sitwell represent shell shock through the narrative tropes of the pastoral and the Bakhtinian carnivalesque; as I will show, this tropological representation is inherently anti-sublime, since it allows quotidian, automatic, and repetitive elements to

---

23   Hazel Hutchison, *The War that Used Up Words: American Writers and the First World War* (London: Yale University Press, 2015) 2.

cancel out the ineffability, immeasurability, and transcendence of traditional war representation. Thus, Borden, Price, and Sitwell put into question one of the most prevalent Great War tropes, namely that of the modern sublime as an "abyss, where verbal logic collapses" and words fail to "denominate a knowable, controllable world."[24] In order to demonstrate in what ways these three narratives perform an anti-sublime representation of Great War and shell shock, this chapter is divided into sections thematically, exposing instances of the tropes of the pastoral and the carnivalesque.[25]

Pastoral

Paul Fussell writes that the English pastoral "invok[es] a code to hint by antithesis at the indescribable," for comfort or measurement;[26] such a definition of the pastoral trope in Great War literature is particularly resonant with the purposes of the sublime. Written as a response to Erich Maria Remarque's *All Quiet on the Western Front* (1929), Price's *Not So Quiet* is not the average pastoral narrative, as the antithesis between what can be described and what cannot be described is lost, and there is neither comfort, nor an exact measurement of the tragedy. The story vividly depicts the war experiences of upper class volunteer ambulance driver Nellie Smith. The novel's hybridity, its being part testimonial and part fiction, avoids the potential solipsism of personal confession and reflects wider issues that relate to Great War shell shock, such as socially-constructed notions of gender and class. To uncover these elements, examining the role of the

---

24   Vincent Sherry, *The Great War and the Language of Modernism* (Oxford: Oxford UP, 2003) 166 and 212.

25   Tracey Loughran writes that there is a difference between shell shock and PTSD, and that shell shock is tied to a specific, albeit contradictory, historical narrative (10). In the same vein, I recognize that shell shock is not one and the same with trauma, insofar as the latter is the general category under which every psychological affliction falls. In this chapter I refer to trauma as war trauma and shell shock to incur the specific symptoms of the disorder.

26   Paul Fussell, *The Great War and Modern Memory* (Oxford: Oxford UP, 1975) 235.

pastoral is of essence, since it is a multilayered trope of narration that, in Jörn Steigerwald's words, performs a "game with the reader," as opposed to a one-way representation and preservation of tradition.[27]

One encounters such nuanced narration of the pastoral at the most intense and climactic moments of Price's novel. As an ambulance driver, Smithy, as everyone calls her, must drive the injured soldiers from the Front Line to a designated hospital. A large portion of the novel is concerned with the constant journeys from the Front Line to the hospital, and what takes place until Smithy drops off the traumatized soldiers. For that amount of time and space, not only are the soldiers and Smithy part of the same predicament, but the narration follows the tangled axes of soldierly trauma and civilian life: when, during one of the fiercest snowstorms, Smithy drives the ambulance to hospital Number Eight, the traumatized men at the back of the ambulance start wailing. In order for Smithy to focus on driving through the snowstorm, she mediates her own shock by thinking about her life as a civilian:

> I must fix my mind on something. . . . What? I know—my coming-out dance. My first grown-up dance frock [. . .] *Did I hear a scream? . . .* Made over a petticoat . . . *don't let them start screaming . . .* a petticoat of satin [. . .] *Was it a scream? . . .* [. . .] my hair up in little rolls at the back . . . *another scream—the madman has started, the madman has started. I was afraid of him* [. . .] Thirty-one little rolls like fat little sausages [. . .] *The shell-shocked man has joined in.*[28]

---

27   Jörn Steigerwald, "Arcadie historique Paul et Virginie de Bernardin de Saint-Pierre, entre classicisme et préromantisme," *Revue Germanique Internationale* 16 (2001):69, translated by Olivier Mannoni and Françoise Mancip-Renaudie, accessed July 22, 2017, https://rgi.revues.org/86016:200.

28   Evadne Price (aka Helena Zenna Smith), *Not So Quiet . . . : Stepdaughters of War* (New York: Feminist Press, 1989) 98-99, emphasis in the original.

Smithy's reminiscing of her peaceful life and the happy event of her coming-out are still narrated through echoes of her current trauma, as if the only language that she can speak is shell-shocked. The "thirty-one little rolls" on her hair are uncannily likened to "fat little sausages:" considering that Smithy and the women on her team have not had enough to eat for weeks, and that the wounded soldiers are described merely as meat, as in the case of a soldier having "a wagging lump of raw flesh on [his] neck, that was a face a short time ago,"[29] this is an abject metaphor. Additionally, the image of Smithy from her peaceful past is a repetition itself, "copied from a picture post card of Phyllis Dare or Lily Elsie."[30] The repetitive structure seeps into Smithy's alternative pastoral reminisce and fails to comfort her. Smithy's flashback is of pastoral nature in terms of tone and theme. For Fussell, "recourse to the pastoral is an English mode of both fully gauging the calamities of the Great War and imaginatively protecting oneself against them."[31] Price's novel refutes this interpretation of the pastoral, since, not only does the pastoral image fail to protect Smithy from her traumatic reality, but more importantly, the trauma trickles into the pastoral image, joining the individual and collective traumas and performing what Cathy Caruth terms "the destruction of experience, which can never be grounded in the unity of a single position or voice."[32]

As opposed to Sassoon's and Owen's pastoral, which for Fussell function as withdrawals from the horrors of the Great War, Price's pastoral scene that alternates with grotesqueness designates the exact opposite. Even if Smithy is called Nellie when she returns to her civilian life, her reality does not change: her family's resoluteness to send her and her sister back to the war is equally traumatizing—"'I think it's the most disgraceful thing I've ever

---

29 Ibid., 95.

30 Ibid., 99.

31 Fussell, 235.

32 Cathy Caruth. *Unclaimed Experience: Trauma, Narrative, and History* (Baltimore: JHU Press, 2016) 121.

encountered,' says Mother" when Smithy reveals she is not going back.³³ This reverse pastoral refutes sublimity, since the remembered image is polluted by the war, as seen by the abject metaphor, thus not being preserved whole even in memory, while at the same time the remembered image bears no mystery. Importantly, Smithy's description is not a product of intensive thinking about her idyllic past, but a habitual technique for her to keep her sanity. This behaviour contradicts the traditional Great War pastoral sublimity, since, as it has been argued, "the anti-sublime is not based on contemplation but on habitual behavior."³⁴

Although Sitwell is generally more faithful to the English tradition of the pastoral containing contemplative elements, her images are again less than wholesome and are filled with the premonition of war. The second chapter of *I Live Under a Black Sun* is the prelude to the war, and is filtered through pre-war country images and womanly presence:

> Under the hot gold rays of the rough fruitful sun, the wisdom and lore of the countrysides sprang from the growth and ripening and dying of the seasons, from the peaceful rhythms of their life, rising and toiling and sowing and reaping in the holy fields, loving and giving birth, growing old and sinking into sleep. This was the life they knew in the countrysides before the dawn of the day that was to change and maim the rhythm of the seasons and of all pulses.³⁵

Sitwell clearly employs this pastoral image to provide measurement for the impending disaster, but, contrary to popular pastoral references during

---

33 Price, 183.

34 Konstantinos Vassiliou, "Sublime and Anti-sublime: Reconsidering the Relation of the Sublime to Technology," *Contemporary Aesthetics* 15 (2017), accessed July 22, 2017, http://www.contempaesthetics.org/newvolume/pages/article.php?articleID=784.

35 Edith Sitwell, *I Live under a Black Sun* (London: Peter Owen, 2007) 19.

the Great War that denote nostalgia for ruralism,[36] her imagery betrays expectation: what Sitwell provides us with is not a mere static representation of landscape, but rather the depiction of a living organism to be mutilated. Her retrospectively bitter imagery is reinforced as the chapter continues, with the light of the countryside concealing instead of revealing:

> An old ragpicker was stooping over a dustbin, searching for treasures left over by the night; her bonnet and hair were like black and filthy cobwebs, her dress seemed as if she had stolen it from the habitations of the dead. But the light, falling like snow upon her, changed her stature and the nature of her rags till she seemed tall and splendid as a queen. The light, falling on the grey waste of cokers in the dustbin had covered it with a sparkle like that of gold.[37]

Not only is Sitwell's peacescape pregnant with death, but its memory is blemished. In both passages, anti-sublimity is ripe, since the depiction focuses on less than haughty imagery: the quotidian habits of poor, anonymous "they," and the haunting and base presence of a homeless woman. For both Sitwell and Price, the traditional irrevocability of Sassoon's and Owen's pastoral heaven is a myth.

Borden approaches the pastoral with similar anti-sublimity in her vignette titled "The Regiment," contained in *The Forbidden Zone*:

> There was no sign of horror in the heavens or upon the earth. The summer world was deep, immense, beautiful. High white clouds were moving slowly towards Belgium, moving without movement through a sky ineffably blue, superb castles of white vapour, floating towards a

---

36 Fussell, 231.

37 Sitwell, 19-20.

land called No Man's Land, and their shadows were flung like banners far below over the green meadows and fields of yellow corn.[38]

Borden's opening of "The Regiment" depicts a peacescape that is not perfect, but seems to have been heading towards destruction all along. The depiction of the scape is almost anachronistic, since the passage refers to the summer before the war, while at the same time depicting No Man's Land as ubiquitous. The contradiction between the introductory sentence and the mention of No Man's Land undermines the sublimity of the peacescape's description, and adds irony and bathos, which are key for anti-sublimity. It is this anti-sublime break in the passage that symbolizes the break that the Great War brought on. Borden uses the pastoral anti-sublimity as yet another means of expressing the horror of the war. The clouds' shadows resembling banners is reminiscent of the defense of nations and becomes literally a foreshadowing of impending tragedy. The whole passage seems to express denial: the words that are used by Borden are reminiscent of war, and yet used in a supposedly peaceful context. "Vapour" alludes to gas, "moving without movement" refers to No Man's Land, "castles" and "banners" point to battle, and in the middle of this first paragraph the word "ineffably" winks at the reader.

Another experiment with the pastoral in *The Forbidden Zone* occurs when the domestic scape and the warscape come together in the tableau vivant of the vignette titled "The Square," in which an unknown, omniscient narrator witnesses the everyday life of a non-descript city from their window:

> Below my window in the big bright square a struggle is going on between the machines of war and the people of the town [. . .] The business of

---

38   Mary Borden, *The Forbidden Zone*, (London: Heinemann, 1929) 21.

killing and the business of living go on together in the square beneath the many windows, jostling each other.[39]

There are two different comparisons taking place in "The Square." Borden stresses the ability of women who have stayed behind and the square of the town becomes for women what the trenches are for men: within the square, "the little women" are busy if bereaved. They seem to be carrying on exhibiting symptoms of shell shock as they perform quotidian tasks: "they scurry," "instinctively dodging," they talk "without smiling," and "they stare in front of them." Borden compares the traumatized experience of men and women by writing that women "are staring at life," while men are "staring at death." Non-combatants' trauma becomes equally important as the realities of busy women and dying men become interwoven, but that is not all: men and women never coincide on the square, as, on Saturdays, the women set up their market in the square and "there is no room [. . .] for the generals, nor for the dying men in the ambulances. The women are there."[40] Borden's description of scape resembles Price's and Sitwell's in that sense, since the square is there to accommodate the spectacle of the war performed by civilians or soldiers: there is no wholesome and harmonious scape prior to the war, but instead, the scape acquires purpose because of the war. The fact that the vignette does not include any other information on the square's whereabouts suggests that perhaps the square has been summoned for the purposes of the war only, just as pastoral images were summoned to escape the war. The parallelism of women and men sharing a scape and a reality and yet being unable to see each other hint at a pastoral image with a characteristic anti-sublimity: by combining an everyday, peaceful activity with the soldiers' dying, Borden uses the shell-shocked women's mundane actions to name and

---

39 Ibid., 13.
40 Ibid., 15-16.

articulate the ineffable war trauma. Much like Sitwell and Price, who refuse to narrate a pure pastoral pre-war past, Borden tells of a Great War trauma that extends into the future as much as it does into the past.

Carnivalesque

The predominant propaganda narratives around the role of women in the Great War revolved around "the patriotic mother and the dutiful nurse," roles which carried the ideal of femininity from civilian life to wartime.[41] There are a number of narratives that seek to actively debunk this idea by telling the stories of women joining the war effort, mostly ambulance drivers, who discover their lesbianism.[42] Price, Borden, and Sitwell contest the official discourse of a unified femininity and an official war discourse by employing carnivalesque tropologies in their war narratives. All three narratives comprise a plethora of voices and paratext: Price's adaptation of Winifred Young's wartime diary creates a female experience of the Great War that is mediated by class structures as much as gender politics; Borden consciously creates fragments, or sketches, as she calls them, of wartime experience, where characters' lives are merged and co-exist in wartime; and Sitwell's carnivalesque allegory comprises images littered with Jonathan Swift's quotations as opposed to clear narration, as well as a merging of the private desolation of her protagonists with the collective black sun that the Great War was.

In *Rabelais and His World*, Mikhail Bakhtin writes that carnival in social life is the "people's second life,"[43] and a time and place during which "the

---

41   Meg Albrinck, "Borderline Women: Gender Confusion in Vera Brittain's and Evadne Price's War Narratives," *Michel de Certeau and Narrative Tactics* 6, No. 3 (October 1998): 274, accessed January 1, 2017, http://www.jstor.org/stable/20107157.

42   Most notably two works by Radclyffe Hall: *The Well of Loneliness* (1928) and *Miss Ogilvy finds herself* (1934).

43   Mikhail Bakhtin, *Rabelais and His World*, transl. by Hélène Iswolsky (Bloomington: Indiana UP, 1984) 8.

suspension of all hierarchical rank, privileges, norms, and prohibitions" occurs.⁴⁴ Even from this partial definition, one sees the relationship between carnivalesque narration and anti-sublimity: the carnival is intended as an experience that is base, bathetic, and measurable to its last detail. Julia Kristeva adds that the carnivalesque tropology is inherently dialogical and "a spectacle, but without a stage," where actor and spectator merge.⁴⁵ What connects the carnivalesque tropology with Price's narration is the annihilation of rank and even the suspension of humanity, since women who are fighting and doing "their bit" turn into automatons.⁴⁶ Throughout her volunteering experience, Smithy encounters many different classes and slowly but surely rejects her own upper class background:

> The B.F.'s father is a motor manufacturer; Etta Potato is a virgin war widow; [. . .] Tosh has been in the picture papers so often she hasn't a shred of private life left; Skinny is the only child of a big pot at the War Office; while I am the nondescript daughter of a nondescript father who made money.⁴⁷

At the frontline, civilian status does not matter, and all women acquire different ranks to the ones they had in their previous lives, along with new names that reflect their roles in the camp: Tosh is the masculine woman, Smithy is an every-woman, the B.F. is a self-righteous advocate of freedom (which is probably why Smithy gives her the most literal nickname, two letters that stand for her own name), and Mrs. Bitch is

---

44   Bakhtin, 10.

45   Julia Kristeva, *The Kristeva Reader*, ed. by Toril Moi, trans. by Léon S. Roudiez and Seán Hand (New York: Columbia UP, 1986) 48-49.

46   Price, 33.

47   Ibid., 23.

the camp's Commandant, who is "punishment-mad,"[48] and treats all the women with "impartial hellishness."[49] As the characters co-exist, they influence each other and function as one well-oiled machine, whose habits and repeated processes are reminiscent of "the comic rites and cults, the clowns and fools, giants, dwarfs, and jugglers, the vast and manifold literature of parody."[50] Price depicts her surroundings as a parody and a contradiction, referring to the "wholesale slaughter" that the ambulance drivers experience, a wholly intense and yet fragmented experience, much like the nature of shell shock.[51] Similarly, Sitwell depicts melancholia as the great equalizer when she "focuses not on a single, culturally-privileged form of melancholia embodied in a creative male subject—as Freud arguably does,"[52] but rather provides stories of melancholy from every social stratum and gender.

For the characters of *Not So Quiet*, the war itself is a parody of the official narrative. Smithy explicitly juxtaposes the two different narrations of the war, as her family understand it and as she experiences it:

> "*It is such fun out here, and of course I'm loving every minute of it*," [. . .] The only kind of letter they want. Father can take it to his club and swank [. . .] "proud to do her bit, God bless her" [. . .] They've made me a heroine, one of England's Splendid Women, and I'm shaking with fright.[53]

---

48   Ibid., 18.
49   Ibid., 124.
50   Bakhtin, 5.
51   Price, 18.
52   Jean Radford, "Modernist Melancholy: Edith Sitwell's Black Sun," in *At Home and Abroad in the Empire: British Women Write the 1930s*, ed. by Robin Hackett, Freda Hauser, and Gay Wachman, (Newark: University of Delaware Press, 2009) 209.
53   Price, 31-34.

Smithy parodies the official narrative in her letter to her parents and the carnivalesque style shows in the exaggeration of the statement, as well as the italics. The self-reflexive polyvocality that is characteristic of the novel counters the "masculine economy" of the Great War.[54] In this sense, Price's war narrative is anti-sublime, since it represents the war by difference and in parody. As Kristeva notes, "On the omnified stage of carnival, language parodies and relativizes itself, repudiating its role in representation; in so doing, it provokes laughter but remains incapable of detaching itself from representation."[55] Price's narration shows its sickened commitment to representation through various gaps and ellipses, but by employing degradation instead of sublimity:

> Mother smug, saccharine-sweet . . . shelves of mangled bodies . . . filthy smells of gangrenous wounds . . . shell-ragged, shell-shocked men . . . men shrieking like wild beasts inside the ambulance until they drown the sound of the engine . . . *"Nellie loves to be really in it"* —no God to pray to because you know there isn't a God—how shall I carry on? . . . *"Proud to do her bit for the old flag."*[56]

Instead of stating that representing the war experience is ineffable, Price employs "the structural dyads" and degrading language found in the carnivalesque tropology, particularly the antithesis between "food and excrement, praise and curses, laughter and tears,"[57] in order to counter what Fussell considers to be the indescribability of the bad news of the Great War.[58] "Saccharine-sweet" and "shelves" allude to food and are directly

---

54   Albrinck, 271.
55   Kristeva, 50.
56   Price, 33.
57   Kristeva, 49.
58   Fussell, 70.

juxtaposed to the soldiers' "gangrenous wounds." From a linguistic point of view, Price employs sets of words that are directly opposing, so that the full meaning can be conveyed. Additionally, if the news from the nurses and ambulance drivers of the war is unwanted in its bleak and obscene truth, then Price's antitheses that showcase the distance between her narrative and the official, "sublime" story would compel one to listen.

A more literal version of dialogism in relation to soldierly and civilian trauma is performed by Borden, particularly in her sketch "The Beach," where an amputee veteran and his wife take a walk on the beach towards the end of the Great War. Although the couple address one another, they are not having a conversation; instead, their individual voices form a complete picture. The woman's repetitive articulations betray her trauma: "The beach is perfect, the sun is perfect, the sea is perfect,"[59] and the man's complaining about his phantom left foot is described in terms of parody:

> The old foot begins the old game, then I look down and it's not there any more, and I'm fooled again. He laughed. His laughter was such a tiny sound in the great murmur of the morning that it might have been a sand-fly laughing.[60]

Equally, the woman's comforting statement seems to be appropriated by nature: "what is it, darling? Are you in pain? Are you tired?[61] The word "darling" seems to be repeated infinitely, "sounding and sounding like a little hollow bell,"[62] being a "faint mocking echo" (44), until the word becomes part of their surroundings: "Darling, darling," far out the bell-buoy was

---

59 Borden, *Zone*, 42.
60 Ibid., 44.
61 Ibid., 43.
62 Ibid., 43.

sounding.⁶³ The displaced laughter and the repetition of the word "darling," which is also placed in quotation marks as if truly spoken by someone, are elements that refute the singularity of the war story and dialogically compile the narrative.

A similar treatment of polyvocality is found in *I Live*. Sitwell writes the mock-biography of Jonathan Swift, using facts from Swift's life and his novel *Gulliver's Travels*, while setting the story in the Great War. The narrative oscillates from the personal, with descriptions of Jonathan Hare's and his lovers' lives, to the collective, with interpolated depictions of the results of the Great War. Whereas Sitwell has every opportunity to not discuss the Great War directly, she interrupts the biography to tell stories of trauma and death, being conscious of the fact that the story of the war cannot be contained in a singular official narrative:

> Eight years had passed since the maelstrom died, and now, when the sun rises over the desecrated earth, no cry is raised by the race that lies beneath it. Under the dawn the betrayed lie patient. We need not fear to hear their voices [. . .] we shall see a shadow in our path, like a ghost from the solemn and revengeful dead, from the loving and pitying dead, arisen to ask us, what have we made from all the oceans of blood that have spilt for us, from all the words that have been laid down for us.⁶⁴

At this point the narrator speaks of voices that haunt the civilian population, arguing that the voices that belong to the deceased contribute to the community's perpetual shell shock. In this sense, not only is civilian trauma an affect that extends into the future, but also a means of communication between the dead and the traumatized. This dialogue

---

63 Ibid., 47.
64 Sitwell, 137.

between the dead and the traumatized, and the past and future culminates into transgenerational trauma: "The dead are beneath the earth and the women who clasped them to their hearts lie in the dawn alone [. . .] hold[ing] to their hearts an alien child grown in their blood but foreign to it."[65] Despite the general nature of the statements, anti-sublimity is achieved through the successful combination of rational representation and imaginative narration.

Degradation is another key concept for the Bakhtinian carnivalesque: "Degradation here means coming down to earth as an element that swallows up and gives birth at the same time."[66] This almost paradoxical statement of killing and burying something in order for something bigger to emerge can be detected in Great War catchphrases such as "a war to end all wars" and "doing one's bit," with the implication being that killing and/or being killed will result in a collective good that transcends individual existence. For Sue Vice, the carnivalesque trope of degradation belongs to the genre of grotesque realism, whose primary purpose is to ground "anything ineffable or authoritarian, a task achieved principally through mockery."[67] This moving towards the earth in a literal and linguistic way but also metaphorical way is symptomatic of the anti-sublime narration: the description of the effects of the Great War on bodies in minutely accurate terms adds to the anti-sublimity of the narrative. In this sense, Bakhtin's degradation and anti-sublimity have a lot in common. If the sublime makes its appearance through reductio ad absurdum techniques to represent an abundance of horror,[68] then Borden's intentional moving away, or rather, downwards, from descriptions of war and shell shock that inspire awe, is fundamentally anti-sublime.

---

65   Ibid., 137.
66   Bakhtin, 21.
67   Sue Vice, *Introducing Bakhtin* (Manchester: Manchester UP, 1997) 155.
68   Fussell; McLoughlin, *Authoring War*, 153.

Borden's vignette "Moonlight" performs a conscious split between sublimity and anti-sublimity through degradation, as it contains the natural world of beauty and the artificial world of the pop-up hospital. The protagonist and narrator, presumably Borden herself, is concerned with the natural environment's awe inspiring traits "polluting" the gruesome environment of her workplace:

> The moonlight is a pool of silver on the linoleum floor [. . .] Everything in my cubicle is luminous. My clothes hanging on pegs, my white aprons and rubber boots [. . .] the big sharp scissors on the table—all these familiar things are touched with magic and make me uneasy.[69]

For the nurse who stays in the pop-up hospital and listens to "the little whimpering voice of a man who is going to die in an hour or two,"[70] her way of managing her own shock is to compulsively remove all hints of sublimity from the reality she is experiencing. Familiar things must not be tinged with sublime elements that upset the nurse's "routine:"[71] "lovely night, lovely lunatic moon, lovely scented love-sick earth—you are not true; you are not part of the routine."[72] In both the excerpt above and the description of the nurse's routine, the dash is used as a fundamental element of grounding the sublimity of the previous part of each sentence. This lexical grounding is repeated in the story when the nurse describes the war as "the Alpha and the Omega" of the world.[73] Borden refrains from using expressions that distance war from conscious representation. Thus, the compulsive manifestation of the nurse's trauma is to ground her responses to the anti-sublime.

69   Borden, *Zone*, 51.
70   Ibid., 51.
71   Ibid., 53.
72   Ibid., 55.
73   Ibid., 53.

Degradation in Price and Sitwell has less to do with volunteer fieldwork and is more related to the fading away of moral and human values. The juxtaposition between Smithy's experience in her letters to her parents and her actual experience performs the twofold task of tricking the reader into half-believing that there are some ineffable truths about the war (which is quickly overruled as Smithy is explicit in her diary), while highlighting the doubt that upper classes want to hear specific details about the war that stretch beyond the ineffable grand statements: Smithy imagines her father bragging to his group of upper-class friends, through his limited vocabulary, that one of his daughters is "pretty well in the firing line [. . .] doing her bit, you know, doing her bit [. . .] proud to do her bit."[74] In this sense, the break between sublime and anti-sublime language designates civilian moral degradation. In the same respect, Sitwell employs already existing language of Swift's writings to narrate the human degradation that takes place during the Great War, degrading Britain's already precarious morals: "For the two nations that alone inhabit the earth, the rich and the poor, walking to their death in opposed hordes, had found the only force that could bind them together, a cannibalistic greed, hatred, and fear."[75] Sitwell narrates that "Thus began the Plague that was to sweep Europe" and uses Swift's novel to show that some took advantage of it: "a man [. . .] imagin[es] in his ferocious hatred, 'twenty thousand of them [horses] breaking into an European army, confounding the ranks, overturning the carriages, battering the warrior's faces into mummy by terrible yerks from their hinder hooves.'"[76] The carnivalesque takes another stance at this point, as its key elements of reproduction and regeneration become literal: Sitwell reproduces Swift's comparison between the Houyhnhnms and humans to show moral degradation.

---

74 Sitwell, 32.

75 Ibid., 29.

76 Ibid., 30.

As discussed earlier, sublimity refers to extraordinary terror that leaves the audience or participant in awe; this is true of some aspects of shell shock, but at the same time does not reflect aspects of psychological trauma that do not necessarily inhibit continuation. Price's, Borden's, and Sitwell's narrations feature images of automata and mechanization that are direct results of shell shock, but instead of breaking communication and progress, they facilitate the war effort. Price's narrative shows that despite Smithy's trauma of witnessing death, she goes on functioning automatically: "Mechanically I sit up straight behind my steering wheel. Mechanically I switch off the lights."[77] The sentence reflects this automatism through the lack of punctuation. Even after Smithy's best friend, Tosh, dies in her arms and Smithy succumbs to family pressure and decides to enlist again as a cook's assistant, her trauma is shown through mechanized composure and not through hysterical collapse:

> I am a slot machine that never goes out of order. Put so much rations into the slot and I will work so long, play so long, and sleep so long. The administration is perfect. Everything is regulated. Even my emotions [. . .] I am not unduly happy, neither am I noticeably unhappy . . . I would not dare be either.[78]

In this excerpt, Price performs a double social commentary, as she hints at both the exploitation of women's labour during the war, as well as the denial that women can exhibit symptoms of shell shock if they have not been under fire. Price's construction and development of Smithy's character as a duty-performing volunteer is a literal and anti-sublime trope that shifts attention from the typical model of the Great War shell-shocked man, who

---

77   Price, 151.

78   Ibid., 214-215.

was seen as a body "twitching, each limb working in a different direction."[79] Price's description corresponds with Frederick Walker Mott, who, in his 1919 treatise *War Neuroses and Shell Shock*, points out that "under intense emotional shock an individual may be deprived of even elemental perceptions; not seeing any more, not hearing any more, not feeling any more, transformed into a simple automaton."[80]

The trope of the shell-shocked woman as automaton appears in Borden's narration as well. Borden's depiction of the shell-shocked woman is performed along Mott's lines in "The Square," where she compares the motors and the women as seen from the narrator's window. Through the comparison, it appears that the motors have acquired life, while women have become motorized:

> The motor cars have all gone wrong. They are queer. [The women] ignore the motors; they do not see the fine scowling generals, nor the strained excited faces in the fast touring cars, nor the provisions of war under their lumpy coverings. They do not even wonder what is in the ambulances. They are too busy.[81]

Borden comments on civilian shell shock by parodying civilian space and switching characterizations of the woman and the motor cars. Perhaps because both war accounts reflect the situation at the French Front, Borden's depiction of the shell-shocked nurse is very close to Price's portrayal of the anaesthetized yet capable ambulance driver. In her sketch "Moonlight," Borden describes a fellow nurse, who tends to wounded soldiers, as "no longer a woman. She is dead already, just as I am [. . .] Blind, deaf, dead—she is

---

79 Ibid., 92.

80 Frederick Walker Mott, *War Neuroses and Shell Shock* (London: Hodder and Stoughton, 1919) 120.

81 Borden, *Zone*, 14.

strong, efficient, fit to consort with gods and demons—a machine inhabited by the ghost of a woman."[82] The machinic made-up of the female volunteer's body is emphasized by Price, too, whose protagonist, Smithy, claims to exist in "a flesh and blood case containing nothing save the machinery that keeps Smith, assistant cook, alive."[83] The trauma of war is manifested through references to automation in Sitwell's novel as well, albeit more subtly, and in a sense, from a collective perspective. For Anna, one of Jonathan Hare's rejected lovers, the years after the war bring an unexpected realization: "this year, the whole of life seemed changed, even the summer was dimmed—was only the mechanical dull action of the light and shadow over a dark world. Grief is like this."[84] Faithful to her covert political commentary, Sitwell alludes to the remembered repetitive lightning of weapons as they must have been seen from the countryside, but also points to repetition as a collective symptom of trauma and grief.

For Borden, Price, and Sitwell, the Great War is not immeasurable, but paved and counted on human bodies and minds. In this chapter, I have presented the tropes through which Borden, Price, and Sitwell stray from the supposed challenges of war writing and contest the supposed sublimity of Great War representations, thus exposing the aporias of the official narratives on shell shock. The terrains of anti-sublime tropology are the pastoral and the carnivalesque. Where other Great War narratives present the war in terms of absence and other-worldliness, Borden, Price, and Sitwell deconstruct the nostalgia that is attached to pastoral narration; dissect the other-worldliness of shell shock and trauma; and reveal, through often subtle instances of repetition, the lasting effects of shell shock and the narrative tropes through which it can be accessed.

---

82 Ibid., 59-60.

83 Price, 217.

84 Sitwell, 176.

Bibliography

Albrinck, Meg. "Borderline Women: Gender Confusion in Vera Brittain's and Evadne Price's War Narratives." *Michel de Certeau and Narrative Tactics* 6, no. 3, October 1998, pp. 271-291. *JSTOR*, http://www.jstor.org/stable/20107157. Accessed January 1, 2017.

Bakhtin, Mikhail. *Rabelais and His World*. Translated by Hélène Iswolsky, Indiana UP, 1984.

Bonikowski, Wyatt. *Shell Shock and the Modernist Imagination: The Death Drive in Post-World War*. Routledge, 2016.

Borden Mary. *Sarah* Gay. London, Heinemann, 1931.

The Forbidden Zone. London, Heinemann, 1929.

Bourke, Joanna. *An Intimate History of Killing: Face to Face Killing in Twentieth Century Warfare*. London, Granta Books, 1999.

Caruth, Cathy. *Unclaimed Experience: Trauma, Narrative, and History*. JHU Press, 2016.

Dodman, Trevor. *Shell Shock, Memory, and the Novel in the Wake of World War I*. Cambridge UP, 2015.

Fussell, Paul. *The Great War and Modern Memory*. Oxford UP, 1975.

Grogan, Suzie. *Shell Shocked Britain: The First World War's Legacy for Britain's Mental Health*. Barnsley, South Yorkshire, Pen and Sword History, 2014.

Hutchison, Hazel, *The War that Used Up Words: American Writers and the First World War*. Yale University Press, 2015.

Hynes, Samuel. *A War Imagined: The First World War and English Culture*. Atheneum, 1991.

Joseph, Tiffany. "Non-Combatant's Shell-Shock: Trauma and Gender in F. Scott Fitzgerald's Tender Is the Night." *NWSA Journal* 15, no. 3, Fall 2003, pp. 64- 81. doi: 10.1353/nwsa.2004.0010. Accessed March 4, 2017.

Kant, Immanuel. *Critique of Pure Reason*. Translated and edited by Paul Guyer and Allen W. Wood, Cambridge UP, 1998.

Kristeva, Julia. *The Kristeva Reader*. Edited by Toril Moi, translated by Léon S. Roudiez and Seán Hand, Columbia UP, 1986.

Loughran, Tracey. *Shell-Shock and Medical Culture in First World War Britain*. Cambridge UP, 2017.

McLoughlin, Kate. *Authoring War: The Literary Representation of War from the Iliad to Iraq*. Cambridge UP, 2011.

---. *The Cambridge Companion to War Writing*. Cambridge UP, 2009.

Mott, Frederick Walker. *War Neuroses and Shell Shock*. London, Hodder and Stoughton, 1919.

Price, Evadne (aka Smith, Helena Zenna). *Not So Quiet . . . : Stepdaughters of War*. Feminist Press, 1989.

Radford, Jean. "Modernist Melancholy: Edith Sitwell's Black Sun." *At Home and Abroad in the Empire: British Women Write the 1930s*, edited by Robin Hackett, Freda Hauser, and Gay Wachman, University of Delaware Press, 2009, pp. 203-221.

Remarque, Erich Maria. *All Quiet on the Western Front*. Putnam & Company Ltd, 1970.

Showalter, Elaine. *The Female Malady: Women, Madness and English Culture, 1830-1980*. London, Virago, 1987.

Sherry, Vincent. *The Great War and the Language of Modernism.* Oxford UP, 2003.

Sitwell, Edith. *I Live under a Black Sun.* London, Peter Owen, 2007.

Steigerwald, Jörn. "Arcadie historique Paul et Virginie de Bernardin de Saint-Pierre, entre classicisme et préromantisme." *Revue Germanique Internationale* 16, 2001, pp. 69-86. Translated by Olivier Mannoni and Françoise Mancip-Renaudie, https://rgi.revues.org/86016:200. Accessed July 22, 2017.

Vassiliou, Konstantinos. "Sublime and Anti-sublime: Reconsidering the Relation of the Sublime to Technology." *Contemporary Aesthetics* 15, 2017, http://www.contempaesthetics.org/newvolume/pages/article.php?articleID-784. Accessed July 22, 2017.

Vice, Sue. *Introducing Bakhtin.* Manchester UP, 1997.

West, Rebecca. *The Return of the Soldier.* Petersborough, Broadview Press, 2010.

Winter, Jay. *The Cambridge History of the First World War: Volume 3, Civil Society.* Cambridge UP, 2014.

Iro Filippaki received her PhD in English Literature and Medical Humanities from The University of Glasgow. She is currently a postdoctoral researcher at the Center for Medical Humanities and Social Medicine at The Johns Hopkins University, where she researches war and trauma, and narrative medicine. In particular, Iro writes on the narrative representations of trauma and affect in a variety of texts and contexts: war narratives and video games; cancer memoirs, horror films, and Greek literature and culture. Her current book project explores the representations of resilience to war trauma in the literary imagination of the twentieth and twenty-first centuries.

REPORTING FROM THE NEUROPATHIC WARD

Eugène Jolas, *transition*, and Psychological Refuge

Jason Parks

Abstract

The following essay argues for a rereading of the transatlantic/Euro-American periodical *transition* (1927-1938) through a lens of psychological trauma, especially shell shock. *Transition*'s responses to the psychological dimensions of art, the psychology of the artist, and the psychological legacies of the war deserve more attention, especially if we are going to fully understand both the influence of shell shock on the shape and reception of transatlantic modernist literature, and on the peculiar form of Jolas' highly eclectic periodical. Starting with Jolas' experiences as a secretary in a psychiatric ward for US veterans, followed by close readings of the psychological and experimental aspects of selections from *transition* (Masson's "Combat De Poissons," Genevieve Taggard's "The Plague," and Kay Boyle's "On the Run"), and concluding with a brief discussion of Jolas's own poetry, I make the case that *transition's* strength lies in its simultaneous resistance to conflating art with trauma (and the artist with neurosis), and its unflinching openness to publishing experimental work that reflected the inexplicable dimensions of the human psyche—often referred to in *transition* as the poetry of "the night mind." *Transition* was, in magazine form, an ideal psychological refuge for the shell shocked veteran-artist. Jolas provided a space where the artist's war trauma was not a prerequisite for understanding or creating art, and, at the same time, *transition* invited its readers and contributors to feel free to create, explore, and express the inexplicable, all in a moment when modernism's political and aesthetic aspirations were increasingly and irrevocably dividing.

Note to Another Civilization

this age is distorted with madness—
fever stalks through the cities of stone,
Through misery-echoing hospitals and police-stations,
Through tenement houses in factory towns,
Through streets lonely with desire-furrowed faces—
And life goes through a metamorphosis of lies
Hidden in the noises of stammering accents
And laughter is dying. . . .

Eugène Jolas, 1926, *Cinema Poems*, p. 59

The Great War and Question of Influence

IN "The Avant-Garde, Madness and the Great War," Annette Becker[1] addresses a paradox in the discourse on madness among the postwar

---

1   See also Audoin-Rouzeau Stéphane, and Annette Becker. *14-18: Understanding the Great War*. Hill

avant-gardes. Why, Becker asks, is there no direct account of psychiatric war trauma in the works of artists such as Breton[2] and Aragon[3]? Despite first-hand combat experiences and sideline encounters with shell-shocked soldiers, she argues, the avant-gardes appeared (in their postwar art) to be circumventing both the collective and personal psychological costs of the Great War. For some artists, she continues, this omission was, perhaps, a conscious resistance to the psychological influence of war trauma upon their art. Citing French psychologist Georges Dumas' 1919 work, "Troubles Mentaux et Troubles Nerveux de Guerre[4]," Becker writes: "For these artists [such as Max Ernst and Paul Klee], the madness or sanity of the artist was beside the point. [As Dumas writes] 'There is hardly more sense in the claim that there is insane art as there is dyspeptic art or the art of those with knee troubles'" (81).

Echoing Dumas' essay, the Alsatian-American writer Eugène Jolas, most well known for his multilingual poetry[5] and his work as editor of *transition* (1927-1938), discusses the absence of the war in the work of postwar artists. In "Literature and the New Man" (*transition 19/20,* June 1930), Jolas states: "The period immediately following the war was one of disquiet and despair. But let us not forget that the war did not particularly influence the arts. It

---

and Wang, a Division of Farrar, Straus and Giroux, 2014.

2   André Breton, a founding figure in the Surrealist movement, was a French writer whose work appears in translation in *transition 12* (March 1928) and *transition 27 (*April-May 1938).

3   Louis Aragon, a French writer who was drafted into and served in both World Wars, was a co-founder of the Surrealist review *Littératur*e. His literary career spanned most of the twentieth century. A translation of his essay "Painting and Reality: A Discussion" appears in *transition* 25 (Fall 1936).

4   The open-source full text of Dumas' work can be found here: https://archive.org/details/39002010600642.med.yale.edu/page/n10

5   See the following articles for more insight into Jolas' multilingualism: Perloff, Marjorie. "'Logocinéma of the Frontiersman': Eugene Jolas's Multilingual Poetics and Its Legacies." In *Differentials: Poetry, Poetics, Pedagogy*, 82–101. Tuscaloosa: University of Alabama Press, 2004; Taylor-Batty, Juliette. *Multilingualism in Modernist Fiction*. Basingstoke: Palgrave Macmillan, 2013; Monk, Craig. "Eugene Jolas and the Translation Policies of *Transition*." *Mosaic: A Journal for the Interdisciplinary Study of Literature* 32, no. 4 (December 1999): 17–34; Kelbert, Eugenia. "Eugene Jolas: A Poet of Multilingualism." *L2 Journal* 7, no. 1 (January 1, 2015). http://escholarship.org/uc/item/9f7486t2.

interrupted temporarily an anti-positivist movement, and I am inclined to believe that we are only now returning to the point where we left off" (262, *Collected Writings*). Drawing from Aragon's *Anicet ou le Panorama, roman,* Becker raises the possibility of this rejection (or denial) of the war-as-artistic-influence as a special form of war protest. She quotes Aragon as follows:

> To ignore the war was for us a system, false without doubt but directed against the war. We thought that to talk of the war, even to damn it, was still to advertise its wares. Our silence seemed to us a way of deleting the war, of arresting it. Don't waste your time by telling me this was puerile, or of telling me about Under Fire (for which we had at least a certain respect). . . . If suppressing the war seemed an efficient way of combating it, this simply expressed our faith in the written word. To us everything written was an advertisement, or what today we would call propaganda. Breton called religion an advertisement for Heaven. (qtd. in Becker 73)

Aragon's statement, published nearly fifty years after the war, must, of course, also be put into perspective, as many of these avant-garde writers and painters, when actively serving as soldiers or medical personnel, consistently fell in line with their compatriots. Becker writes, "The future surrealists were, during the war, neither bloodthirsty combatants nor pacifists, dedicated, as Paul Eluard put it in 1916, to 'do their duty.' As such they were representative of the vast majority of those who fought in the war" (74). In Jolas' case, this dedication was equally evident during his service in the U.S. Army during WWI and WWII. Drafted into the U.S. Army in 1917, Jolas, a conscientious objector, served as the secretary to the chief psychiatrist in a U.S. military hospital. Later in his career, Jolas also served as part of the Allied efforts towards the denazification of the German press (Kiefer and Rumold 514). Long before his service in WWII, in which he fully devoted himself to training German newspaper reporters in a more objective approach to journalism, Jolas spent over a decade working on his magazine, which provided very different but equally important type of service to many postwar artists. Namely, a devotion to supporting and humanizing the work of experimental artists, some who did suffer greatly with psychological conditions, but also many who simply wanted to seek new paths and depths for artistic expression.[6]

In "The King's English is Dying: Long Live the American Language," from *transition 19/20* (June 1930), Jolas expresses his anti-psychological perspective on artistic creativity more thoroughly, while also clarifying a sharp distinction between *transition*'s mytho-poetic "Revolution of the Word" project and that of the surrealists. Jolas (who was one of the first English language and American translators of psychologist Carl Jung) writes:

> I agree with Dr. Jung in rejecting the theory that the artist is per se a neurotic one . . . This seems to me also the error of the surrealistes [sic], which I have point out several times. The surrealiste [sic] tries to evoke the subconscious in its raw and absolute state "without the intervention of reason." He does not try to organize [sic] the symbolic mechanics. He fails to see that here is a difference between the symbols of the dream and those of art. The dream is a biologic function of the instinctive. Art demands, however, that the entire personality be in play and that a conscious action follows the movement of the symbolical images [sic]. ("The King's English," 144)

---

6 While I do not have time to elaborate fully on how *transition* supported numerous artists, whose lives also ended in suicide, I recommend looking at Djuna Barnes' forward to "Selections from Letters" by Elsa Von Freytag-Loringhoven in *transition* 11 (Feb. 1928), p. 19, and "In Memoriam: Harry Crosby," *transition 19/20* (June 1930), pp. 218-233. The way that *transition* counters the narratives of the popular press regarding the suspected and/or confirmed suicides of various writers and artists provides a fascinating insight into how *transition* embraced an alternative and dignifying response to mental illness among artists.

Breton and Jolas, interestingly, had a similar experience working in military hospitals. As Becker points out, Breton was transformed by his experiences at the St. Dizier military hospital in the fall of 1916, particularly through his observations of shell-shocked soldiers (Becker 77-78).

"The Spectacle of Human Malady"

While he did not experience combat, Jolas was deeply transformed by his close contact with war trauma, specifically that of young American soldiers, both black and white, who had returned home after fighting in Europe. Jolas writes of one of his early experiences as a secretary to the chief psychiatrist at a base hospital in Virginia:

> The spectacle of human malady which I watched at close range in Ward 33 was an overwhelming experience. Here both Negroes and whites from Southern and Northern states passed through the ward for mental examination, cases of schizophrenia, alcoholism, dope addiction, psychopathic conditions of all kinds came to our attention. Sometimes the patients were kept under observation for a long period, at the end of which they were either discharged as incurable or returned to their regiments with specific recommendations. My duty consisted in typing their case histories. I had to listen to *fantasies* and *hallucinations*, to *frantic screams*, to *incessant weeping*. I heard paranoiacs crying out against a hostile world. (35-36, *Man from Babel*, emphasis added)

Although Jolas' expressions of an anti-psychological attitude towards war trauma in relation to modernist aesthetics should be considered, his recall of these experiences in his autobiography also give us another lens for understanding *transition*. In short, *transition*'s responses to the psychological dimensions of art, the psychology of the artist, and the psychological legacies of the war need far more attention, especially if we are going to fully understand the influence of shell shock on the shape and reception of American and transatlantic modernist literature, and the peculiar form of Jolas' pluralistic/heterogeneous interwar periodical.[7]

Transition's enduring value lies foremost in its explicit resistance to conflating art with trauma (and the artist with neurosis), and its equally unapologetic openness to publishing experimental works that reflected the inexplicable dimensions of the human psyche—including those dimensions sometimes referred to in *transition* as the poetry of "the night mind."[8] In his foundational study of *transition*, Dougald McMillan writes:

> *transition*'s contributors were not a close-knit literary cabal, but a loose alliance of writers whom Eugène Jolas attempted to bring together under the aegis of a theory partly imported from European movements, partly derived from the practice of important English-language innovators, and partly simply asserted out of the exigencies of his own personal background . . . Together the contributors of *transition* define an important wave of literary thought and practice that passed over Europe and America in the late 1920s and '30s. It was *transition* that proclaimed the poet's right to more direct presentation of the unconscious, greater linguistic experimentation, and freer development of personal mythic structures. And it was primarily *transition* that re-established the importance of "the word" which had suffered so much in the exaltation of the image in the first quarter of the century. (5)

---

7   For further discussion of *Transition*'s eclectic form, see the following: Setz, Cathryn, "Transocean: *transition's* anachronistic zeitgeists." *Modernist Cultures*, vol. 11, no. 1. 2016, pp. 65-85. doi: 10.3366/mod.2016.0126.

8   See Jolas, Eugene. "Night-Mind and Day-Mind." *Transition*, vol. 21, 1932 (March), pp. 222-223.

While this chapter cannot account for how many of *transition*'s over 400 contributors directly experienced shell shock, it is well documented that many of the artists/writers published in the magazine were closely connected to combat trauma, and as representatives of various factions within the conflict—including contributors such as Harry Crosby, Elliot Paul, Malcolm Cowley, Kay Boyle, Andre Breton, André Masson, Paul Klee, Carl Einstein, and Ernest Hemingway.

In the following pages, I will use close readings of the psychological and experimental aspects of just a few selections from *transition*'s four thousand pages of multilingual, multi-disciplinary contributions. My discussion will involve André Masson's painting, "Combat De Poissons" (*transition 3,* June 1927), Genevieve Taggard's short story, "The Plague" (*Transition* 5, August 1927), and an excerpt from a novel-in-progress from Kay Boyle, entitled, "On the Run" (*Transition* 16/17, Jun. 1929). To draw attention back to Jolas' editorial influence and the historical interwar context of the magazine, I will also include additional discussion of Jolas' interwar poetry. *Transition* was, in magazine form, an ideal example of how art and literature could serve as a psychological refuge for the shell-shocked veteran/artist. Jolas and his co-editors and translators provided a space where the artist's war trauma was not a prerequisite for understanding or creating art. At the same time, *transition* also invited readers and contributors to feel free to create, explore, and express the inexplicable, all in a moment when modernism's political and aesthetic aspirations were increasingly and irrevocably dividing.

In the opening issue, Jolas expresses the aspiration of the magazine as follows:

> TRANSITION wishes to offer American writers an opportunity to express themselves freely, to experiment, if they are so minded, and to avail themselves of a ready, alert and critical audience. To the writers of all other

countries, TRANSITION extends an invitation to appear, side by side, in a language American can read and understand. The result should be mutually helpful and inspiring. Contributions will be welcomed from all sources and the fact that an author's name is unknown will assure his manuscript a more favorable examination. . . . No rigid artistic formulae will be applied in selecting the contents of TRANSITION. If the inspiration is genuine, the conception clear and the result artistically organized, in the judgment of the editors, a contribution will be accepted. Originality will be its best recommendation. Neither violence nor subtlety will repel us. (Jolas, "Introduction", 137)

The idea that neither "violence nor subtlety will repel [them]," is especially pertinent with respect to postwar trauma, and the level of "violence" (which could be interpreted not just as gore, but also psychological violence in various ways) that ends up being alluded to in many of the creative contributions within the periodical.

One additional perspective I will also consider is how *transition* embodies certain aspects of Lutz Koepnick's recent theorization of "slow modernism." Through its publication of certain cubist and futurist paintings and sculptures, such as Juan Gris "Still Life" (*transition 4*, July 1927) and Boccioni's "Movement of a Bottle in Space" (*transition* 23, July 1925), and, in light of its psychological discourses, *transition*'s slowness is also an integral part of its status as a modernist refuge.

Experiment vs. Experience

While *transition* was open to all forms of experiment, it was not necessarily open to all forms of experience.[9] As one of the interwar era's

---
9   I would like to credit Sean Weidman, Penn State University, for providing me this exact phrasing

longest running "little magazines," one might expect to find at least one assemblage of WWI-themed texts. On the surface, however, very few works make overt references to the war. A complete digital search of the entire index of stories, critical essays, and artworks (based on the Charles Silet index) reveals only a single poem entitled "Postwar," one painting with the French word "Poissons (Combat)," and no titles using the words "trench," "battle," "fight," "bomb," or "soldier."

A closer reading of the stories and poems, published between 1927 and 1938, and populating the nearly four thousand pages of text, also reveals an apparent deflection away from any type of war or war trauma story—although there are occasional appearances of veterans as characters and, in the case of one story, the appearance of a physically-wounded veteran (see Laurence Vail's *Murder, Murder, transition 16/17*, June 1929). Due to Jolas' experiences in the Virginia military hospital, and other contacts with his own family following the war, Jolas' ability to empathize with war trauma may also be linked to a heightened sensitivity to the shell-shocked dimensions of avant-garde art, especially art created by veterans which invoked war trauma without speaking overtly about the war itself.

Transition's Biographical Omissions and the War Artist

A primary example of the kind of omission of a war reference included in *transition*, and one that Becker also cites in her discussion of madness and the avant-gardes is the painter Andre Masson. In *transition 3* (June 1927), Jolas included Masson's unsettling, violent painting "Combat De Poissons." A full color image of this painting can be found at: https://www.moma.org/collection/works/79309. As of April 2019, the MoMA website describes it as follows:

for describing the magazine. In a presentation of an early draft of this chapter, presented at the 2018 *Louisville Conference on Literature and Culture since 1900*, Mr. Weidman provided invaluable feedback and suggested these specific terms.

Masson made *Battle of Fishes* by freely applying gesso to areas of the canvas, throwing sand on it, then brushing away the excess. The resulting contours suggested forms "although almost always irrational ones," according to the artist around which he rapidly sketched and applied paint directly from the tube. The image that emerged suggests a savage underwater battle between sharp–toothed fish. Masson, *who was physically and spiritually wounded during World War I* (emphasis mine), joined the Surrealist group in 1924. He believed that, if left to chance, pictorial compositions would reveal the sadism of all living creatures." (https://www.moma.org/collection/works/79309)

Unlike the description attached to the painting in the twenty-first century, however, *transition* makes no mention of Masson's war experience. As the miniature biography in *transition* 3 (June 1927) states: "Andre Masson is a young French painter belonging to the Surrealist group, living in Paris, and deriving his recent inspiration from the wonders of the submarine world. He has translated the textures, colors and rhythms of undersea creatures and vegetation into a series of paintings now on view in the Galerie Simon" (110).

Despite including one of Masson's most evocative war paintings, *transition*'s editors have clearly made it part of their contrarian agenda to avoid categorizing artists in terms of their war experience. At first glance, Masson's painting actually appears more like a battle map than an underwater battle of sea monsters. In fact, because it is printed in black and white in *transition*, the blood pouring from the eyes of the fish, which is in red in the actual painting, could be interpreted as bodies of water or as outlines of other landmarks. For the soldier-reader of *transition*, I would argue that both images, the battle map and the sea battle, would be equally visible; however, the ambiguity of the painting, coupled with the black and white and reduced size in the magazine, will transform the reader's encounter in significant ways. Moreover, because the biography of Masson in *transition* does not mention his war experience, *transition* sends a clear message that it will avoid using the war as a way of mediating a reader's understanding of experimental works (even, and perhaps especially, with the most directly war-related ones).

This ironic rejection of the war, consequently, invites readers (then and now) to see *transition* as a special form of refuge. There is no direct editorial statement alluding to the fact that *transition* will not print war poems or war art. However, the content itself demonstrates an effort to de-sentimentalize and to separate its inclusion of experimental, and sometimes brutal art, with psychological trauma. A close reading of the absence (and subtle appearances) of war texts and images, then, reveals war trauma as a previously-unacknowledged explanation for *transition*'s longevity.

The Plague and/of War

One story that represents a combination of physiological and psychological disease that is also characteristic of shell shock (without direct reference to the war) is Genevieve Taggard's "On the Run" (*transition 5, August 1927)*. Genevieve Taggard's odd, naively colonialist narrative, "The Plague," while less stylistically fragmented than other experimental texts in *transition*, foregrounds the traumatized body through an extended focus on the effects of brain fever on one's psychological/mental perception of reality—particularly the colonialist's real or perceived relationship to another and, to an extent, the orientalized Other. In relation to the strange, untenable politics, if not outright racist or sexist works of many of the avant-garde (Dada and Surrealist) contributions in *transition*, Taggard's story is in familiar company. Nevertheless, the narrative perspective (of a young girl) and the rural location (colonial Hawaii) invites us to consider a range of topics related to, but not explicitly referencing, the soldier's traumatized mind/body—from a nationalistic, racial, and gendered perspective—that few other stories in *transition* even approximates.

Highly autobiographical, Taggard's "The Plague" follows a young American girl's experience of the bubonic plague at a Christian Mission in Hawaii. The story begins with the sickness of a Japanese servant, Hayashida, who had developed what the narrator describes as a "beubo" (inflamed lymph node) under his arms. Because he is also the school's janitor, there is (an unacknowledged but clearly racially-motivated) fear that the school has been contaminated. So, everyone is required to evacuate the area while it is fumigated. The narrative then follows the young girl's family to the coast where the entire family becomes ill. The girl then describes her psychological and bodily experience of "the plague."

Taggard's narrative is mostly straightforward. There are no elaborate similes in the opening paragraphs and the characters are all described with simple adjectives. Given *transition*'s emphasis on experimentation and innovation, one would have to question the inclusion of this story as one that exemplifies a revolution of language. But in its prominent use of a feverish dream (and some might also argue colonialist fantasy), "The Plague" partakes of *transition*'s employment of narrative to render anew the unceasing dialectics of mind/body, thought/action, brain/skin that is such an important part of the legacies of shell shock.

Before the story reaches its climax, in Genevieve's nightmare, it establishes the interlinking of sickness and health in the body of the character Hayashida. Taggard's narrator describes Hayashida as follows: "He was a big, raw-boned Japanese, gaunt and yellow, and very merry" (78). In young Genevieve's mind, "gaunt and yellow" and "merry" are meant to encapsulate the image of a healthy Japanese man. "Gaunt" and "Yellow," of course, may also have resonance for ones who suffered or witnessed the effects of mustard gas as well. Following Taggard's Orientalist feminization of Hayashida, Genevieve, the narrator, then describes his talents for gardening and general carpentry. Unfortunately for our understanding of the colonial perspective, the story of Hayashida drops off quickly in favor of Genevieve's experience. This erasure of the Other, of course, may also be read as a sign of the disposable attitude toward Hayashida and his compatriots. Though Hayashida's body is quickly erased from the story, however, the disease that afflicts him follows the colonials/missionaries. One might consider, here, how the shell-shocked soldier, upon returning home from the war, may also be "quickly erased" or "disposable" in the eyes of his/her community. Would a shell-shocked reader, perhaps, see affinity between the disposable attitude towards Hayashida and towards veterans (who may also be "gaunt" and "yellow")?

When Hayashida becomes sick, he is examined by a team of doctors and then hauled away in what the narrator describes as the "death wagon" (79). Through young Genevieve's eyes, one easily recognizes that Hayashida is some sort of infected rat that the community has to get out of sight immediately. When Genevieve is forced into quarantine with her family, however, one will see a connection between Hayashida's outsider status and Genevieve's family. Genevieve's mother even describes the children running up together from the shore as "wild things," which reinforces the colonial language in the earlier sections of the story. Considering *transition*'s European context, this also suggests additional correlation with the longstanding nineteenth-century literary depictions of the healthy European versus the body of the unhygienic "other."

The experience that seems to link Genevieve and Hayashida, and that perhaps momentarily levels the world out a little, however, is the sickness of the plague. One might also consider the leveling effects of the war experience as well. When talking about her experience of the illness that night, Genevieve uses the phrase "we were sick together" in reference to herself and her mother. Being "sick together," however, is also an important element of this story because the plague itself lived inside of all who experienced it. So, in that sense, a biological connection, even beyond the familial/genealogical connection becomes possible. Though readers never fully learn of Hayashida's fate, the line "we were sick together," which seems to unite Genevieve and her mother, also clearly reaches back to the earlier connection between Hayashida and Genevieve and her siblings. In numerous ways, Hayashida performed a traditionally motherly role, including "keeping [the children's] swings going" and singing "very sweet songs in a high silly voice" (78). Thus, the mother-daughter link via sickness can and should be extended to our reading of the connection between Hayashida and Genevieve's bodily experiences, and the vision she has as she lays under the mosquito net. Genevieve states, "I lay under the thick mosquito net as if I were as wide as the Pacific Ocean and the fever took one arm off to the east, the other to the west, my legs stretched into dimness, I gazed flat upward, fixed, at some immensity—I immense and facing immensity." Following this geographical expansion of her body, Genevieve then looks over at a lamp and describes it as a "yellow torment" (82). Since the only other item described as "yellow" to this point in the story was Hayashida, it is clear that Genevieve is absolutely "infected" by colonialist racist ideologies.

While Genevieve cannot name what torments her about the flame, one must not overlook the way that her mother's highly influential colonial perspective might be reinforcing a specific view of the "other," in this case, the "other" Orientalist/feminized mother-figure Hayashida. Since Genevieve is just a young girl, it is possible to see her as more impressionable, yet, as soon as the sickness is over, it is her actual mother who brings an end to her "torment." Taggard writes, "She fanned me and called out that I was her first born, and rubbed the wet hair from my head and chafed my feet. Her hand on my legs made them limited again at the bottom of the bed, not so long that they had no feet as a moment before" (83). After her mother "rubs" and "chafes" her sick body, erasing the "yellow torment," Genevieve eventually minimizes the horror and concludes with a simple thought: "It ended—fear and a sick headache and a little fever—that was all. And I did not die except in some experience of the mind" (83). Her mother has saved her from the "yellow fever," which, as I see it, was the nascent idea that Hayashida was, in some substantial way, a real human being.

As part of *transition*'s quest to "cure" the malady of banal language and conventional narrative, Taggard's story is one that could easily be passed over in our critical discussions for more grotesque or scholarly treatments of sickness and the Other.

In the opening issue to *transition*, Jolas, speaking for the editors, writes: "We believe, that although art and literature are, in many quarters, growing more definitively racial and national in coloring and texture, their appeal is becoming distinctly international" ("Introduction" 137). Taggard's story, then, can stand in as an example of how a narrative focus on the body in particular can highlight and reinforce these racial constructs or divisions, despite *transition*'s claims to the contrary for their own magazine. To extend this further, however, parallels may also be drawn between the marginalizing of the mentally and physically ill veteran. Though *transition* was proclaiming an international or pluralist-nationalist mission, and drew a vast number of contributions from veterans from all over Europe and America, stories like Taggard's remind us that stylistic and formal experimentation did not always equate with progressive ideological positions.

De-sentimentalizing the Sick Soldier's Body: Kay Boyle's Tubercular Collage

The purpose of the *papier collé* was to give the idea that different textures can enter into composition to become the reality in the painting that competes with the reality in nature. We tried to get rid of "trompe l'oeil" to find a "trompe l'esprit.". . . If a piece of newspaper can become a bottle, that gives us something to think about in connection with both newspapers and bottles, too. This displaced object has entered a universe for which it was not made and where it retains, in a measure, its strangeness. And this strangeness was what we wanted to make people think about because we were quite aware that our world was becoming very strange and not exactly reassuring.

Pablo Picasso (qtd. in Perloff, *The Futurist Moment*, 44)

If for Pablo Picasso collage brought materials from the physical world into new contexts where they were representational tools while remaining irreducibly themselves, Kay Boyle, through a specific contribution in *transition*, further adapted collage, using such found materials to evoke and thereby integrate sensual, bodily experience into her literary work. In the following section, I will demonstrate how Boyle's story "On the Run" resembles collage to de-sentimentalize the death scene, a common sentimentalized trope in pre- and post-war fiction. In crafting a literary collage of the tubercular body through object-based imagery, I argue, Kay Boyle allows readers to contemplate this disease (and the male soldier's dying body) in radically unconventional ways, both in relation to and apart from the "softer" physicality and sentimentality of the typical death scene.

We might be reminded here of Virginia Woolf's question about the ways that Western literature had ignored the body and why illness "has not taken its place among the prime themes of literature" (193). Woolf writes, "Novels, one would have thought, would have been devoted to influenza; epic poems to typhoid; odes to pneumonia; lyric to toothache" (193). While certainly no ode to tuberculosis, or to shell shock, Boyle's style re-embodies a modernist aesthetic that had come to see the male body as either steel-and-girders or essentially transparent. As part of *transition*'s status as a psychological refuge, this story is important because it provided an alternative model for creatively writing about and contemplating the emotions of watching the physical demise of a loved one that did not fall into conventional narrative methods. For any *transition* reader experiencing trauma or a sense of alienation, whether brought on by the shock of war or other shocks of modernization in the interwar era, stories like this, I believe, model and anticipate a therapeutic possibility for writing in a modernist (in this case cubist) mode.

"On the Run," set primarily in a hotel room in St. André-les-Alpes, and published in *transition 16/17* (June 1929), is a short story that recounts two lovers' final moments together as the male partner dies of tuberculosis. "On the Run" follows a compact, mostly linear structure of just thirteen paragraphs. The experimental narrative style includes a blend of realistic dialogue, surrealistic description, and free indirect discourse. While the dying man (who is based on Ernest Walsh, who was involved in a plane crash during flight training for the First World War, and who was also the father of Boyle's daughter, Sharon, although he died of tuberculosis five months prior to Sharon's birth) is the central figure, his companion, also referred to as Madame, is also at his side as he takes his final breaths. Aside from the human characters, the dismal descriptions of the surrounding landscape also reflect the physical features of a dying and diseased body. Considering the trauma of losing Walsh just months before their daughter's birth, one can also see how this story might have functioned as a way of writing about that loss without explicitly making it into autobiography.

As this brief summary of the story and its context should imply, the story might easily have fallen into a common trope of sentimental, travel-based fiction: two lovers, a bedside death scene, and an exotic locale. The tubercular death, of course, was nothing new to literature or life in America or Europe in the early twentieth century. In relation to the nineteenth-century novel, one is as likely to find a tubercular death as not. Furthermore, critics have typically cited this story in terms of its emotional intensity, and for its autobiographical resonance with Boyle's experience of Ernest Walsh's death (Clark 135).

In Boyle's "tubercular death" scene, however, formal experimentation overrides and reimagines the sympathetic, sentimental identification with physical and psychological breakdowns—for the lover and the beloved. Additionally, in reimagining the male body in this unsentimental fashion, Boyle's story provides a direct contrast to the idealized, hyper-masculine images of modern bodies in the Futurist works, such as those by Joseph Stella and Laurence Vail, which populate the pages of *transition*.

Although charged with emotion, the story's representation of sickness is moving precisely because it resists conventional sentimentality. Boyle's stylistic fragmentation, or "sick" form, and her use of multiple analogies between the dying body and the landscape of St. Andre, creates what should be understood foremost as a collage of the male tubercular body (which, in the context of my argument here, might also be analogous to the shell shocked body). While Boyle's fiction never departs from the familiar literary scene of sentimental fiction, her story distorts and reorders the man's dying body into a highly unsentimental collage, with a special emphasis on the stoma (oral cavity), including ropes of smoke as breath, a gaping sky as mouth, pigs' feet as a tongue, and rosary beads as decaying teeth. If the Futurist's response to "sentimental" fiction was to erase the feminine, Boyle's story provides an alternative response, which places focus directly on the reality of modern psychological theory's inability to provide an answer to the biological-pathological forces of nature. In other words, Boyle's story brings mortality back without the violence of the futurists or the sentiments of late-Victorian fiction.

In the opening paragraph, Boyle presents four key images: a mouth full of smoke, a "pink tide" of pigs, a gaping sky, and a crumbling finger. Each of these images heightens the reader's awareness of the male protagonist's sick body. The first three, in particular, are related to actions associated with the mouth, gustation and breathing in particular, while the "crumbling finger" places special emphasis on decaying flesh.

The first image, train smoke, serves as a layered metaphor for the choking and loss of breath that accompanies tuberculosis. In the opening lines, Boyle writes, "These little mountains ran in a sharp sea in the windows and the smoke from the engine twisted in strong white ropes through the car. He opened his mouth to say 'St. André-les-Alpes' and when he had opened it the smoke came in and filled it with bitterness" ("On the Run," 83). The first, immediate equation with the tubercular body is the relationship between smoke and choking. Instead of an image of smoke as a vapor or mist, though, the "breath" of smoke coming from the train and entering the protagonist's mouth is imagined as a solid material, a rope. In using white instead of black, sooty train smoke, which would be far more hazardous to one's physical body, this smoke is chemically much less dangerous to respiratory health. In depicting the ropes of smoke entering into the protagonist's mouth, the implication of choking associated with ropes also reinforces the association between choking and cigarette smoke that is carried on throughout the story. It also remind us of Wilfred Owen's poetry and the choking brought on by the nerve gas on the battlefield. Boyle's literary collage begins, then, by using a solid image of train smoke as a rope as a complex metaphor for the battlefield strangulation, and tubercular strangulation.

As the protagonist initially breathes in, however, he is not choked, but, at this moment, only tastes bitterness. While the bitterness can be read to indicate a mood or disposition, there is also the literal implication of flavor. Following the use of the word "bitterness" to place emphasis on the taste buds, Boyle's next sentence in the opening paragraph provides the visual, visceral image of a "soft pink tide of pigs" rushing underneath the train (83). She writes, "As the train stopped a soft pink tide of pigs rose out of the station-yard and ran in under the wheels of the wagon" (83). The pigs, in this moment, become important parts of the literary body-collage in multiple ways. Through Boyle's description of "pink tide," the tongue's texture becomes part of the mouth image, which is the central image of the tubercular body, and the choking soldier—an all too familiar experience for medical personnel.

The second material association with the pigs, aside from the wet, pink tide, reinforces another aspect of bodily health. As the story continues, pigs' feet become a food that can only be digested by healthy and strong bodies. This is seen when the protagonist thinks about ordering pigs feet as he is trying to cover up his illness: "A sick man would not want pigs feet grilled in batter and bread crumbs" (84). In order to try and convince the hotel owners that he is healthy enough to stay, the protagonist attempts to order food to cover up his illness. Unfortunately, however, it is nearly impossible to stop the fits of coughing. In a similar way, one might be reminded here of the stigmas that could be associated with war trauma, and how the soldier or nurse returning from battle may also try to cover his or her illness in other ways.

To complete the opening set of images and set the backdrop for her "collage" of the tubercular body, Boyle then describes a "crumbling finger" and a "white," "hot," and "gaping" sky. She writes: "The crest of the little alps was burning across the roofs of the town, with the dry crumbling finger of the church lifted and the sky gaping white and hot upon decay" (83). In ending the opening paragraph with the image of "crumbling finger," which symbolizes physical touch and skin, and a sky that is "gaping white and hot," the story has laid out a literary canvas of startling, fragmented, and, most importantly, solid images to illustrate and reimagine the dying body.

The story's body collage technique is not, of course, merely isolated to the opening paragraph. As the story continues, additional bodily analogies are presented. The Alps are "closed like a dry fist" and the rosary by the bed is "hanging like false teeth" (84). The protagonist also refers to Saint André as a "hole that dries the guts in you" and a "blue eye painted at the bottom of a piss pot." If a reader pulls these various images out of the story and places them onto a canvas or inside of a frame, the assembly of the sky as a mouth, breath as smoke, crumbling steeple as finger, "pink tide" as tongue, rosary as teeth, and the blue eye in the urine (which indicates the yellowed eyes often accompanying sickness), we can see that Boyle assembles solid objects into collages that provide insight into the formal/stylistic fragmentation in the text, which is the other way that this story represents an (un)wholesome male body.

"On the Run" is subsumed by fragmented sentences; the narrative jumps around, and multiple shifts in perspective are constant, seen most vividly in the story's progression from an omniscient narrator to internal monologue. As the story progresses, readers move closer and closer into the mind and thoughts of the dying man to the point that, in the end, his thoughts become blurred as he slips out of consciousness.

Boyle concludes the story as follows:

"Saint-Andre," he said into the pillow, "I'm a sick man. I'm afraid. This time I'm afraid to go on."

You you afraid listen here packing the bags again the hairy-legged brushes pointed ampoules as beautiful as earrings bottles of ergotine and striped pajamas we're going on somewhere else and have pigs' feet grilled and champagne and peaches with flames running on them this hole dries the guts in you do you remember Minton last February and everythime you read Umbra the cabinay flushed may the Gods speak softly of us in days hereafter

> And the very small sausages for breakfast at the Ruhl
> St. André-les-Alpes you're a perfectly ordinary piss-pot
> With a blue eye painted in the bottom of it
> Fit only to be put in a cheap room under the bed
> With education refinement and all the delicate belly-aches
> Here's to bigger and better pigs' feet
> Keep on keep on keep on he said maybe I'm going to bleed
>
> (Boyle 85)

While sentimental in setting, and its evocation of personal memory, "On the Run" is uneasily sentimental. The ending is highly grotesque, particularly in its final bodily images of urine ("piss pot") and undigested pigs feet ("belly-aches"). If one were to take the suggestion of possible bleeding a bit further, one might also imagine the possibility of blood gushing out of the speaker's mouth, which, due to the damage in the character's lungs, could be implied by his final words: "I'm going to bleed." In relation to the discourse on war trauma, this story adds a significant counter-perspective on the male body as either a masculine machine or as simply weak. It is also significant to note that the space in which this collage is built is not an urban space, but is above (in elevation) and away (in distance) from the metropolis, more closely aligning it, perhaps, with the dusty scene of the battlefield, although there was plenty of combat in the urban spaces as well.

While just one example, Boyle's innovative story shows how *transition* was directly engaged with post-traumatic life-writing, and, thus, had the potential to invite engagement from specific readers like the shell-shocked soldier, the traumatized medic, and the hospital secretary, among other broader readerships.

More than Politics

Transition was a periodical created for artists and critics. It was ambitious and did not always live up to its ideals. Under Jolas' strong direction, *transition* championed aesthetics over politics far into the thirties, when most other artists and publications were becoming increasingly interested in overtly political art. Yet, somewhere along this modernist continuum, we have psychological reality (or, as Jolas might say, superreality), which, of course, is a part of both aesthetics and politics. To say that *transition*'s omission or possible suppression of the war, and the legacies of shell shock, might be connected to its anti-political agenda/pro-aesthetic agenda, however, is inaccurate. If an audience for *transition* was to be found outside of the interwar artistic/literary establishments, I would argue that its aesthetically, formally-disruptive nature would have resonated most fully with readers deeply interested in human psychology and trauma, both physical and psychological, particularly the shell-shocked soldier, whose mind and world had been inexplicably distorted by the war experience. Jolas' experiences in the Virginia military hospital, and other contacts with his own family following the war, allowed Jolas to empathize with war trauma, and suggests a strong connection between his magazine and a heightened sensitivity to the "shell-shocked" dimensions of avant-garde art, including art created by veterans (or others traumatized by war) that invoked war trauma without always speaking directly about the war itself.

In my early research phase for my dissertation on *transition* magazine, I ordered an ex-library copy of *Transition Stories* (1929) from eBay. When I received this artifact in the mail, I was baffled and intrigued by something I found stamped in the back of the book: "Remotivation Library." Apparently, someone at a New Jersey mental hospital thought a collection of experimental stories from this wildly eclectic, quasi-mystical, Euro-American periodical might offer a reprieve or 'remotivation' for its psychiatric patients. Unfortunately, I have been unable to track down the name of the librarian (or, perhaps, psychologist) who might have ordered this particular collection of *transition* stories for the Remotivation Library; however, I have continued to ponder the relationship between *transition*'s (and Jolas') aesthetic projects (i.e., "the revolution of the word"/verticalism) and interwar psychology more broadly.

What this research project has lead to, for me, is a reconsideration of another dimension of modernism and war: its obsession with speed. This, in turn, has lead me to question whether an under-recognized, but significant aspect of modernism, slowness, might also be part of what makes *transition* resonate so well with the distorting psychological effects of war. "Modernist slowness," Lutz Koepnick writes, "opens our senses and minds to experiences of space as more than merely a container for movement and of time as a dimension that exceeds the opposition of teleological progress and circular repetition" (41). "Modernist slowness," Koepnick continues,

> expands the space of the present, not simply in order to make us hesitate and become contemporaneous with various speeds and temporalities, but in so doing to reflect on alternate models of mobility and uphold visions of indeterminacy, newness, and aesthetic playfulness . . . To go slow and practice what Siegfried Kracauer, in the early 1920's, called "hesitant openness" instead meant nothing less than to encounter the

present as a space charged with the virtuality of various possible futures and the durations of multiple pasts, remembered and forgotten. (42)

As a slow modernist magazine, *transition* gathered up paintings, sculptures, photos, film stills, and more, and put them in a material space that also (re)printed poetry, essays, and art criticism (often in translation), which, I think, ultimately enabled what I would call a freeze-framing of modernism, but not for the sake of glorifying its recent past (and its potential future value—despite *transition*'s own clever self-promotion), but imposed, in part, a negative acceleration onto modernism (i.e., the aesthetic response to modernity), ultimately enabling a deeper view into what D. H. Lawrence called "the pure present."[10]

To conclude, I would like to return to an excerpt from Jolas' poetry collection, *Cinema*, published separately from, but just prior to the start of *transition* in 1927.

In "Challenge of the Age," Jolas presents readers with a series of unnerving images that call to mind both the failure of words and, in light of the war, a failure of humanity itself to find any sense of hope.

"Challenge of the Age"

your earth is sick with longings
blood trickles from all its wounds
come heal its searing pain
beat our veins into visions
our hopes lie in reeking hospitals
asylums stretch out withered wishes

---

10 This phrase, "the pure present" is actually a phrase used in 1920 by D.H Lawrence but was cited within *transition*'s final, 1938 issue in Herbert Read's essay "Myth, Dream, Poem."

men whimper on operating tables
women lie with slashed breasts
hatreds sputter across sinister borders
a great hunger wails from dawn to dusk
nerves drop lacerated
hearts beat into mists
do you not hear the weeping of the soil
night thoughts veer towards mountains
a stake dies into crackling ashes
our words sink into ruins
(Jolas, *Cinema*, 40)

If this malady of language, as Jolas alludes to in the final image of the poem, was part of "challenge of the age," perhaps one could argue that *transition*, through its open and heterogeneous form also represented part of a larger attempt, by numerous American poets and editors, at home and abroad, to offer, if not hope, at least a place where those affected by mental illness—whether brought on by war trauma or through many other inexplicable conditions— could, at least for a time, find a refuge.

Bibliography

Becker, Annette. "The Avant-Garde, Madness and the Great War." *Journal of Contemporary History*, vol. 35, no. 1, 2000, pp. 71–84.

Boyle, Kay. "On the Run." *Transition*, no. 16/17, Jun. 1929, pp. 83-85.

Clark, Suzanne. *Sentimental Modernism : Women Writers and the Revolution of the Word*. Indiana University Press, 1991.

Jolas, Eugène. *Cinema*. Adelphi Company, 1926.

---. "Introduction." *Transition,* no. 1, April 1927, pp. 135-138.

---. "The King's English is Dying: Long Live the American Language." *Transition*, no. 19/20, Jun. 1930, pp. 141-146.

---. *Man From Babel.* Eds. Andreas Kramer and Rainer Rumold, Yale University Press, 1998.

Jolas, Eugène, Klaus H. Kiefer, and Rainer Rumold. *Eugene Jolas: Critical Writings, 1924-1951.* Northwestern University Press, 2009.

Koepnick, Lutz. *On Slowness : Toward an Aesthetic of the Contemporary.* Columbia University Press, 2014.

Masson, André, "Combat de Poissons." *Transition ,* vol. 3, June 1927, 114.

McMillan, Dougald. *Transition: The History of a Literary Era, 1927-1938.* G. Braziller, 1976.

Silet, Charles. *Transition: An Author Index.* SJK Publishing Industries, Inc., 1980, pp. 1–175.

Setz, Cathryn. *Primordial Modernism*: *Animals, Ideas, Transition (1927-1938).* Edinburgh University Press, 2019.

Taggard, Genevieve. "The Plague." *Transition*, 5, August 1927, 77-83.

Thacker, Andrew. "Poetry in Perspective: the Melange of the 1920s: *The Measure* (1921-26), *Rhythmus* (1923-4), and *Palms* (1923-30)." Eds. Peter Brooker and Andrew Thacker, *The Oxford Critical and Cultural History of Modernist Magazines,* vol. 2, Oxford University Press, 2012. 330-333.

Jason Parks is an associate professor of English at Anderson University (Indiana). His courses include Shakespeare, Medieval British Literature, Contemporary Global Literature, and Rhet/Comp. He holds a Ph.D. in literature, with an emphasis on Transatlantic Modernism, from Ball State University. He has published essays on the use of digital technology in the literature classroom, and he also writes about modernist periodicals. His essay on translation and multilingualism in Wyndham Lewis's *The Enemy* was published in the 2017 issue of the *Journal of Wyndham Lewis Studies*. He is an active member of the Modernist Studies Association.

MODERNISM, SHELL SHOCK, AND TRANSATLANTIC PERIODICALS

Louise Kane

Abstract

This chapter charts discussions and debates about shell shock that emerged in British and American periodicals during and after World War I. Beginning with medical journals like *The Lancet*, the chapter explores how shell shock first appeared as a barely-understood illness that was documented only through objective scientific case studies and remained largely invisible to a wider public. However, as the War continued, the advent of literary representations of shell shock in poetry magazines like *The Egoist, The Nation,* and *The Crisis* resulted in a more widescale legitimization and exposure of the affliction to a public consisting of readers from different parts of the globe. The chapter explores the differing nature and forms of these representations, before considering how they worked in a post-war context not only to express outrage and fear about the ravages of modern warfare, but also to emphasize the importance of unity and international cohesion, rather than division and isolation. The chapter draws on the

Medical Humanities to explain how these periodical representations of shell shock ultimately codified the affliction as an integral part of wartime illness narratives, which in turn catalysed its development from a private, subjectively experienced condition which sufferers often felt compelled to hide or unable to "voice," into a public, universal trauma trope symbolizing the collective horror of World War I and its unprecedented loss of life.

IN January 1916 an article titled "Men at War" appeared in the British little magazine *The New Age*. Its focus was a strange set of physical and mental symptoms seen uniquely in soldiers fighting in World War I, which had been raging for the previous eighteen months. At this point, the mysterious phenomenon was largely imponderable. As the article's anonymous writer, known only by the pseudonym "B," observed, "In former times, it was put down to funk. Now we call it shell shock."[1] The article did not coin the term "shell shock;" rather, the first recorded usage of this nomenclature appears in the English physician Charles Myers' "A Contribution to the Study of Shell Shock," published in the *Lancet* in February 1915. However, it marked a definitive point at which attempts to pin down and define "shell shock" gained momentum, not just within the medical field, but also in discourse written for and read by the general public. The writer of "Men at War" frames shell shock as a collective experience, one demanding narrative devices and literary language that transcend medical diction. Describing it in epic language reminiscent of the Romantic sublime, "B" attempts to verbalize the terror of shell shock, only to be unable to bridge

---

1 "Men at War," *The New Age* 28.12 (Jan. 20 1916), 276.

the epistemological gap between sensory experience and the ability to comprehend or communicate it:

> It is impossible to give any idea of the roar of the great guns and the explosions of their shells. It is so tremendous that it passes beyond the comprehensible [. . .] The effect on one's sensory apparatus, when first experienced, is so overpowering that to do anything, much less run away, is impossible. I sat stupefied in a motor-car with a most peculiar feeling running up and down my spine, after a large shell had hit a building . . . and blown it with terrific noise into the street. On one side was a lorry with its driver hanging over his steering-wheel dead, and overhead shells were screaming like angry demons.
> Another shell burst within sight . . . But what of the man who has to stand it, to live in it, to fight in it, and to be brave in it? Shell shock, indeed! I should think so.[2]

The publication of this short but pivotal narrative in *The New Age,* a London-based weekly originally established as a socio-political journal in 1894 that entered a new era in the early 1910s as a thriving literary magazine under the editorship of A. R. Orage, encapsulates two key claims that form the basis of this chapter. The first is that early twentieth-century periodicals, little modernist magazines, and other serial forms of print media played definitive yet over-looked roles in the representation and construction of shell shock as a "real," definite affliction. These representations countered contemporary dismissals of shell shock as a psychosomatic problem, an act of malingering or cowardice, or even outright fraud. Shell shock, then, was made "real" by magazines. This process of legitimization relates to the second claim of this chapter: that periodicals were central in converting shell shock

---

2   Ibid.

from a singularly felt and oft-disputed private experience into a widespread, validated, public experience that novelists, poets, and journalists (and indeed the general public) soon began to coopt as a symbol of the ubiquitous "shock of the new," wider hostilities, and antagonisms that accompanied the simultaneous continuation of World War I and encroachment of early twentieth-century modernity.

Medical Humanities has highlighted how the rise of literary modernism coincided with the "massive 'turn inward'" which saw psychologists, scientists, and philosophers alike develop a profound interest in the internal workings of the human mind.

> It is commonplace to observe that the cultural transformation of Modernism produced the most radical and far-reaching changes in Western culture since the Renaissance. Less widely remarked is the fact that these changes occurred precisely when the distinctly modern disciplines of psychology, psychiatry, and psychoanalysis began to establish their scientific foundations. . . . The cultural affinities between aesthetic and psychological modernism are . . . striking and varied.[3]

As a result, modernist short stories, along with other genres such as the late Victorian "Sensation" novel, are recognized as texts which encode, explore, and interrogate the uncertain boundary between public and private, boundaries including the physical and the psychological, nerves and neurosi, and the external self and internal mind. Scholars have highlighted how conditions like nervous hysteria, phobias, and sexual repression provide material for uniquely-modernist utterances of collective trauma. Vike Plock,

---

3   Mark Micale, "Introduction, The Modernist Mind—A Map" in *The Mind of Modernism: Medicine, Psychology, and the Cultural Arts in Europe and America, 1880–1940*, ed. Mark Micale (Stanford, Calif.: Stanford University Press, 2004), 1-2.

for example, has shown how agoraphobia underwent the transition from a private "medical entity" to a public "cultural signifier" symbolizing unease and anxiety about an era in transition.[4] Yet few studies have explored the way periodicals converted shell shock from private affliction to public cultural signifier. Extending Tracey Loughran's assertion that shell shock embodies "an essentially timeless manifestation of trauma," this chapter argues that modern periodicals facilitated this manifestation in increasingly public ways through their recording, documentation, and discursive representations (in both literary and non-literary forms) of shell shock several years before poems and novels like Wilfred Owen's "Mental Cases" (1918) or Woolf's *Mrs. Dalloway* (1925) began to explore the condition.[5]

As Sara Wasson notes, "illness narrations achieve normative work, demonstrating modes of being ill that have moral authority within particular cultural milieu."[6] Many of the earliest illness narratives about shell shock appear in periodicals. Periodicals were vehicles that, through their status as serially-issued texts, offered writers—both medical and non-medical—unique, recurring possibilities for documenting and giving medical authority to shell shock, and for using it creatively to communicate with unmatched immediacy widespread fears, disgust, and confusion about ongoing warfare. While shell shock was, of course, a global phenomenon documented in newspapers and magazines from all over the world, this chapter limits its focus to the literary representations of shell shock published in magazines like *The Egoist* and *The New Age* with a transatlantic reach from their issuance in Britain to their strong American readerships; and *Scribner's Magazine*,

---

4   Vike Plock, "Introduction: Fearful States, the emergence of Modern Phobias." *Journal of Literature and Science* 3.1 (2010), 2.

5   Tracey Loughran, "Shell Shock, Trauma, and the First World War: The Making of a Diagnosis and Its Histories," *Journal of the History of Medicine and Allied Studies* 67.1 (2012), 94.

6   Sara Wasson, "Before Narrative: Episodic Reading and Representations of Chronic Pain," *Medical Humanities* 44 (2018), 107.

which though published in America featured many European writers. This focus allows for a clearer examination of the ways shell shock emerged gradually from a misunderstood illness into a collectively-experienced phenomenon understood by a public on both sides of the Atlantic. The final part of the chapter focuses on this strangely "collective" quality of shell shock by examining how post-war periodicals like the British *Athenaeum* and American *Crisis* represented it as a phenomenon that could also encapsulate post-war ideals of peace, international cooperation, and reconstructivism.

Neurasthenia, Hysteria, Shock: Shell Shock's Vague Outlines in *The Nation* and *The Egoist*

The few early descriptions of shell shock are, unsurprisingly, primarily medical in their focus and register. Charles Myers's "A Contribution to the Study of Shell Shock" exemplifies this approach. This first scientific case study of shell shock appeared in *The Lancet* in February 1915. It documented "three cases of loss of memory, vision, smell, and taste," and provided various charts recording retinal damage, the results of hearing tests, and patients' responses to various strong scents, such as peppermint and ether.[7] Myer believed that the study's conclusion was straightforward enough as to make any comment seem "superfluous:" the "close similarity" between cases constituted a "definite class" of wide-ranging symptoms that could commonly be referred to as "shell shock."[8]

It would be a few months before the term "shell shock" became commonplace. Physicians and policymakers in the early years of the War instead used a variety of terms, such as "neurasthenia," "nervousness," or "hysteria," to diagnose soldiers—often as means of casually relegating the

---

7   C. S. Myers, "A Contribution to the Study of Shell Shock," *The Lancet* (Feb. 13 1915), 316.

8   Ibid., 320.

physical symptoms of shell shock to an apparently-psychological cause. Arthur Slogett, Director of the British Army Medical Services, issued a directive dividing war casualties into two main groups: those bearing visible wounds relating to "effects of explosion," and those bearing no visible wounds whose condition was classed dismissively as "nervousness."[9] Shell shock victims were inevitably placed into this second category. Myers himself elided shell shock with psychological illness, declaring that "[t]he close relation of these [shell shock] cases to those of "hysteria" appears fairly certain."[10]

Three months after the publication of Myers's article, in May 1915 *The British Medical Journal* published a piece that specifically used the word "shock" to encompass the wide range of symptoms displayed by soldiers arriving at British and French war hospitals. Written by W. A. Turner, a War Office physician, the article explained how

> [c]ases of nervous and mental shock . . . began to arrive in England shortly after the commencement of hostilities in which British troops were engaged . . . It was soon recognized that one type of case was due to the explosion of big shells in the immediate vicinity of the patient.[11]

These early attempts to define the "shock" resulting from exposure to shells evince the gap between medical observation and clinical understanding then obtaining. Physicians like Turner and Myers could *see* shell shock, but they could not rationalize or comprehend it.

This epistemological "gap" also characterizes some of the first explorations of shell shock in non-medical literature. Discussing visual art, Karen

---

9   Edgar Jones, Nicola Fear, and Simon Wessley, "Shell shock and mild traumatic brain injury: a historical review," *American Journal of Psychiatry* 164.11 (2007), 1642.

10 Myers, 320.

11 W. A. Turner, "Remarks on Cases of Nervous and Mental Shock Observed in Base Hospitals in France," *British Medical Journal* 1.2837 (May 15 1915), 833.

Jacobs asserts that "what distinguishes the modernist literary response from its predecessors stems from a crisis of belief in the continuity between seeing and knowing."[12] This distinctly modernist "crisis" is evinced in the Georgian poet Wilfrid Wilson Gibson's "The Messages." Published in the London-based magazine *The Nation* (*The Nation and Athenaeum* from 1921) in October 1914, this poem is one of the earliest literary narratives of shell shock. It depicts a speaker who does not possess the language (or full knowledge of what shell shock is) to adequately articulate the affliction affecting the unnamed soldier. This deficit is, in turn, represented in the soldier's inability to remember or utter sensible speech:

Back from the trenches, more dead than alive,
Stone deaf and dazed, and with a broken knee,
He hobbled slowly, muttering vacantly:
"I cannot quite remember . . . There were five
Dropped dead beside me in the trench—and three
Whispered their dying messages to me."[13]

The speaker can only gesture toward the soldier's shell shock through vague descriptions of his "muttering vacantly," memory loss, and being "[s]tone deaf," and "dazed." The soldier's ultimate inability ("I cannot quite remember") to relate the "dying messages" replicates the confusion and mystery characterizing shell shock and early attempts to explain or document it. "The Messages" provides a war narrative-cum-illness narrative: Gibson's depiction of the soldier as "back from the trenches, more dead than alive" shows how shell shock becomes the vehicle for an implicit yet definite critique of a war barely underway but already resulting in largescale casualties

---

12   Karen Jacobs, *The Eye's Mind: Literary Modernism and Visual Culture*, (Itacha: Cornell UP, 2001), 19.

13   Wilfrid Wilson Gibson, "The Messages," *The Nation* (Oct. 17 1914), 16.

with both psychological and physical injuries. It is unsurprising that Gibson published this poem in a largely pacifist journal like *The Nation*, which also published such anti-war pieces as Wilfred Owen's "Miners," a poem Owen wrote while recovering from shell shock at Craiglockhart Hospital.

At this early stage in the War, not all poets followed Gibson's subtle encoding of shell shock as a microcosm of war trauma; instead, many preferred to espouse patriotic sentiments about a war they assumed would soon end. The publication of the American poet John Gould Fletcher's "The Orange Symphony" in the British little modernist magazine *The Egoist*, then edited by Harriet Shaw Weaver and Richard Aldington, epitomizes this espousal through the defiant, epic tone with which it relates martial imagery: "I will race between the grey guns, / And the clouds, like shrapnel exploding, / Flinging their hail through the tumult, / Bursting, will melt in cold spray."[14] Such exultant descriptions of warfare were not to last in *The Egoist*. Its "Special Imagist Number," appearing on May 1, 1915, included many of poems imagining wartime battles—and, tellingly, shell shock—through troubling language. D. H. Lawrence's "Eloi, Eloi, Laba Sabbachthani" depicts a soldier whose constant exposure to shelling elicits a perversely pleasurable, intensely masochistic self-awareness of his bodily fragility:

God, how glad I am to hear the shells
Droning over, threatening me!
It is their threat, their loud, jeering threat,
Like screaming birds of Fate
Wheeling to lacerate and rip up this my body.[15]

---

14   John Gould Fletcher, "The Orange Symphony," *The Egoist* (Nov. 2, 1914), 411, ll. 40-43.

15   D. H. Lawrence, "Eloi, Eloi, Laba Sabbachthani," *The Egoist* 5.2 (May 1 1915), 75. Translated as "My God, my God, why have you forsaken me," Matthew, 27: 46-49, Lawrence's title is the original Aramaic version of this phrasing.

The Egoist's publication of its Paris Correspondent Muriel "Madame" Ciolkowska's "Fighting Paris" column marks a turning point in periodical representations of war trauma. Running from November 1914 through April 1915, the column appeared in diary format and is ostensibly one of the first pieces of frontline journalism from World War I. It chronicled in graphic terms the everyday horrors of trench life and incessant shelling:

> Some German shells came to disturb the gaieties. When the little shower was over, the usual count was made of the survivors [. . .] There is a monotony in horror, and our daily life has become horribly monotonous. News, conversation, anxiety, vary but in degree—the fundamental theme is the same, from morning to night, wounds, deaths, nursing, Germans, military tactics[. . .]you hear descriptions of wounds, of tetanos [sic], gangrene, amputations, hemorrhages [sic]—the whole scale of physical suffering is run over.

Shell shock appears as an inevitable part of this physical suffering. One young soldier is "lamed for life, not because the shrapnel wounded him seriously but because the shock sent him stumbling into a ditch."[16] Shell shock is not only made strikingly "real," but also presented as something commonplace, an everyday experience that, through being witnessed, becomes a shared affliction. James Mussell has noted that, usually, periodicals inevitably possess a sort of built-in obsolescence as they "address a moment that is provisional and is destined to pass."[17] However, the repeat serialization of Ciolkowska's "Fighting Paris" meant that even if each issue of *The Egoist* became obsolete, the concerns expressed in her column did not. Instead, the recurrence of the

---

16 Muriel Ciolkowska, "Fighting in Paris," *The Egoist* 22.1 (Nov. 16 1914), 428-9.

17 James Mussell, "Of the making of magazines there is no end": W.T. Stead, Newness, and the Archival Imagination," *ESC: English Studies in Canada* 41.1 (Mar. 2015), 70.

column reminded readers that the War was not something that would "pass." This continued exposure to disturbing descriptions of warfare and shell shock codified both as legitimate, increasingly pressing concerns for readers who could no longer imagine them as distant problems played out overseas.

Along with documenting shell shock as a newly-emergent syndrome, periodicals also chart changing societal attitudes to it. The March 1916 publication of Wyndham Lewis's short story "The French Poodle" in *The Egoist* evidences how, eighteen months into World War I, writers were still largely unable to explain or describe shell shock in precise terms but were nonetheless keen to disrobe it of the suspicions and scepticism it often prompted. Lewis would, of course, spend time on the battlefront, and his presentation of the story's protagonist, Rob Cairn, a shell-shocked British Army Officer on convalescent leave, is, unsurprisingly, a sympathetic one. Haunted by the knowledge that he must return to the "monotonous and malignant missiles," Cairn is "arrested in a vague but troublesome maze of discomfort and ill-health" but cannot understand the cause of the ailment that afflicts him. He spends his days "drifting about London in mufti, by no means well, and full of anxiety, the result of his ill-health and the shock he had received at finding himself blown into the air and painted yellow by the unavoidable shell."[18] As time passes, Cairn and his friend, James Fraser, ponder the nature of his illness:

> I'm sure there's something wrong, Rob. How do you feel exactly; physically, I mean? What can happen to a man inside who is blown up in the air? What do the doctors exactly say?
>
> They can find nothing. I don't believe there is anything. But I don't feel at all well. It's something in my brain, rather, that's dislocated: cracked, I think, sometimes. I shall never be any good out there again.[19]

---

18 Wyndham Lewis, "The French Poodle," *The Egoist* 3.3 (March 1 1916), 39.

19 Ibid., 40.

Cairn's questioning whether there is "anything" wrong with him shows how epistemological disjunct continued to hinder improvements to the treatment of shell shock: the doctors cannot "find" or understand the cause of Cairn's condition because they cannot see his psychological symptoms, and Cairn's inability to see his own psychological injuries evokes feelings of self-doubt and guilt. As Jay Winter has noted, towards the end of the 1910s some physicians were slowly beginning to consider shell shock an affliction of the brain (the "something in my brain" Cairn's describes) as well as the body, but this shift failed to end accusations of fraud from other camps:

> On one hand there were those who believed that such individuals suffered from lesions we cannot see: thus all such injuries were physiological in character, and could be treated as such. On the other hand, some physicians and psychologists took the view that there were disabilities which were psychogenetic in character, and they had to be treated in a different way . . . Most physicians and serving officers believed that the entire category of psychogenic disability was a cover for fraud . . . To such sceptics, a more likely explanation . . . was cowardice or dissimulation; in short, acting disabled was a tactic to avoid facing the enemy.[20]

"The French Poodle" reflects these problems of diagnosis and legitimization, and Lewis's message is clear: far from "acting disabled," Cairn is in the grip of a real affliction, even if he cannot explain it and is considered as "painted yellow" (a reference to cowardice) by others. Fraser's question—"What can happen to a man inside who is blown up in the air?"—offers one of the most profound contemporary comments on the reality of shell shock: the unique and unprecedented nature of shelling in World

---

20   Jay Winter, "Shell Shock," in *The Cambridge History of the First World War*, vol. *Civil Society*, ed. Jay Winter (Cambridge: Cambridge UP): 310-33.

War I meant that there was simply no way of knowing how extensively it impacted the human body and mind and no established medical precedent for investigating this impact.

Recent revisionary accounts of the materiality of modern periodicals and their status as media alert us to the ways in which magazines and newspapers documented and recorded shell shock through their commitment to bring "news" to readerships. As Faye Hammill explains, "media theory has long been central to the theorization of the periodical as a form," and the process of "reading periodicals as, and in relation to, media" reminds us that in the early 1910s, periodicals like *The Egoist* were not just responsible for promoting new literary trends, but also for reporting wider *news*: current affairs, political developments, "hot" topics and trends for wide audiences.[21] Yet, periodicals also offered something beyond a documentary function: the publication of pieces like "The French Poodle," with its implicit critique of treatment of the war-injured, shows how periodicals possessed another function: the ability to shape public opinion and beliefs about shell shock and the ongoing War.

With their transatlantic readerships, *The Nation* and *The Egoist* conducted this shaping on both sides of the Atlantic. Besides being distributed to the USA and Canada, many of *The Nation*'s foreign readers often wrote into the periodical to express their admiration for its pacifist stance and thought-provoking articles.[22] Equally, *The Egoist* may have been a London-based little modernist magazine with only 2000 subscribers in 1914 (and only 400 by 1919), but Harriet Shaw Weaver, assisted by Ezra Pound, was careful to cultivate its international contributor network. Pound brought American writers like Fletcher into the magazine (Pound reviewed Fletcher's *The Dominant City* and *Fool's Gold* in September 1913 when *the Egoist* was

---

21 Faye Hammill, Paul Hjartarson, and Hannah McGregor, "Introducing Magazines and/as Media: The Aesthetics and Politics of Serial Form," *ESC: English Studies in Canada* 41.1 (Mar. 2015), 15.

22 See "From a Canadian Reader," *The Nation and The Athenaeum* 28 (Feb. 19 1921), 714.

still *The New Freewoman*). By 1915, when the magazine began to publish Imagist poets in earnest, its contributors included both American poets, like Amy Lowell, Pound, William Carlos Williams, and British poets, like May Sinclair, D. H. Lawrence, F. S. Flint, as well as writers from countries like Japan and India, Yone Noguchi and Rabindranath Tagore, respectively. Magazines therefore held the potential to familiarize audiences from all over the world with shell shock and its impacts.

A Shift in Attitude: *The New Age* and *Scribner's Magazine*

The New Age and *Scribner's Magazine* are two periodicals that played a key role in this familiarization. Critics have pointed to the publication of Frederick Mott's *War Neuroses and Shell Shock* in 1919 as a turning point in attempts to understand and treat shell shock, but both *The New Age* and *Scribner's* made concerted attempts to investigate shell shock long before World War I ended.[23] In *The New Age*, the publication of B's "Men at War" piece presented shell shock in a sympathetic manner and praised the fact that "[n]othing has changed so much as the military attitude to the poor devils who break up under the great strain of deafening noise and surrounding death."[24] In May 1916, another *New Age* piece, "A Visit to the Front," continued the curious vogue for magazine features describing physicians' accounts of visits to shell-shocked soldiers at military hospitals. The writer, the Spanish journalist and political theorist Ramiro de Maeztu, concludes after his visit to a "convalescent hospital" that shell shock is "one of the commonest illnesses of the war.... The modern man's nerves are always strained ... Science will yet discover, if it has not already done so,

---

23 See Edgar Jones, "'An atmosphere of cure': Frederick Mott, shell shock and the Maudsley," *History of Psychiatry* 25.4 (2014): 412-21.

24 "Men at War," 276.

what precisely shell-shock is. Good."[25] The piece also explains how "soldiers are treated as a mother treats a frightened child. They are entertained. They are amused . . . They play all kinds of games, and have plenty to eat."[26] Around this time, the British periodical *The Athenaeum*, a weekly journal that reported on politics, science, economics, and current affairs, also pushed for greater recognition of shell shock as mental trauma. Shell shock was "a popular but inadequate title for all those mental effects of war experience," a "vague" term that, thankfully, was receiving medical reconsideration.[27]

The publication of a series of articles in *Scribner's Magazine* "globalized" shell shock for a much larger readership. In 1918, *Scribner's Magazine* had been in existence for over thirty years. Established in 1887 after the closure of *Scribner's Monthly* in 1881, the magazine was designed to compete with such established popular magazines as *Harper's Monthly* and *Atlantic Monthly*. Its mixture of literary stories and poems; non-fiction articles on subjects such as decorative arts, politics, and cookery; and reproductions of color photography and richly-illustrated front covers produced a familiar, comfortable reading experience for its 270,000 readers. The first shell shock article—"Caring for American Wounded in France"—appeared in May 1918. Its author, C. L. Gibson, a Major and Medical Services Director for the US Army, describes two weeks he spent at a Casualty Clearing Station in France and lauds the emergence of "specialist branches" of medical teams specifically designated to treat shell shock.[28] Gibson's article belies Hans Pols' observation that "it was only in World War II that military psychiatrists, particularly those in the USA, began to implement treatment methods for this phenomenon in a systematic way."[29]

---

25 Ramiro de Maeztu, "A Visit to the Front," *New Age* 19.22 (Sept. 28 1916), 510.

26 Ibid.

27 "The Nature of Shell-Shock," *The Athenaeum* 4615 (Mar. 1917), 130.

28 C. L. Gibson, "Caring For American Wounded in France," *Scribner's Magazine* (May 1918), 598.

29 Hans Pols, "Waking up to shell shock: psychiatry in the US military during World War II,"

As the War continued with no sign of a ceasefire, *Scribner's* extended its focus to provide more politicized articles and commentary on shell shock. In July 1918, an advertisement announced the publication of a new article series by M. Allen Starr, Emeritus Professor of Neurology at Columbia University, exploring "Shell-shock: the new terror of this war."[30] Beginning the next month, the series initiated a revisionary exploration of shell shock and emphasized its physiological and physical aspect. Shell shock, Starr argued, could no longer be dismissed as anxiety but resulted from pathological "changes to the cells of the brain."[31] Additionally, Starr posited that shell shock was caused by the gas emitted from exploding shells:

> a TNT shell sets free a large amount of carbon monoxide which . . . causes sensory and motor paralysis . . . The underlying conditions therefore are not always the same. There may be actual damage; there may be exhaustion and disintegration; there may be merely a temporary suspension of brain activity. The final result will vary in accordance with these various conditions, and these conditions will, therefore, determine the different lines of treatment.[32]

While it may not have been the intention of magazine editors to legitimize shell shock, the publication of articles like Starr's inevitably challenged scepticism toward the condition. In today's world, media is central in influencing attitudes toward mental health; the periodicals of the late 1910s worked in a similar fashion, contributing to shell shock's conversion from a "new condition never observed in any previous war"

Endeavour 30.4 (2006), 144.

30   Advertisement, *Scribner's Magazine* (July 1918), 2. In a typical example of its juggling popular commodities and erudite content, this advertisement appeared adjacent to another for Tiffany & Co.

31   M. Allen Starr, "Shell Shock," *Scribner's Magazine* (May 1918), 183.

32   Ibid., 186-7.

into a scientifically-documented disorder demanding funding and specialist treatment.[33] Many months after the Armistice of November 1918, articles detailing scientific accounts of shell shock appeared in periodicals all over the globe.[34] The appearance of the British Government-issued *Report of the War Office Committee of Enquiry into "Shell-Shock"* in 1922, followed by the "Neuropsychiatry" volume of *The Medical Department of the United States Army in the World War* (1929) series, paved the way for the publication of more literary illness narratives of shell shock during the interwar years, including lesser-known examples like Irene Rathbone's *We That Were Young* (1929).

Shell Shock as Aftershock?

The end of World War I in late 1918 brought about undoubted relief but also a profound awareness of the devastation caused by over four years of fighting. It was against this backdrop that shell shock began to emerge most clearly as a collective trauma trope symbolizing wider anxieties about war and modern life. The first evidence of this emergence appears in the way "shell shock" began to be used as an everyday expression. Of course, in today's society "shell-shocked" is a commonly-used idiom whose "extended and hyperbolical" meaning signifies a feeling of surprise or horror at an unexpected event, but in the late 1910s this usage was completely novel.[35] A comment in a 1918 *Washington Post* article—"Your maid comes in and gives you a touch of 'shellshock' by announcing that she's going to be a conductorette or a munitions worker"—epitomizes this new use of the term.[36] Periodicals

33   Ibid., 183.
34   See, for example, the account of Major Colin Russel, a Consultant of Neuropsychiatry, which argues for the recognition of "shell-shock" as a "clinical" condition frequently manifesting as "organic anatomical lesions" to the brain. Colin Russel, "The Management of Psycho-Neuroses in the Canadian Army," *The Journal of Abnormal Psychology* 14 (1919), 27.
35   "Shell shock, n1b," *OED Online*. Oxford University Press, June 2017. Web. 11 July 2017.
36   Ibid.

naturally reflected this sense of the War as something universally endured. In Britain, 1919 saw the establishment of several little magazines like *Coterie,* an Oxford-produced poetry magazine mentored by T. S. Eliot; *Voices,* a short-lived literary magazine edited by Thomas Moult; and John Middleton Murry's *Athenaeum* (edited by Murray between 1919-21), which aimed to promote post-war camaraderie and "revelatory, reconstructive enthusiasm."[37] One of Murry's early editorials implicitly draws on the language of shell shock as an emblem of the widespread trauma of the War:

> Our heads ache too much from the bludgeoning of war to count our wounds . . . we are somehow maimed, yet how we do not know . . . Our catastrophe has been far more intimate and perilous than this. Wherein, then, does it lie? . . . The earthquake has happened and we have to live amid the debris. We had better make the best of it.[38]

Another example of shell shock being presented as a cultural signifier appears in a poem by the well-connected English socialite Lady Margaret Sackville, "The Women to the Men Returned," published in *The English Review* in July 1920. The poem provides a timely reminder of the collective impact of warfare. The female speaker's bitter lament at her returned partner's inability to mesh back into the usual rhythms of family and societal life hint at shell shock as the cause of his malaise:

> Oh you can love us still, laugh with us, smile,
> But in your haunted spirits all the while,
> Tortured and throbbing like a nerve laid bare,

---

37 David Goldie, *A Critical Difference: T.S. Eliot and John Middleton Murry in English Literary Criticism, 1919-28* (Oxford: Oxford UP, 1998), 35.

38 John Middleton Murry, "Prologue" *The Athenaeum,* 4640 (Apr. 4 1919), 1.

Lie sleepless memories we dare not share.
Your secret thought—what is it? We do not know.[39]

Long before the relatively recent turn in psychiatry which has seen Post Traumatic Stress Disorder (PTSD) become a medically-recognized side-effect of warfare, Sackville's poem uses shell shock as a trope through which to express keenly-felt concerns about the "price" of war, especially as soldiers returned to families as forever altered men.

Recent literary criticism has emphasized the "several forms of speechlessness associated with the war experience—from mouth trauma to shell shock, censorship, the divide between the front lines and those at home," and "The Women to the Men Returned" can be read through this frame of reference.[40] The poem's speaker displays an almost angry frustration with the inability of the soldier to communicate his wartime experience. In an era when many soldiers were unwilling or physically unable (due to the mutism that frequently accompanied shell shock) to give utterance to private experiences, the publication of poems like Sackville's gave voice to such experiences in a more public forum. Of course, it was a concern that T. S. Eliot would explore two years later in *The Waste Land*, with the now infamous scene in which the female speaker begs her male counterpart to reply to her, only for him to provide a response that has widely been interpreted as a reference to the horror of trench warfare:

"Speak to me. Why do you never speak. Speak.
"What are you thinking of? What thinking? What?
"I never know what you are thinking. Think."

---

39   Margaret Sackville, "The Women to the Men Returned," *The English Review* (July, 1920), 3.

40   Alec Marsh and Patrick R. Query, "Pound and Eliot" in *American Literary Scholarship: An Annual, 2013* (Duke: Duke UP, 2013), 178. 145-62. See also Ezekiel Black, "Mouthlessness and Ineffability in World War I Poetry and The Waste Land," *WL&A* 25, 1–17.

I think we are in rats' alley
Where the dead men lost their bones.⁴¹

The *Waste Land* was published in both British and US periodicals, the October 1922 inaugural issue of Eliot's *Criterion* and the November issue of *The Dial*, respectively. Magazines were thus outlets for poets and writers to publish work which, in the interwar years, dealt with the lasting trauma and shadow of World War I in new and increasingly public ways.

Yet periodicals also offered a space for writers to use World War I and the trope of shell shock as a means to promote community, cooperation, and a spirit of post-war cohesion. Indeed, as David Goldie has recognized, the British magazine *The Athenaeum* soon became recognized as a "Journal of Reconstruction" owing to its publication of literary works promoting post-war cohesion.⁴² At the exact same point at which *The Athenaeum* was in its reconstructivist "hey-day," U.S. periodicals evince a similar unifying impulse, particularly through depictions of shell shock. The publication of Joseph Seamon Cotter Jr.'s "On the Fields of France: a One Act Play" in the June 1920 issue of *The Crisis* exemplifies this call for post-war unity in its representation of shell shock as a form of "common ground" between two very different soldiers. *The Crisis* had been founded some ten years previously in New York as the official organ of the National Association for the Advancement of Colored People (NAACP) and published works by African-American writers who, like Cotter, were associated with the Harlem Renaissance movement. Appearing on a single page of the magazine, Cotter's play uses the trope of shared trauma to unite a "colored officer" and "white officer."⁴³ Opening "on the battlefields of Northern France," the play begins

---

41   T. S. Eliot, "The Waste Land" in *Collected Poems 1909-1962*. New York: Harcourt, Brace and World Inc., 1963: 55, ll.111-6.

42   Goldie, 15.

43   Joseph Seamon Cotter, Jr. "On the Fields of France," *The Crisis* 20.2 (June 1920), 77.

with "both mortally wounded" men crawling toward one another in the sodden grass. The white officer tells the black officer "a shell has gone through my body" and begs for water. While the action is limited, the few lines of dialogue serve as a moving vignette of the everyday terrors of combat. The black officer, stunned by the shell and struggling to breathe, tells the white officer that he "got this—far and decided to—stop and close my eyes—and wait for the—end here." The white officer is equally disoriented: unable to hear or comprehend his surroundings, he begins to cry. The final action shows the officers come together and hold hands. "Why couldn't we live like this at home?" the white officer questions, "It is one country she will some day be, in truth as well as in spirit . . . The country of the whites and the country of the blacks. Our country!" "America!" the black officer replies, as they "fall back hand in hand as their life blood ebbs away."[44]

The remedial power of shell shock is clear in Cotter's play. Shell shock and warfare is a collective trauma that Cotter uses as a transformative agent to break down barriers of race and background: if the two men can be united on the lonely plains of France, surely they can be united on the green grass of home? Shell shock, in both Sackville's poem and Cotter's play, serves both to divide and to unite. Although the soldier's shell shock separates him from his wife in "The Women to the Men Returned," his wife is united with a wider community of suffering women who waited on the home front and now must deal with shell shock and other post-traumatic conditions as a permanent legacy of the War. In "On the Fields of France," the confusion and fear brought about by the shell attack unifies the officers in an attempt to heal the chasm-like racial divides that plagued 1920s America.

The representation of shell shock in transatlantic periodicals is by no means universal in its manifestations. In *The Nation* and *The Egoist*, poets like Gibson and Lawrence used shell shock to voice looming anxieties about

---

44   Ibid.

a war which was still in its relatively early stages. Wyndhgam Lewis's 1916 representation of shell shock as something Rob Cairn can no longer deny symbolizes the more widespread recognition that shell shock received as warfare continued: two years into World War I, physicians and the general public alike could no longer dismiss it as a figment of the imagination, a message that *Scribner's* and *The New Age*'s frontline dispatch articles reiterated as the war rumbled on into 1918. In the years after the War, periodicals like *The Washington Post* recorded how shell shock began to be used as a colloquialism, a now-accepted "norm" that could serve as the basis for witty comments and jesting remarks. And in The *Athenaeum*, *The English Review*, and *The Crisis*, shell shock and war trauma became symbols of a sort of post-war collectivism, a desire to stand united, rather than divided. As Fiona Reid has argued, however, a battle still rages:

> [o]ne hundred years after the war the diagnosis of PTSD has not resolved the issues initially raised by First World War shell shock. The stigma of mental illness remains strong and it is still difficult to commemorate and remember the mental wounds of war in a culture which tends to glamorise military heroes.[45]

Looking back at some of the periodicals explored in this chapter, it becomes apparent that in their efforts to record the physical battles of World War I, magazines, newspapers, and medical journals were crucial catalysts in the process of destigmatizing mental illness, a battle that, through the continually-evolving power of print, digital, and mass media forms, may yet be won.

---

45   Fiona Reid, "Shell shock, History, and the Memory of the First World War in Britain," *Endeavour* 38.2 (2014), 91.

Bibliography

"From a Canadian Reader." *The Nation and The Athenaeum*, 28, 19 Feb. 1921, p. 714.

"Men at War." *The New Age*, vol. 28, no. 12, 20 Jan. 1916, p. 276.

"The Nature of Shell-Shock." *The Athenaeum*, 4615, Mar. 1917, pp. 130-32.

"Shell shock, n.1b." *OED Online*. Oxford University Press, accessed 11 July 2017.

Black, Ezekiel. "Mouthlessness and Ineffability in World War I Poetry and the *Waste Land*." *WL&A*, 25, 2013, pp. 1–17.

Ciolkowska, Muriel. "Fighting in Paris." *The Egoist*, vol. 22, no.1, 16 Nov. 1914, pp. 428-9

Cotter, Jr., Joseph Seamon. "On the Fields of France." *The Crisis*, vol. 20, no. 2, June 1920, p. 77.

De Maeztu, Ramiro. "A Visit to the Front." *The New Age*, vol. 19, no. 22, 28 Sept. 1916, pp. 510-11.

Eliot, T. S.. "The Waste Land." *Collected Poems 1909-1962*, Harcourt, Brace and World Inc., 1963, pp. 51-82.

Goldie, David. *A Critical Difference: T.S. Eliot and John Middleton Murry in English Literary Criticism, 1919-28*. Oxford UP, 1998.

Gould Fletcher, John. "The Orange Symphony." *The Egoist*, 2 Nov. 1914, pp. 411-12.

Jones, Edgar. "'An atmosphere of cure': Frederick Mott, shell shock and the Maudsley." *History of Psychiatry*, vol. 25, no. 4, 2014, pp. 412-21.

Jones, Edgar, Nicola Fear, and Simon Wessley. "Shell Shock and Mild

Traumatic Brain Injury: a Historical Review." *American Journal of Psychiatry*, vol. 164, no. 11, 2007, pp. 1641-45.

Gibson, C. L. "Caring for American Wounded in France." *Scribner's Magazine,* May 1918, pp. 594-607.

Hammill, Faye, Paul Hjartarson, and Hannah McGregor. "Introducing Magazines and/as Media: The Aesthetics and Politics of Serial Form." *ESC: English Studies in Canada*, vol. 41, no. 1, Mar. 2015, pp. 1-18.

Havighurst, Alfred F.. *Radical Journalist: H. W. Massingham (1860-1924).* Cambridge UP, 1974.

Jacobs, Karen. *The Eye's Mind: Literary Modernism and Visual Culture*. Itacha, Cornell UP, 2001.

Lawrence, D. H. "Eloi, Eloi, Laba Sabbachthani." *The Egoist*, vol. 5, no. 2, 1 May 1915, pp. 75-6.

Lewis, Wyndham. "The French Poodle." *The Egoist,* vol. 3, no. 3, 1 Mar. 1916, pp. 39-40.

Lougran, Tracey. "Shell Shock, Trauma, and the First World War: The Making of a Diagnosis and Its Histories." *Journal of the History of Medicine and Allied Studies*, vol. 67, no. 1, 2012, pp. 94-119.

Marsh, Alec and Patrick R. Query. "Pound and Eliot." *American Literary Scholarship: An Annual, 2013,* Duke UP, 2013, pp. 145-62.

Micale, M. "Introduction: The Modernist Mind--A Map." *The Mind of Modernism: Medicine, Psychology, and the Cultural Arts in Europe and America, 1880-1940,* edited by Mark Micale, Stanford UP, 2004, pp. 1-20.

Murry, John Middleton. "Prologue." *The Athenaeum*, no. 4640, 4 April 1919, p. 1.

Mussell, James. "Of the making of magazines there is no end": W.T. Stead, Newness, and the Archival Imagination." *ESC: English Studies in Canada*, vol. 41, no. 1, Mar. 2015, pp. 69-91.

Myers, C. S.. "A Contribution to the Study of Shell Shock." *The Lancet*, 13 Feb. 1915, pp. 316-20.

Plock, Vike. "Introduction: Fearful States, the emergence of Modern Phobias." *Journal of Literature and Science*, vol. 3, no. 1, 2010, pp. 1-9.

Pols, Hans. "Waking up to shell shock: psychiatry in the US military during World War II," *Endeavour*, vol. 30, no. 4, 2006, pp. 144-9.

Reid, Fiona. "Shell shock, History, and the Memory of the First World War in Britain." *Endeavour*, vol. 38, no. 2, 2014, pp. 91-100.

Russel, Colin. "The Management of Psycho-Neuroses in the Canadian Army." *The Journal of Abnormal Psychology*, no. 14, 1919, pp. 27-33.

Sackville, Margaret. "The Women to the Men Returned." *The English Review*, July 1920, p. 3.

Starr, M. Allen. "Shell Shock." *Scribner's Magazine*, May 1918, pp. 183-7.

Turner. W. A.. "Remarks on Cases of Nervous and Mental Shock Observed in Base Hospitals in France." *British Medical Journal*, vol. 1, no. 2837 15 May 1915, pp. 833-35.

Wasson, Sara. "Before Narrative: Episodic Reading and Representations of Chronic Pain," *Medical Humanities*, no. 44, 2018, pp. 106-12.

Wilson Gibson, Wilfrid. "The Messages." *The Nation*, 17 Oct. 1914, p. 16.

Winter, Jay. "Shell Shock." *The Cambridge History of the First World War*, vol. 1. *Civil Society*, edited by Jay Winter, Cambridge UP, 2014, pp. 310-33.

Louise Kane is assistant professor of Global Modernisms at the University of Central Florida. She has published widely on modern periodicals and historical print cultures, and she is currently working on a monograph about modernist magazines and the emergence of global literature.

NO WAY BACK

War Trauma in Richard Aldington and Virginia Woolf

Elisa Bolchi

Abstract

After fighting as a soldier in World War I, the poet, writer and co-founder of imagism Richard Aldington was so shattered that he had to wait ten years before he was able to write about his experience at the front. His 1929 novel *Death of a Hero*, praised by George Orwell as "much the best of the English war books," tells the story of a young, talkative painter, George Winterbourne, who undergoes a deep change after joining the army and experiencing the horror of war. While home on leave after several months in the trenches, George is amazed to find himself unable to communicate and interact with people, feeling "remote" from everyone and no longer belonging to his "old life." Focusing on this sense of remoteness and marginalization, This chapter analyzes how George Winterbourne is connected to—if not inspired by—Septimus Warren Smith, a character from *Mrs Dalloway* who is the archetypal shell-shocked veteran. By means of a comparison between George Winterbourne and Septimus Smith, this study examines how Aldington and Woolf depict the impossibility of restoring routine and recovering from the "debilitating emotions" (DeMeester) of war trauma. Back home, both George and Septimus are misunderstood by the people around them, find interaction impossible, annoy their women. In short, they are no longer the men they used to be and become the means "to criticise the social system, & show it at work" (Woolf, *Diary*).

We are those that Dante saw
Glad, for love's sake, among the flames of hell,
Outdaring with a kiss all-powerful wrath;
For we have passed athwart a fiercer hell,
Through gloomier, more desperate circles
Than ever Dante dreamed:
And yet love kept us glad.

(R. Aldington, *Che son contenti nel fuoco*)

IF it is true, as George Mosse argued, that for "the cultural historian, shell-shock provides an excellent example of the fusion of medical diagnosis and social prejudice,"[1] then for the literary scholar shell shock represents an even more useful instrument to read and understand the relationships between the individual and society. Jay Winter beautifully pointed out how "individual memories fade away, but cultural representations endure,"[2] and this is why a character like Septimus Warren Smith in Woolf's novel *Mrs.*

---

1   George Mosse, "Shell-Shock as a Social Disease," *Journal of Contemporary History*, 35, no. 1, Special Issue: Shell-Shock (2000): 101.

2   Jay Winter, "Shell-Shock and the Cultural History of the Great War," *Journal of Contemporary History*, 35, no. 1, Special Issue: Shell-Shock (2000): 10.

Dalloway is still so powerfully emblematic of the psychological damage European society underwent during the Great War.

In her essay *Trauma and Recovery in Virginia Woolf's Mrs Dalloway*, Karen DeMeester illustrates how Septimus's war trauma is "perpetuated and its psychological damage aggravated by a culturally prescribed process of postwar reintegration that silences and marginalizes war veterans."[3] Recent psychiatric studies[4] have indeed shown how this marginalization, this inability to communicate their experience to others, together with the inability of those at home fully to understand the psychological damage of the shell-shocked veterans, makes their recovery difficult, if not impossible. These feelings of marginalization and estrangement are a cause of great distress, and eventual suicide, in both Woolf's Septimus Smith and in the protagonist of Richard Aldington's 1929 novel *Death of a Hero*, George Winterbourne, a character with many similarities to Septimus. By comparing Septimus Warren Smith and George Winterbourne, this paper examines on one hand how Woolf and Aldington succeeded in describing incomprehension and marginalization as the main causes for the failed recovery from war trauma and, on the other, how both writers used shell shock as a mental state mirroring not only a personal and social disease, but a national degeneration as well.

Literary Embodiment of Trauma

Military psychiatry, and the recognition of psychiatric injury in general,[5] is typically regarded as having begun in World War I in the

---

3   Karen DeMeester, "Trauma and Recovery in Virginia Woolf's *Mrs Dalloway*," *MFS Modern Fiction Studies*, 44, no. 3 (1998): 649.

4   See for instance Dan J. Stein, Metthew J. Friedman and Carlos Blanco, *Post-traumatic Stress Disorder* (Oxford: Wiley-Blackwell, 2011).

5   See Edgar Jones and Simon Wessely, *Shell Shock to PTSD: Military Psychiatry from 1900 to the Gulf War* (Hove and New York: Psychology Press, 2005), Kindle.

United Kingdom, but it was not until the 1980s that post-traumatic stress disorder (PTSD) gained the status of a psychiatric injury with diagnostic and therapeutic guidelines. Yet, modernist writers were surprisingly accurate in their descriptions of the symptoms of the psychological injury of shell shock, as if they had drawn inspiration for their characters directly from diagnostic manuals. In his book *Shell Shock and the Modernist Imagination*, Wyatt Bonikowski explains the relevance of shell shock in the context of modernist literature. "Soldier's symptoms of amnesia, mutism, anxiety, and various bodily dysfunctions with no apparent organic cause demonstrated that war's effects were not limited to bodily wounds", writes Bonikowski; "war also disrupted the mind and the individual's capacity for ordering and making sense of experience."[6]

The description of such mental states could not but become a central issue for modernist artists, who were most concerned with the need for "ordering, of giving a shape and a significance to the immense panorama of futility and anarchy which is contemporary history."[7] It is with regard to this concern that Bonikowski identifies the experimental modernist prose as the perfect vehicle for epitomizing shell shock and war trauma, underlying how, "in taking up symptomatic memory loss and speechlessness into the fabric of their novels," writers like Ford Madox Ford, Rebecca West, and Virginia Woolf "turned the figure of the shell-shocked soldier into the embodiment of anxieties the war had brought to England, particularly anxieties about the ability to represent experience to oneself and communicate it to others."[8]

World War I was not the first conflict to cause psychological trauma in soldiers, of course, but it was the scale of the problem that was

---

6   Wyatt Bonikowski, *Shell Shock and the Modernist Imagination: the Death Drive in Post-World War I British Fiction* (London and New York: Routledge), chap. 1, Kindle.

7   Thomas S. Eliot, "Ulysses Order and Myth," in *Selected Prose of T.S. Eliot*, ed. Frank Kermode (London: Faber&Faber): 177.

8   Bonikowski, *Shell Shock and the Modernist Imagination*, chap. 1.

unprecedented: the number of soldiers involved in warfare was higher than it had ever been and, on the battlefields, soldiers were devastated by new machine guns and an artillery barrage that was the result of industrial production. In particular, gas and chemical attacks exacerbated the horrors of life at the front. For all these reasons, during World War I "the effects of psychic attrition, fright and exhaustion were seen more drastically and in far larger numbers than before."[9] The term shell shock became "a metaphor for the nature of industrialized warfare, a term which suggests the corrosive force of the 1914–18 conflict *tout court*."[10]

Coined by soldiers themselves and first employed in a medical publication by Charles Samuel Myers in February 1915,[11] the term shell shock soon attained popular usage as the issue became more and more dominant in military psychiatry. This was so much the case that "by 1916, the British army was suffering from an epidemic of shell shock and, with losses incurred on the Somme, faced a manpower crisis."[12] Edgar Jones and Simon Wessely explain that, when traumatized soldiers were brought to hospitals, doctors had "the greatest difficulty understanding and therefore treating was shell shock. There was no accepted definition of the disorder as patients suffered from a range of unexplained symptoms and disabilities."[13]

In 1980, PTSD was eventually included in the third edition of the *Diagnostic and Statistical Manual of Mental Disorders* (DSM-III). Its definition in the DSM-III is particularly enlightening in helping us understand how much modernist literature was able to give "form and representation to a

---

9   Jones and Wessely, *Shell Shock to PTSD*, chap 1.
10 Winter, "Shell-Shock and the Cultural History of the Great War," 8.
11 Jones and Wessely, *Shell Shock to PTSD*, chap 2.
12 Ibid., chap 1.
13 Ibid., chap 1.

psychological condition that psychiatrists would not understand for another fifty years."[14]

The DSM-III description of PTSD symptoms involve: "reexperiencing the traumatic event; numbing of responsiveness to, or reduced involvement with, the external world; and a variety of autonomic, dysphoric, or cognitive symptoms."[15] Such symptoms are further explained as "recurrent painful, intrusive recollections of the event or recurrent dreams or nightmares during which the event is re-experienced." Also dissociative-like states have been reported in combat veterans, during which "components of the event are relived and the individual behaves as though experiencing the event at that moment." Other symptoms include "diminished responsiveness to the external world, referred to as 'psychic numbing' or 'emotional anesthesia.'" In such cases the person "may complain of feeling detached or estranged from other people, that he or she has lost the ability to become interested in previously enjoyed significant activities, or that the ability to feel emotions of any type, especially those associated with intimacy, tenderness, and sexuality, is markedly decreased." Many patients also present symptoms such as "hyperalertness, exaggerated startle response, and difficulty falling asleep" accompanied by recurrent nightmares. Some also complain of "impaired memory or difficulty in concentrating or completing tasks. In the case of a life-threatening trauma shared with others, survivors often describe painful guilt feelings about surviving when many did not, or about the things they had to do in order to survive."[16]

Anyone familiar with Virginia Woolf's *Mrs Dalloway* would recognize the character of Septimus Warren Smith in these symptoms. Septimus suffers from nightmares, dissociative-like states, emotional anaesthesia,

---

14 DeMeester, "Trauma and Recovery," 649.

15 *Diagnostic and Statistical Manual of Mental Disorders - 3rd edition*, (American Psychiatric Assoaciation, 1980), 309.81, 236, http://displus.sk/DSM/subory/dsm3.pdf. From now on: DSM-III.

16 Ibid.

hyperalertness, and estrangement from other people and from everyday life activities, with all manifestations causing great distress not only to him but to his wife, Rezia. Some of these symptoms are also visible in the protagonist of Richard Aldington's *Death of a Hero*. Like Septimus, George Winterbourne suffers from dissociative-like states, emotional anaesthesia, hyperalertness and above all estrangement from other people and from everyday life activities, with a "difficulty concentrating or completing tasks."

Karen DeMeester observes how, for many years, critics read Septimus's malady more as a "psychological pathology" than as a "psychological injury," thus failing to understand how his "identity as a war veteran makes him a particularly powerful tool with which 'to criticise the social system, & show it at work, at its most intense' (Woolf, *Diary*, 248)."[17] Some critics noted, for instance, that he does not experience a mental breakdown until four years after the Armistice,[18] in discord with the notions of shell shock that were known at the time. Yet the DSM-III clearly states that symptoms may begin "immediately or soon after the trauma," and it underlines how it is not unusual for the symptoms "to emerge after a latency period of months or years following the trauma." When this happens, "the chronic or delayed subtype is diagnosed," and the prognosis for remission is much harder.[19]

Through the character of Septimus, Virginia Woolf shows an almost innate understanding of the interior experience of trauma, an understanding that can extend to traumatized soldiers; how was it possible for her to have such a precise knowledge of the symptoms of PTSD well before the psychiatric disorder had been correctly diagnosed?

---

17 DeMeester, "Trauma and Recovery," 653.

18 Peter Knox-Shaw, "The Otherness of Septimus Warren Smith," *Durham University Journal*, 87, no. 1 (1995): 99-110.

19 DSM-III, 309.81, 237

"We have known the terror."
Twenty Traumatized Authors, Traumatized Characters

In *Septimus Warren Smith, Modernist War Poet*, Vara S. Neverow presents some hypotheses of men who could have inspired Woolf in the creation of Septimus. Elaine Showalter, for instance, argues how he could have originated from contact with Siegfried Sassoon;[20] Karen Levenback suggests that he might have been inspired by the writer's brother-in-law Philip Sidney Woolf.[21] Neverow's point, however, is that "Woolf does not rely on just a single person in her description of Septimus and sees him as a composite of all the war poets of the era,"[22] claiming that his rants as well as his drawings "can be aligned with the actual writings of Sassoon, Wilfred Owen, Robert Graves, Edward Thomas and Isaac Rosenberg."[23] Woolf had not been on the front then, but still she had first-hand knowledge of shell-shocked veterans and of the symptoms of war trauma. Moreover, as Reina van der Wiel explains in *Literary Aesthetics of Trauma*, Woolf herself was a trauma survivor and thus had authentic experience of such feelings.

If Virginia Woolf had obviously never fought at the front, Richard Aldington had. Although he thought war "an insanity" and had "the deeper suspicions about the motives of the combatants,"[24] he enlisted in the army as soon as he could,[25] because he thought "it was a plain duty to be in the army,

---

20 Cfr. Elaine Showalter, *The Female Malady: Women, Madness and English Culture* (London: Virago Press, 1987).

21 Karen Levenback, *Virginia Woolf and the Great War* (Syracuse: Syracuse University Press, 1999).

22 Vara S. Neverov, "Septimus Warren Smith, Modernist War Poet," *South Carolina Review*, 48, no. 2 (2016): 59.

23 Neverov, "Septimus Warren Smith, Modernist War Poet," 59.

24 Richard Aldington, *Life for Life's Sake. A Book of Reminiscences* (London: Cassell, [1968] 1941): 155.

25 As he wrote to his Italian translator, he was rejected in August 1914, because of a severe abdominal operation he underwent in 1911. However, when men became more and more necessary at the Front, he was accepted "and fought in the campaigns of 1916, 1917 and 1918, as a front-line soldier, and was promoted from private to Lieutenant, and for a time commanded a Company" (Richard Aldington,

and cowardly to be out of it."²⁶ These are the same feelings that lead George Winterbourne to enlist. *Death of a Hero* is actually a quite autobiographical novel in this sense, and Aldington explains that he had said in it "everything or almost everything" he had to say about the war of 1914–1918.²⁷ Because of the many connections and similarities between George Winterbourne and Septimus Warren Smith, however, one could venture to consider the character of Septimus, epitomizing the shell-shocked veterans, as a further inspiration for Aldington.²⁸

Apart from the most obvious difference, namely that Septimus Warren Smith is a war veteran whereas George Winterbourne dies at the front, the two share a number of similarities. Not only were they both artists before joining the army (Septimus, a poet; George, a painter), thus representing the psychological "type" that is more likely to "break down" during the war, they were also both born in provincial towns and then moved to London to follow their vocation. Moreover, they are both married to women who do not understand them. In fact, although Rezia and Elizabeth are very different women who cannot easily be compared to one another, they both serve to intensify the sense of loneliness and extraneousness felt by the protagonists. Vara Neverow claims that

---

Letter to Alessandra Scalero dated 16.7.1933. © The Estate of Richard Aldington.)

26   Aldington, *Life for Life's Sake*, 155.

27   Ibid., 163.

28   While it is certain that Aldington had read *Jacob's Room*, as he wrote to Woolf to express his appreciation, there is no "proof" that he read *Mrs Dalloway*. Yet, it is not unlikely that he had. He was a close friend of T.S. Eliot, and he was directly in contact with Virginia Woolf for the so-called "Bel Esprit," the Eliot Fund created by Pound and Aldington, with the help of Woolf and Lady Ottoline Morrell. He surely knew about the novel's publication, because when it came out it was (anonymously) reviewed in the TLS, where Aldington worked as a reviewer. Moreover, in January 1926, Aldington asked Virginia Woolf to write an introduction to his recent translation, an invitation that she declined claiming to have "too much work on hand" and to be "entirely ignorant of French 18*th* century memoirs" (Woolf, 26.01.1926). It is thus likely that, before asking Woolf to write an introduction for his work, he had read the novel she had just published.

Septimus serves as the doppelgänger of all the war survivors and for all the war dead from all social classes and all ranks, for all those who voluntarily joined the armed forces in patriotic euphoria in August 1914 and all those who were conscripted as the war progressed.[29]

If Aldington actually read *Mrs Dalloway*, he might then have seen his own experience reflected in this character, and the possibility of giving voice to what he had felt after his return from the front. Like Septimus and Aldington, George Winterbourne voluntarily enlists in the army in 1914, only to receive the most cruel and ferocious disappointment when he understands that warfare is useless and pointless: "The élan of his former life had carried him through a good many months of the Army; but after about two months in the line, he saw that intellectually he was slowly slipping backwards."[30] After having fought at the front, Septimus perceives he has become incapable of feelings; in the same way, George, still on the battlefield, understands "that his mind degenerated; slowly at first, then more and more rapidly."[31] It is when he realizes that he is incapable of concentrating or achieving any of the things he had been able to achieve previously that he feels "that even if he escaped the War he would be hopelessly handicapped in comparison with those who had not served [. . .]. These lost War months, now mounting to years, were a knock-out blow from which he could not possibly recover."[32] The gap between those who fought and those at home is as clear in George's mind as it was in Aldington's.

---

29 Neverov, "Septimus Warren Smith, Modernist War Poet," 59.
30 Richard Aldington, *Death of a Hero* (London: Penguin, [2013] 1929), chap. 3, Kindle.
31 Aldington, *Death of a Hero*, ch. 3.
32 Ibid., ch. 3.

Aldington also examines in detail the sense of estrangement that Septimus begins to perceive at the end of the conflict, using his protagonist to portray feelings he had himself experienced:

> he felt a degradation, a humiliation, in the dirt, the lice, the communal life in holes and ruins, the innumerable deprivations and hardships. He suffered a feeling that his body had become worthless, condemned to a sort of kept tramp's standard of living, and ruthlessly treated as cannon-fodder. He suffered for other men too, that they should be condemned to this; but since it was the common fate of the men of his generation, he determined he must endure it. His face lost its fineness and took on the mask of "a red-faced Tommy" [. . .].[33]

In order to endure the horror, George has to alienate his mind from his body, and his consciousness from everything around him. Yet, alienation was not enough. After a severe battle, in which Winterbourne had "lost completely the sequence of events," he understood that

> he was profoundly affected by it, that it made a cut in his life and personality. You couldn't say there was anything melodramatically startling, no hair going grey in a night, or never smiling again. He looked unaltered; he behaved in exactly the same way. But, in fact, he was a little mad. We talk of shell-shock, but who wasn't shell-shocked, more or less? The change in him was psychological, and showed itself in two ways. He was left with an anxiety complex, a sense of fear he had never experienced [. . .]. And he was also left with a profound and cynical discouragement, a shrinking horror of the human race . . .[34]

---

33 Aldington, *Death of a Hero*, ch. 3.

34 Ibid.

In this symptom described by Aldington as "a shrinking horror of the human race," I glimpse the same horror Septimus feels for Dr. Holmes, whom he refers to as the embodiment of human nature, a human nature that soldiers had seen at its ugliest on the battlefield and by which they could not but be disgusted.

Another element that needs to be remarked upon is that the only comrade with whom "Winterbourne was brought into much closer intimacy,"[35] the one assuming a fundamental role for him on the battlefield, is called Evans. It is quite impossible not to think of Septimus's friend who died by his side at the front and haunts his nightmares.

Eventually, both Septimus and George commit suicide, and although Septimus kills himself four years after the war, while George decides to let himself be killed on the battlefield, I believe they are both led to suicide not only by their "debilitating emotions,"[36] but also by the marginalization and lack of understanding of a society that looks at their disease as a threat to its stability. Back home, be it during home leave for George, or after the Armistice for Septimus, what they find is incomprehension, together with a feeling that they are jeopardizing the facade of patriotism and the social solidity of their nation, so that they become unable to speak about what they experienced or interact with people.

Communication is Health

Kate McLoughlin argues that "Frequently encountered in war writing is the proposition that war defeats language, as though words themselves have been blasted to smithereens or else suffer from combat fatigue."[37] This

---

35 Ibid.

36 DeMeester, "Trauma and Recovery", 650.

37 Kate McLoughlin, "War and Words", in *The Cambridge Companion to War Writing*, ed. Kate McLoughlin (New York: Cambridge University Press, 2009), 15, LION e-book.

"language fatigue" was experienced not only by the two characters here under analysis, but by Richard Aldington himself. Like other writers and poets who had fought in the war, Aldington needed some years to pass before he was able to write about what he had seen on the battlefield. In a letter to his Italian translator, Alessandra Scalero, Aldington explains how war left him "very unwell and shattered," so much so that he had to leave the city and move to the country and, for nearly ten years, he "found it impossible to do much creative work."[38] In fact, Aldington also suffered from a slight form of shell shock, as can be inferred from his autobiography *Life for Life's Sake*—in which he makes reference to his "nervous malady and insomnia"[39]—but also from the above-mentioned letter he writes to Scalero, in which he confides to her that

> the long years of War not only broke all my plans and ended the career I had begun, but for a long time made me incapable of creative writing. I had to start all over again, re-educate myself (I forgot my Greek and Italian, and had to re-learn them) and earn a living.[40]

He never lost hope, however, and although nobody read the war poems he wrote right after the Armistice, "since everyone was sick of the War," he always believed that he should be able to write something, that his "creative spirit was still there."[41] In the aftermath of the first world conflict, Aldington writes that he was actually jeered at by journalists for his "obsession with the war,"[42] as if it were odd for a poet who had fought at the front to write about his experience instead of wanting to forget about it. In his review to *All*

---

38 Aldington, letter to Scalero, 16.7.1933.

39 Aldington, *Life for Life's Sake*, 189.

40 Aldington, letter to Scalero, 16.7.1933.

41 Ibid.

42 Aldington, *Life for Life's Sake*, 146.

Quiet on the Western Front, Herbert Read writes of the public's unwillingness to know in terms of "shame-neurosis: . . . it must have been the experience of many men, when the war was over and they came back with minds seared with the things they had seen, to find a civilian public weary and indifferent, and positively unwilling to listen."[43]

Similarly, Aldington comments, in his autobiography, on how the nation was split in two after the Armistice. On the one side was the increasing number of "turbulent, impatient" young men "confident that a grateful country would be eager to find them out jobs for which they were often quite incompetent;"[44] on the other side was a civilian population "frayed in its nerves, crushed with taxation" with its "benevolence and emotional sympathy long since exhausted."[45] A civilian population that only realized what the young men had endured with the "flood of war books" that came ten years after the war ended. From Aldington's words two key problems related to veterans emerge: the society's desire to forget the war and the necessity for, but initial inability of, the veterans to communicate their experience.

"Communication is health; communication is happiness,"[46] mutters Septimus, who would like to be able to tell others what he thinks he knows, what he has learnt out there, but remains incapable of uttering. Like all trauma survivors, he wishes to convey his emotions and experience but knows that they will not be understood: people cannot comprehend what these front-line soldiers actually experienced and felt. Yet communication is a key factor in recovery after trauma, and for this reason communication, or lack of it, is a key issue in both *Mrs Dalloway* and *Death of a Hero*.

---

43 Herbert Read, "Review of *All Quiet on the Western Front*," *Nation & Athenaeum*, (27 April 1929): 544.
44 Aldington, *Life for Life's Sake*, 187.
45 Ibid.
46 Woolf, *Mrs Dalloway*, (Orlando: Harcourt, [2005] 1925): 104.

Woolf emphasizes Septimus's symptoms of detachment and estrangement throughout her novel. "Look, look," continuously repeats Rezia to Septimus, "Look," she implores, in order to force him to "take an interest in things outside himself,"[47] as Dr Holmes suggested, believing that "a nice out-of-door game" could cure Septimus, given that he had "nothing whatever seriously the matter with him."[48] As a response to his wife's often reiterated request, Septimus, on the contrary, "shut his eyes; he would see no more."[49] He is not only completely estranged from the world, but also misunderstood by those who are supposed to take care of him; his doctors, in the first place, treat him according to the common medical prescriptions of the period "like a stubborn child."[50] A harsh treatment was actually reserved for shell-shocked soldiers "in order to cure men of their weakness and send them back to the front,"[51] and the same harsh treatment was used for shell-shocked veterans once the war ended. Since their excessive sensitivity was considered to threaten the English ideal of "true men," who should be committed to "moderation and self-control,"[52] doctors often minimized their problem by simply suggesting some rest and more resolution to go back to their pre-war lives.

George Winterbourne is likewise forced to react with and connect to people by his wife: on his second day of leave she organizes a night out to dine with friends, inciting him to "take an interest" in the world around him. At the dinner, George, who used to be extremely—not to say excessively—talkative before the War began, "set very silent" being "amazed to find how

---

47 Woolf, *Mrs Dalloway*, (London: The Hogarth Press, [1958] 1925): 25.
48 Ibid.
49 Ibid., 26.
50 Mosse, "Shell-Shock as a Social Disease," 107.
51 Ibid., 106.
52 Ibid., 101.

remote he felt, how completely he had nothing to say."⁵³ This feeling is worsened by the comments of Elizabeth's friends that show their complete incomprehension of the reality of war, such as when they ask him how did he spend his leisure in France—"still reading and painting?"⁵⁴—or when Mr. Upjohn points out to George how he looks "most grotesque in those clothes" and then asks him if he is "still writing for periodicals." George answers his questions with a sardonic smile: "No. I've been rather busy, you know, and in the trenches one—,"⁵⁵ but he cannot finish his sentence as Mr. Upjohn interrupts him. Most of George's utterances are interrupted during the dinner: his interlocutors prevent him from saying anything about the war, even though they pretend to be there to ask him about it. As a result, these pages become quite representative of how misunderstood, silenced and marginalized soldiers and veterans must have felt. Feeling this way, George ceases to listen to the conversation and starts thinking about Evans, who, as for Septimus with his Evans, represents the last sympathetic relationship he was capable of having. At the end of the dinner, in the taxi taking them home, Elizabeth "reprove[s] him with gentle dignity for drinking too much" and scolds him for his hands and fingers being terribly dirty: "did you forget to wash them? And you were rather rude to everybody."⁵⁶ DeMeester states that "the principal way Septimus could give meaning and purpose to his war experiences is by communicating" and, when he tries to, he "encounters resistance from members of the community."⁵⁷ In the same way, George tries to tell Elizabeth about some of his war experiences, but right when he is describing the horror of "gas bombardment and the awful look on the

---

53 Aldington, *Death of a Hero*, ch. 3.
54 Ibid.
55 Ibid.
56 Ibid.
57 DeMeester, "Trauma and Recovery," 660.

faces of men gassed" he notices her mouth is "dried by a suppressed yawn"[58] and he stops abruptly. Both characters thus show how the "personally reconstitutive act"[59] that communication might represent for the victims of shell shock becomes unattainable in the post-war society.

Elizabeth and Rezia are significantly different characters: Rezia is herself a victim of the war, one of those "war brides who were brought to Britain as a symbol of male triumph, power, egotism, and romanticism" who now "suffers from loneliness, anxiety, and horror" and, like Septimus, "has nobody to tell her agony except her husband, who finally feels nothing for her pain."[60] By contrast, Elizabeth and Fanny (George's lover) represent the "lack of knowledge about the war, sustained by the censorship and propaganda of the government and media,"[61] identifiable as those women who worshiped men when they were "heroes, wounded in mentionable places"[62] but had no real idea of what war was like. Regardless of their differing disposition, the role of their characters is similar, as they serve to emphasize a lack of empathy from the person who is supposed to better understand the soldier, or the veteran: his wife. This lack of empathy is represented through their paying more attention to what people may think of their husbands than to what their husbands actually feel. Elizabeth is worried because George was rude to everybody during the dinner, and Rezia is preoccupied by what people might think in watching her husband's exaggerated reactions: "People must notice; people must see."[63]

---

58   Aldington, *Death of a Hero*, ch. 3.

59   Kali Tal, "Speaking the Language of Pain: Vietnam War Literature in the Context of a Literature of Trauma," in *Fourteen Landing Zones: Approaches to Vietnam War Literature*, ed. Philip K. Jason (Iowa City: University of Iowa Press): 230.

60   Masami Usui, "The Female Victims of the War in *Mrs Dalloway*," in *Virginia Woolf and War. Fiction, Reality and Myth*, ed. Mark Hussey (Syracuse: Syracuse University Press): 152.

61   Bonikowski, *Shell Shock and the Modernist Imagination*, ch. 1.

62   Sigfried Sassoon, *Collected Poems 1908-1956*, (London: Faber&Faber, [1984] 1961): 79.

63   Woolf, *Mrs Dalloway*, 18.

Shame is indeed a fundamental aspect related to shell shock. While in *Mrs Dalloway* it is Rezia who feels shame when considering what people might think of her husband, and of herself, in *Death of a Hero* it is George who feels scared by and ashamed of his shell-shock symptoms. He first notices the symptoms while home on leave, when he confronts his house, his friends, his job, and a community that "wants him to be the man he was before the war,"[64] and he notices that he no longer is what he used to be: "An immense effort of imagination was needed to link himself now with himself then."[65] He had become like "Septimus, who wasn't Septimus any longer,"[66] and "grown stranger and stranger,"

> he went back to his room with paper and pencil and began to sketch. He was astonished to find that his hand, once as steady as the table itself, shook very slightly but perceptibly. The drink last night, or shell-shock? [. . .] Both his hand and brain failed him—he had even forgotten how to draw rapidly and accurately.[67]

While Virginia Woolf never gives a name to Septimus's illness in her novel, Aldington mentions Winterboune's shell-shocked condition more than once, mainly to explain how ashamed he feels of it: "To his shame he found the shell-fear come back as the Archies opened up, and he started each time he heard the thud of a bomb."[68] Elaine Showalter famously showed how shell shock was affected by an ideology of gender that classified any kind of mental disease or hysteria as effeminate, and was therefore a condition true men should try to overcome. Thus, although

---

64   DeMeester, "Trauma and Recovery," 661.
65   Aldington, *Death of a Hero*, ch. 3.
66   Woolf, *Mrs Dalloway*, 73.
67   Aldington, *Death of a Hero*, ch. 3.
68   Ibid.

George could feel his mind collapsing, "yet his pride would compel him to urge himself far beyond the point where another man would merely have collapsed."[69]

As George Mosse explains, "War was the supreme test of manliness, and those who were the victims of shell-shock had failed this test."[70] This is why Septimus tried to resist, why he "would shut his eyes" and "see no more"[71] so as not to go mad, and this is also why George tries as hard as he can to "repress shell-shocked nerves:"

> His state of mind, what with sleeplessness and worry and shock and ague—which came back as soon as he was in the line again—and physical exhaustion and inhibited fear, almost fringed dementia, and he would have collapsed but his strength of will and pride. He was a wrecked man, swept along in the swirling cataracts of the War.[72]

He becomes more and more hallucinatory and, similar to Septimus, "every incident seemed to beat on his brain Death, Death, Death. All the decay and dead of battlefields entered his blood and seemed to poison him."[73] In his last days, his mind is "so dulled that he could scarcely comprehend and write down [. . .] orders. He mis-spelled words as he scrawled down notes in shaking, deformed hand-writing,"[74] until the last moment, when he felt "he was going mad" so that he "sprang to his feet" in the front line, and "the line of bullets smashed across his chest like a

---

69   Ibid.
70   Mosse, "Shell-Shock as a Social Disease," 104.
71   Woolf, *Mrs Dalloway*, 26.
72   Aldington, *Death of a Hero*, ch. 3.
73   Ibid.
74   Ibid.

savage steel whip. The universe exploded darkly into oblivion."⁷⁵ George chooses death as a desperate act of escape from the nightmare of war, facing a dark explosion "into oblivion" which once again is reminiscent of Septimus's end: "There he lay with a thud, thud, thud in his brain, and then suffocation and blackness."⁷⁶

Conclusions

Karen DeMeester explains how "Septimus's psychological pain does not cause his suicide. It is caused by society's refusal to let him give meaning to that pain."⁷⁷ He feels he knows something he should reveal to others: "he knew everything. He knew the meaning of the world, he said."⁷⁸ War gave him awareness, an awareness he feels compelled to share, yet trauma makes it difficult for him to express it, and society is, however, unwilling to listen and understand. Quoting DeMeester again, Septimus "is an extreme example of the struggle all trauma survivors experience in trying to create a means of describing their traumatic experiences so that others will fully comprehend them."⁷⁹ This is further emphasized by Rezia continually asking herself "why" all this is happening to her. She does not understand nor recognize him any longer: "why had he gone, then, why."⁸⁰ In a similar way, it is during his home leave that George realizes how his own life has collapsed, and this gives him the feeling "that even if he came out alive he would never be able to rebuild his life."⁸¹ As Bonikowski explains, "the

---

75 Ibid.
76 Woolf, *Mrs Dalloway*, 202.
77 DeMeester, "Trauma and Recovery", 653.
78 Woolf, *Mrs Dalloway*, 74.
79 DeMeester, "Trauma and Recovery", 655.
80 Woolf, *Mrs Dalloway*, 74.
81 Aldington, *Death of a Hero*, ch. 3.

intensely private experience of war cuts the individual soldier off from those who have no experience of war, creating an unbridgeable gap between combatants and non-combatants." He suggests the existence of "a silence within the experience of war, a sense of something that cannot be spoken or represented either to oneself or others;" a silence which manifests itself "most emphatically upon the soldier's return from war, in his encounter with a home that has become strange."[82]

Before the composition of *Death of a Hero*, Aldington had already dealt with this aspect in his review of Herbert Read's *In Retreat*, where he had written of the "torturing sense of something incommunicable" in war, explaining the struggle of the veteran "trying to communicate the incommunicable" and concluding that "there was no ration between the two races of men—those, I mean, in the line and those who had never touched it."[83] Both Septimus and George's suicides, to which they were led by social marginalization and incomprehension, represent a last and extreme act of communication with a world which is unable to accept, listen, and heal. It is Clarissa Dalloway who, eventually, feels genuine empathy for Septimus, feeling "somehow very like him," feeling "glad that he had done it; thrown it away" because, as she added in the U.S. edition, "he made her feel the beauty."[84] Although she can only empathize with Septimus in an abstract way, as she does not share his shell-shock, it is thanks to his suicide if the two become connected, and if Clarissa can understand the deep feeling of trauma. Quite significantly, pondering on Septimus's suicide, she thinks: "Death was defiance. Death was an attempt to communicate."[85]

---

82 Bonikowski, *Shell Shock and the Modernist Imagination*, intro.
83 Richard Aldington, "Review to *In Retreat* by Herbert Read," *The Criterion*, 4, no. 2 (1926): 363.
84 Woolf, *Mrs Dalloway* (Orlando: Harcourt): 182.
85 Ibid., 202.

Bibliography

Aldington, Richard, "Review to *In Retreat* by Herbert Read." *The Criterion*, vol. 4, no. 2, 1926, pp. 363-367.

Aldington, Richard, *Death of a Hero*. Penguin, 1929, 2013.

Aldington, Richard, *Life for Life's Sake. A Book of Reminiscences*. London, Cassell, 1941, 1968.

Aldington, Richard, "Terror," *The Complete Poems of Richard Aldington*, London, Allan Wingate, 1948.

Aldington, Richard, "Letter to Alessandra Scalero, 16.7.1933." *Archivio Scalero*, Biblioteca Civica di Mazzé, © The Estate of Richard Aldington.

Bonikowski, Wyatt, *Shell Shock and the Modernist Imagination: The Death Drive in Post-World War 1 British Fiction*. Routledge, 2013.

DeMeester, Karen, "Trauma and Recovery in Virginia Woolf's *Mrs Dalloway.*" *MFS Modern Fiction Studies*, vol. 44, no. 3, 1998, pp. 649-668.

Diagnostic and Statistical Manual of Mental Disorders (Third Edition), American Psychiatric Association, 1980, http://displus.sk/DSM/subory/dsm3.pdf.

Eliot, Thomas S., "Ulysses Order and Myth," in *Selected Prose of T.S. Eliot*, ed. Frank Kermode. London: Faber&Faber 1975: 175-178.

Jones, Edgar and Simon Wessely, *Shell Shock to PTSD: Military Psychiatry from 1900 to the Gulf War*. Psychology Press, 2005.

Knox-Shaw, Peter, "The Otherness of Septimus Warren Smith," *Durham University Journal*, vol. 87, no. 1, 1995, pp. 99-110.

Levenback, Karen, *Virginia Woolf and the Great War*. Syracuse University Press, 1999.

McLoughlin, Kate, "War and Words." *The Cambridge Companion to War Writing*, edited by Kate McLoughlin, Cambridge University Press, 2009, pp. 15-24.

Mosse, George L., "Shell-Shock as a Social Disease." *Journal of Contemporary History*, vol. 35, no. 1, Special Issue: Shell-Shock, 2000, pp. 101-108.

Neverow, Vara S., "Septimus Warren Smith, Modernist War Poet." *South Carolina Review*, vol. 48, no. 2, 2016, pp. 58-65.

Read, Herbert, "Review of *All Quiet on the Western Front*," Nation & Athenaeum, 27 April 1929.

Sassoon, Sigfried, *Collected Poems 1908-1956*. Faber and Faber, 1961, 1984.

Showalter, Elaine, *The Femaly Malady: Women, Madness and English Culture*. Virago Press, 1987.

Stein, Dan J., Matthew J. Friedman and Carlos Blanco, *Post-traumatic Stress Disorder*. Oxford, Wiley-Blackwell, 2011.

Tal, Kali, "Speaking the Language of Pain: Vietnam War Literature in the Context of a Literature of Trauma," *Fourteen Landing Zones: Approaches to Vietnam War Literature*, ed. Philip K. Jason, University of Iowa Press, 1991, pp. 217-250.

Usui, Masami, "The Female Victims of the War in *Mrs. Dalloway*," in *Virginia Woolf and War. Fiction, Reality and Myth*, ed. Mark Hussey, Syracuse University Press, 1991.

Winter, Jay, "Shell-Shock and the Cultural History of the Great War," *Journal of Contemporary History*, vol. 35, no. 1, Special Issue: Shell-Shock, 2000, pp. 7-11.

Woolf, Virginia, *Mrs Dalloway*. London: The Hogarth Press, 1925, 1958.

Woolf, Virginia, *Mrs Dalloway*. Orlando FL: Harcourt, 1925 [2005].

Elisa Bolchi is founding member and vice-president of the Italian Virginia Woolf Society. She has taught English literature at Università Cattolica del Sacro Cuore, Milan, for several years. Her research focuses on Anglo-Italian relationships; she studied the reception of Virginia Woolf in Italian literary periodicals during Fascism, publishing the book *Il paese della bellezza* (Milan 2007). Her last book, *L'indimenticabile artista* (Milan 2015), tells the background of the first Italian editions of Virginia Woolf's books, starting from unpublished editorial letters. Other subjects of research include Richard Aldington, Ian McEwan, and Jeanette Winterson, mainly investigating such themes as Italian reception, re-writing, and ecocritical writing.

THREE ITERATIONS OF SHELL SHOCK

Mary Butts and Modern Violence in Interwar Dorset

Ria Banerjee

Abstract

The shell shocked soldier appears repeatedly in literature of the period as an uncanny figure who is like and yet profoundly unlike the rest of the population, a mind full of war in a time of peace. This essay takes up two interrelated questions regarding the depiction of shell shock by civilian women writers in the interwar era: first, the ways that such writers incorporated war experience into their fiction, and second, the attitudes towards shell shock that emerges in their fiction. The essay contrasts Mary Butts's depictions of shell shock with more famous works by Virginia Woolf and Rebecca West. Ultimately, I suggest that Butts's novelistic vision, which has many xenophobic and regressive elements, presents a view of shell shocked war veterans that is unexpectedly positive. Rather than seeing them as a symbol of larger social problems, Butts restore them some measure of their humanity and agency as fictional operatives who contest and complete the novels in which they appear.

The shell shocked veteran in the years between the First and Second World Wars presents an epistemological puzzle for the civilian woman novelist: as a locus of past violence whose proportions are documented and yet unknowable; as a victim who is simultaneously revered as a hero; and, as figures present in peacetime yet inassimilable with attempts to re-establish a previous normalcy because of their recurring experiences of trauma. The shell shocked soldier appears repeatedly in literature of the period as an uncanny figure who is like and yet profoundly unlike the rest of the population. The presence of this figure in interwar society raises a specifically-gendered question about the relationship between authenticity and representation: who can write about war and to what extent? The English novelist Mary Butts, like her more famous contemporaries Virginia Woolf and Rebecca West, had not experienced combat and held vigorous anti-war views (although unlike her first husband John Rodker, she never identified as a pacifist[1]). The ability to talk openly about war and international political action was severely restricted during wartime under the Defence of the Realm Act; but even after the war, the shell shocked veteran is a persistent reminder of the simultaneous accuracy and inefficacy of anti-war opinions held by women writers like Butts, Woolf, and West who protested it through civilian political work, pamphleteering, and novel writing.

My thanks to the New York Public Library for use of the Shoichi Noma Research Study Room during the preparation of this essay.

1   She writes in her memoir, *The Crystal Cabinet* that during war, the "nation was driven past reflection" and in those circumstances, she joined the London City Council to "perhaps stammer a reminder that, in no matter what crisis, society is based upon certain liberties and certain contracts between the individual and the state" (94). However, she declares, "Did I ever believe in absolute pacifism? Not a bit" (94).

What follows is an examination of three iterations of shell shock in characters written by Butts that appear in her Dorset novels: Peter Amburton from *Ashe of Rings* (1925), and Clarence Lake and Picus Tracy from *Armed with Madness* (1928). (Picus marries another recurring character, Scylla Taverner in the novel, *Death of Felicity Taverner*, 1932, which I'll refer to in passing; however, the violence in this later novel is not attributed to veterans of the First World War and is therefore less relevant to the present discussion.) The 1925 and 1928 novels have, at their heart, the shell shocked ex-soldier as motivator and agent, an active force that the narrative contains but cannot control. Butts's shell shocked war veterans are damaged and unpredictable, familiar figures in literary convention. However, they are not victims in her representation but characters whose growth and development, and in one case full recuperation, are crucial to the novels' structure overall. Thus, these novels present an alternative picture of the shell shocked vet in interwar English society, as a man shaped by the War but not limited to that experience. Picus, Clarence, and Peter are shown to have childhood psychological wounds that are exacerbated by modern warfare, and in the aftermath of war experience, they struggle for self-definition with different levels of success. Their journey to selfhood, conceived by the civilian feminine imagination that was restricted from direct experience of war (but, importantly, not of total war), recuperates the outsider status of the shell shocked vet. The novels present the vet as a normal part of a still-violent peacetime world instead of a damaged, distanced reminder of an episode in the past.

Mary Butts in Context: Women Writers and Shell Shock

Reviewing the literature on shell shock and British modernist fiction in the interwar years of the 1920s and '30s reveals the central importance of two civilian women writers: Rebecca West and Virginia Woolf. Nearly every recent literary and historical study of shell shock and the First World War refers to *The Return of the Soldier* (1918) and *Mrs. Dalloway* (1925) as touchstones for the imaginative life of the period, particularly since the novels speak to one another in key ways. However, in the face of war, these works outline the horrific end of experience, ultimately restricting themselves to the home front and drawing key distinctions between civilian and soldierly experiences. The question of who wrote about war experiences was fraught in the interwar period and remains so now. Jonathan Atkin notes that it was important for many well-known writers and poets to engage directly with war work despite some strongly held anti-war views; in common with these men, "direct experience of the war was also regarded by some women as having a serious role to play in their conveying of its essential truths" (Atkin 160). Despite the insistence of some women civilian writers that war experiences could be represented without direct experience of trenches at the front, that dogma persisted and extended into the interwar period. Shell shocked veterans often figure in interwar era literature as cipher-like and unavailable to civilian imaginations of the writer, the woman, and the pacifist. In response, women writers of World War I often confine themselves to stylistic experiments to depict scenes of battle and its human aftermath because of the purportedly ungraspable nature of their material—a brief example of this is West's highly cinematic impressionistic account of Jenny's dreams of the front in *The Return of the Soldier*.

The belief in the primacy of experience when confronted with the enormity of modern warfare can be seen impelling many key figures of British modernism into peripheral war work despite their anti-war politics. E. M. Forster, for instance, went to Egypt to work for the Red Cross because he, along with Edward Carpenter, Duncan Grant, David Garnett and others "believed that experience of war (even from a distance) was important in the formation of a reaction to it" (Atkin 79). Despite the obvious power of antiwar theater and poetry like in Edna St. Vincent Millay's *Aria da Capo* (1920) or Nancy Cunard's *Parallax* (1925), such works were not thought to share the authenticity of, say, published accounts written by war nurses. Despite protests by authors like Storm Jameson, authority in speaking about war and veterans was presumed to be bestowed by authorial experience and not based upon, for instance, the author's grasp of facts and the power of their poetics.[2] Notwithstanding the frequency with which Woolf and West are quoted in later studies of World War I, civilian women writers of the interwar era display an anxiety about their subject that results in very few depictions of battle, and a tendency to view shell shocked soldiers as representatives of type.[3]

Butts, who hovered on the edges of Bloomsbury without becoming a part of it, also took a strong anti-war stance in the 1910s. Although civilian women hesitated to write scenes of direct combat, shell shocked ex-soldiers proliferate in their fiction; in her portrayal of Picus, Clarence, and Peter, Butts is following the massive readerly interest in war-related fiction that drove so much publication in the 1920s and '30s. Simultaneously, contemporary psychology encouraged the desire to explain, label, and thereby contain the multifarious experiences of shell shocked veterans into recognizable categories of damage. In *Shellshock and its Aftermath* (1926), the American

---

2   In a detailed account of writing produced by war nurses in the 1920s and '30s, Atkin writes about the novelist Storm Jameson, who "took to task critics who viewed a war novel as naturally inferior to a 'truthful' memoir" (153). Jameson remains in the minority, however, despite the validity of her point of view, and the admittedly constructed nature of many war memoirs, which Atkin notes often repeated the tropes of faithful nurses and tragic hospital scenes in acknowledgement of reader preferences in the voracious interwar market for memoirs of heroism and wartime valor (142).

3   Bazin and Lauter comment on this aspect of Woolf's fiction, saying that her focus "shifted in her later work from a concern for the survival and mental health of the individual to a concern for the survival of a culture" (24). As I argue later in this essay, this transition from the individual experience of war to the individual-as-trope can be tracked in the progression from *Jacob's Room* to *Three Guineas*; focusing on the shell shocked veteran in broader terms allows Woolf a clarity of argumentative vision that the early novel does not (cannot) have.

psychologist Norman Fenton classifies degrees of shell shock in over 700 American troops who had been hospitalized in France during 1914-1918, and his labels reflect a pervasive interwar cultural anxiety about the status of the veteran in interwar peacetime. Fenton observes that the most severe sufferers are easiest to recognize: the "psychotic" and "disabled" needed to be institutionalized or were unable to get jobs in peacetime. "Fatigued" men had jobs but worked regular hours with great difficulty, and thus were also demarcated from the rest of the population. "Neurotic" and "normal" ex-troops had the least trouble reintegrating with civilian society. These men were declared "cured for the purposes of everyday living, but always with the possibility of relapse" (Leese 136). Shell shock lurks around the corner like a monster or a shade in interwar Britain, tinting civilian expressions of sympathy with a suspicion that the ex-soldier could be at the mercy of hidden internal symptoms like headaches, memory lapses, dizzy spells, and restlessness. As historian Peter Leese writes, "A dropped screwdriver or a newspaper article could provoke an outburst of anger or excitement" that would rend apart the peacetime reassimilation project (135).

Despite evidence that politicians and the press called for greater sympathy and support for the shell shocked, the British War Office and Ministry of Pensions in the 1920s and '30s wrangled incessantly over the degree and severity of shell shock and resultant compensatory payouts, motivated possibly by poor economic conditions in Britain in that period. The conviction, reiterated in several official reports, was that most cases of shell shock could be controlled with hard work and a cheerful attitude, a view that greatly compounded the damaging effects of war in thousands of ex-soldiers and their families. In Butts's *Armed with Madness*, a country doctor replicates this attitude towards Picus, a character who had been in the War and who suffers mysterious ailments indirectly indicating shell shock. When his friend Scylla asks about Picus's condition, the doctor replies: "Everything is wrong [with him], and nothing . . . I don't mean by that that he invents it. His aches and pains are a mask that conceals something. What that is, I've never been able to find out . . . [or] shouldn't care myself to know too much about" (30). The doctor exits the scene without any intervention, and leaves behind only this ambivalent expression of reserved sympathy and squeamish withdrawal (that he "shouldn't care [him]self to know too much about" Picus's nightmares). The doctor's ambivalent reverence for, and withdrawal from, shell shocked veterans is emblematic of the cultural attitude in interwar England and is at odds with the opinions held by Picus's friends in the novel. Instead, the novel pitches its sympathies against the doctor and with the band of friends who define themselves at odds with modern society, and display an unusual sensitivity to, and acceptance of their friends' traumatic experiences.

Public health debates and social attitudes to shell shock are encapsulated on both sides of the Atlantic in literary representations of the veteran, who is often the narrative trigger for meditations on pacifism and the immorality of war. Such musings, while sympathetic to the plight of the returned soldier in general, leave aside the question of the shell shocked individual as an agentic force in his own right. Consider the following passage from Woolf's *Jacob's Room* (1922), a novel that in many ways serves as a useful interlocutor to Butts's interwar fiction. In a rare depiction of battle, Woolf's narrator describes what feels like a dreamscape, or rather a nightmare conjured up from newspaper reports. "The battleships ray out over the North Sea" and "at a given signal . . . a dozen young men in the prime of life descend with composed faces into the depths of the sea." These troops are properly stoic, displaying the complete obedience and commitment of perfect soldiers as they die in an unnamed encounter. Other battalions of young men sweep down on a field like "blocks of tin soldiers." At the end of the maneuver, seen from the far distance at which the generals stand, "one or two pieces still agitate up and down like fragments of broken match-stick" (155-156). Woolf's outrage at modern violence is evident even in these snippets; by highlighting the toy-like stature of the troops, the narrative also underscores its own position of comparative (civilian) safety and concurrent helplessness. Despite their oppositional politics, the narrator unavoidably shares her distant view of the "tin soldiers" with the military generals that she despises. West's *The Return of the Soldier* ironizes a similar restriction and forced alliance with the wartime status quo. West's women, Jenny, Kitty, and Margaret, are inexorably drawn into the project to return Chris Baldry to the war front to perform a socially acceptable version of heroism. Their adherence to notions of Chris's bravery and duty are enacted with a view to what people will say about Baldry Court and its heirs, a collaboration with masculinized public opinion that is analogous to Woolf's narrative circumspection.

Such narrative positions cannot offer much imaginative space to a shell shocked ex-soldier. As if reiterating the narrative constrictions faced by civilian women writers, the shell shocked vet is bound to the circumstances of his wartime experience in Woolf's later fiction as well. Butts's Picus, Clarence, and Peter exist at a tangent to such a narrative position, different from other depictions of shell shock because of their author's conviction, albeit problematic in itself, that the trauma of everyday life is not distinct from that of war. Here it is worth pausing to make one further comment before turning more fully to Butts. I've suggested thus far that in the typical literary view, depictions of shell shock overlook the subjectivity of returning soldiers and distance them from the mass of civilians, women, and pacifists who make up the peacetime population. The effects of this narrative position can be detected in today's academic conversations, even a century later. For instance, Leese provides a historically inflected summary of the development of shell shock as a term that ends by generalizing about the veteran as a symbol while overlooking the individuality and agency of the men described:

> Looking back across the twentieth century, in one sense, the meanings of the Great War viewed through the prism of shell shock have remained wholly stable. The injustice of the capital courts-martial [in which shell shocked soldiers were accused of malingering or cowardice] becomes the injustice of the Great War itself; the "unmanned" warriors of wartime become the unemployed, poverty-stricken and neurotic ex-servicemen of peacetime; the desperate, neurotic, compensation claimant becomes the symbol of lifelong war damage inflicted on millions of veterans. . . . In another sense, though, the memory of shell shock is an entirely unstable condition . . . because it has become the first and most powerful expression of the destructive effects of industrial warfare on the mind, of the war generation's tragedy. (176)

Here Leese echoes a Woolfian rage at the tragedy of a generation, a civilian's authentic response to violence they have not experienced. And yet, this response presupposes a mass of Septimus Smiths observed in the plural as unstable but essentially passive victims of a series of shocks. The import of their psychological illness remains firmly social, so that the focus turns away from individual suffering and towards the difference between one group of people (the damaged) and another (supposedly undamaged civilians). In Woolf and West's accounts as well as in Leese's, illness "measures the extent to which the social order has slipped from its own notion of the normative" (Kavka 154). The shell shocked soldier is rarely shown to transcend the limits of his trauma; his "experiences remained unassimilable, social blemishes that deface the summer scene" in, for instance, the peacetime world of *Mrs. Dalloway* (Schaefer 144). In such literary terrain, Mary Butts presents an alternate vision of shell shock in peacetime that usefully complicates the figure of the ex-soldier by asserting his agentic potential.

Mary Butts is herself difficult to place, presenting something of a critical challenge in the context of her peers. Her biographer relates that although she was at first hoping to be published by the Woolfs' Hogarth Press, she ultimately defined herself against the Bloomsberries stylistically, socially, and politically. Of contemporary writers, she appears to have consistently admired T. S. Eliot and compared her own writing to his High Modernist, classics-infused poetic idiom. Eliot, for his part, wrote that he had "always been interested" in Butts and in a letter to the journal *Time and Tide* from 1935, he publicly defended her work from a negative review by A. A. Milne. This letter reveals the parallels in Eliot's and Butts's views, that economic failures and religious/spiritual hollowness are the two main factors impelling modern warfare. Despite other differences between these writers, the simultaneous attention to materiality and spirituality is a pervasive and important aspect of Butts's idiosyncratic narrative vision.

Butts was born in Dorset on her family's estate and her monied, happy childhood was interrupted by the early death of her father. Subsequent troubles with her mother meant that she had money problems for most of her adult life. Her heroines usually reflect their author's precarious financial state: they grow up in wealthy families with a lot of literary and artistic exposure, only to face unpaid bills and emptying larders as adults. An extreme materiality pervades Butts's fiction, as it does much modernist writing of the era. However, the attention given to darned socks, the price of mead, and the number of fish served at dinner time, is in striking contrast to the otherworldly power accorded to spiritual magic in her literary world system. Hence in *Ashe of Rings*, Vanna Ashe has to steal and scrounge for food and warmth in war-torn London, and experiences bodily comfort and spiritual strength when she returns to her Dorset family home. In *Armed *with Madness*, Scylla and her brother Felix live in their isolated familial manor with an old nurse who keeps house for them, and a rotating series of visiting friends. The luxury of an inheritance and domestic help is offset by the extreme sparseness of their meals and material possessions, which their guests also notice. Offsetting this, both Vanna and Scylla are depicted as Classical priestesses who are intimately tied to their estates, drawing power from the earthworks and forests that surround them. Their quasi-druidic depiction is always tempered by the harsh financial realities of their wartime and postwar existences.[4] The novels repeatedly position their protagonists as displaced souls: women who ought to remain on their family estates and who suffer when they have to be away, priestesses of antiquity who are constricted in a secular world. When shell shock adds to the imbalance of modernity, the narrative appeals to the power of place to set things aright; however, as I show below, close attention to causality reveals a more complicated interplay between magic, modernity, and shell shock.

The author's stated belief in mysticism, particularly the magic of place, has presented some critical difficulty in categorizing these novels as modernist, or even modern. Contemporary critics tend to take Butts at face value for her belief in magic, perhaps in part because she was associated with Aleister Crowley in the early 1920s and shares author credit on one of his books, although she had disassociated from Crowley by the time her first novels were published. *Ashe of Rings* was written during the tail end of World War I, published in an US edition in 1925 and in the U.K. in 1933. The novel accords much mystical power to place, as when the heroine Vanna (Van) and her brother Valentine (Val) draw spiritual strength from an ancient earthwork enclosed in their familial estate, known as "Rings" and modeled on the real Badbury Rings in Dorset. There is almost no factual

---

4 Jed Esty names this impulse to imagine and fetishize a storied English past a recurrent feature of British late modernist narratives (39-50); Butts writes her novels in the '20s and '30s, anticipating the cultural shift that Esty pegs to the late '30s and '40s and the dissolution of the British Empire.

historical information about Rings in the novel. Instead, *Ashe of Rings* insists that "the house laid down its subtle spears [before the child Van]. Before she could walk, the arrows of the sun, the arrows of the moon and rain, were ribbons to keep her upright" (27). The militaristic elements of the passage are by design—Van is a child at war with her time, longing for the past while growing up in the twentieth century. The estate as a whole, the manor as well as the surrounding Rings, fields, even the skies, respond to Van; her father's first son died, he thinks, for being "a young dog who turned up [his] nose at the pretty ladies of Rings Hill" (8), but Van is as committed to the Rings as they appear to her. The repeated personification of the estate as possessed with magic that directly affects the Ashe family makes it difficult to read against the grain of Butts's fictional construct. But to what extent does irony operate in the narrative and complicate the straightforward allocation of power to place? How far does shell shock interrupt the smooth functioning of personification in the novel?

Critical responses have typically seen little room for paradoxes or incongruities in Butts's fiction. When modern violence in the form of the shell shocked Peter threatens Van physically, the narrative insists that she escapes rape and death at his hands through the protection of Rings. A similar connection between Scylla and her estate against the deranged Clarence is emphasized in *Armed with Madness*. However, the mythic/magical elements in Butts's fiction are ultimately red herrings in the plot. For example, *Armed with Madness* is most obviously an elaborate retelling of the Grail Quest for its first half; however, the last chapters show the so-called Grail Cup to be an elaborate hoax or shaggy dog story that has little ultimate impact upon the novel's conclusion. The narrative depends upon the resolution of two mirrored arcs, Scylla's developing love affair with Picus and her confrontation with the shell shocked Clarence, who loses his mental balance out of jealousy over Picus. An elaborate plot line about the friends trying to figure out whether a cup they found at the bottom of a well is (or is not) the real Grail, a fake from India, or a chalice from a church takes up a lot of the novel and has received plenty of critical attention. However, this is typical of Butts's fictional method: narrative attention to the question of the magical cup diverts from the material realities of her fiction.

Butts's use of the legends from Classical and English mythology is familiar modernist fare, and reveals her own childhood training—according to her memoir, *The Crystal Cabinet*, childhood games with her father and her aunt often involved figures like Artemis and Hermes, and she seems as familiar with Norse mythology as with the layout of her childhood home at Salterns close to Poole Harbour in Dorset. The presence of Classical mythology in her novels also points to her admiration of Eliot as contemporary and rival. However, whereas Eliot's references to Classical myth dovetail and complement his vision of the modern world, Butts's use of them in her novels are more complicated and contradictory. Shell shocked and damaged young men and impoverished post-WWI young women populate her novels, but resist becoming straightforward mythic figures. Paying attention to material details in the novels—who ate what, and also what characters did, said, and saw—reveals an alternate sequence of causality than that endorsed by the narrative. Like the shell shocked soldier himself, Butts's novels prove difficult to categorize. Their interest in magic is ultimately superficial, and the novels undercut their own regressive mystical systems for a credible view of shell shocked soldiers coping with modern life after war experience. No longer a symbol of social malaise, this view of shell shock restores individuality to such men who largely occupy symbolic roles in contemporary eyes.

Butts's novels have not been extensively written about for their views on shell shock or other social issues, but a number of critics have rightly pointed out her fixation with "blood-lines and racial purity . . . resonate with fascist rhetoric" (Garrity 209). This "flaw in her feminist and patriotic agenda" could account for her near erasure from anthologies of British women's fiction from the 1930s, and indeed, her belief in the purity of her heroines because of their bloodlines presents a real obstacle to any contemporary critical evaluation of the novels (Radford 157). Van and Scylla hardly ever interact with servants, tenant farmers, villagers, or others outside their social class; their loyalty is to the geographic parameters of their estates at the expense of the people for whom they are presumably responsible. Striking details from Woolf and West's fictions—Mrs. Ramsay's hampers for the villagers and lighthouse-men, or Kitty Baldry's flannel covered work table, "clothes for the cottagers" as she explains to her husband—are completely omitted in Butts's novels (West 29). The butler of the Ashe estate, Clavel, cares for the Ashes and the nurse Nanna keeps house for the Taverners, but neither plays any major part in the novels. Clavel has little interiority, and although "it is to be doubted if anyone since Ursula Ashe [a famed ancestress] knew more than he" about the secrets of the estate, he is denied any potency or defining characteristics beyond mute loyalty (*Ashe of Rings* 53). This decision to endow the landscape with psychology but deny psychological space to all but landed gentry sets Butts in opposition to progressive trends in literary and critical thought in the twentieth century which has paid renewed attention to the small, the poor, and the overlooked.[5]

Indeed, *Death of Felicity Taverner* is an extended diatribe against Felicity's intruding, scheming, devilish Russian widower who intends to disrupt the isolated English rurality of her estate by buying up the surrounding land

---

5   British modernism's interest in the small, the poor, and the normally overlooked does not need further demonstration, but Bazin and Lauter make the point in relation to an analysis of war in Woolf's work (18). The opening sections of *Mrs. Dalloway*, they note, are exemplary for attention to women whose losses in the War have been forgotten in the general frenzy of Victory Day parades and public relief over the end of hostilities. Woolf's narrative begins with Clarissa recalling these women in a gesture that opens to the experience of others, in contrast to Butts's use of stream of consciousness narratives that emphasize the uniqueness of her heroines and their stark difference from other women.

at exorbitant rates to build tourist resorts. Nick Kralin, the widower, has the enthusiastic support of the local farmers for this scheme of economic renewal; but when he is murdered by Scylla's friend, the narrative approves this violent crime. Scylla and the Taverner family are delivered from their existential crisis and left to mourn the death of their cousin in peace, without Kralin's body being recovered.[6] Eliding ethics, the narrative equates the evil of Kralin's death with the "death" he would have brought on the countryside, ignoring the real economic benefits of his plan. Material needs are only given credence when they are Scylla's or Van's, and English places are sacrosanct in Butts's world system. She avoids all direct depiction of war scenes, and her novels are primarily set in isolated post-WWI Dorset villages that seem to have scarcely been affected by total war. Indeed, it seems to me that Butts recursively writes about these coastal places precisely because they appear as a kind of spatial antidote to the upheavals generated by modern violence. Even the war-affected cityscapes like Paris or London that she knew well, and lived in for most of the 1920s, are barely alluded to in her fiction.

The unsavory xenophobia of Butts's thinking is allied with another idea, her sense of twentieth-century modernity as a kind of extended decadence, an approach to the end of days. In *Armed with Madness*, Scylla echoes the author's thoughts from autobiographical notes thus: "[E]verywhere there was a sense of broken continuity, a dis-ease . . . There was something wrong with all of them, or with their world. A moment missed, a moment to come. Or not coming. Or either or both. Shove it off on the war; but that did not help" (9). In Butts's view, many of her more well-known and vocal contemporaries "shoved off" their sense of dis-ease on WWI, in that they

---

6   Rochelle Rives argues that "empathic connections between animate and inanimate worlds only develop from some degree of attached and private ownership of objects" in Butts's narrative system (608). Rives is correct to point out that "Butts sees the basis for collective forms of empathy in a particular style of private ownership" (609). However, both private ownership and empathetic sophistication is reserved in her works for cultural and economic elites; as I suggest elsewhere in this essay, everyone outside Van Ashe or Scylla Taverner's milieu functions as novelistic conveniences and little else.

saw the conflict arising out of, and expressing, existing social problems that needed to be addressed, rather than sharing in Butts's apocalyptic, quasi-Decadent view of civilizational rot. Woolf was one influential voice calling the First World War a "preposterous masculine fiction" of gigantic proportions (Woolf *Letters* 2:76), but she did not share Butts's sense of the overall decline of Western Civilization. West's wartime writing similarly presents the war through an ironic lens that eschews apocalyptic thinking. Hope Mirlees's *Paris* (1919) presents a feminine poetic voice who disparagingly notices that "President Wilson grins like a dog and runs about the / city, sniffing with innocent enjoyment the diluvial / urine of Gargantua," but the Rabelaisian reference is employed to call for recuperation, not to indicate the hopeless dissolution of society (8).

Their gendered view of war led Woolf and others (but not Butts) to represent in their work what Karen Levenback calls a "kind of commerce between the civilian experience of the war and the soldiers' [experience]" (45). The back-and-forth dynamic of this exchange had another result, however: shell shock was often depicted as a primarily social ill as authors' attention turned away from concern with individual psychological iterations. This differs significantly from Butts's position. For her, a war vet suffered psychologically as all victims of violent modernity; as she says using the third person plural, "There was something wrong with all of them, or with their world". This view implicates both masculine and feminine subjects, and sees modernity itself as essentially bankrupt. In contrast, even though so much of Woolf's work seeks "to explore and make clear the connections between private and public violence . . . between male supremacy and the absence of peace", in her view, modernity itself is not inherently broken or irredeemable (Hussey 3).

In contrast to Woolf, Butts's political thinking can appear simplistic for overstepping gender dynamics, and politically regressive for endorsing a *fin-de-siècle* disaster mentality. However, this essay is an attempt to think through the ramifications of such a political and literary position using the figure of the shell shocked veteran as an analytic base. Butts's first husband, John Rodker was a Conscientious Objector to the War and like Woolf et al., Butts herself was vocally anti-war in the 1910s. Despite this, her fiction displaces gendered blame for modern violence in favor of a pervasive "something wrong" with everyone, man and woman and time. In *Ashe of Rings*, Van discusses her friend Judy's peculiar attraction to pain and suffering, presenting the war as a symptom of general social malaise: "There is the war. There is Judy and her kind. The individual state bred the general state, that bred the catastrophe" (149). Upturning the prevalent narrative method, Van prioritizes the "individual state" over the structures that create and sustain them. She dismisses direct causes of the First World War—"Oh, I know tribal instincts and heroism, and love of a row, and coal and duty and obedience and too many people," she lists casually. Political machinations and faulty cultural norms are beside the point, or too short-term in this vision of human existence; instead, civilization is itself ending, driven towards an "abnormal" end by women and men, "who are attracted to not-making and to spoiling; to the other side of life, to what we call death" (149).

Consider the novelty of this position: war creates shell shock, but if war itself is a symptom of social disintegration, of individuals consumed by the death drive, then shell shock loses its abnormal status *vis-à-vis* civilian society in peacetime. Butts's fiction does not normalize war but sees it as pervasive in all aspects of modern life. By overstepping the distinction of gender, it erases the division between civilian and soldier, war front and home front. It thus achieves a different integration between shell shock and everyday trauma. In *Death of Felicity Taverner*, older and younger characters are described thus: "Picus and Scylla were of a generation before the war; Felix [her brother] of the half generation after it. And at the bottom of that dry gulf between half a generation there are corpses, who did not notice the gulf was there" (174). Although Picus has been to war and Scylla has not, the same divide stretches between them and the younger Felix, upturning extant distinctions of gender and experience. Further, there is no end to this violence with the signing of peace treaties. The switch between present and past tenses in the second sentence declares that the corpses remain (they "are") well after the fact, insensate but divisive in the communal imagination. Finally, convention itself is overturned: instead of focusing on Picus, Scylla, or Felix, the last clause fixates upon the corpses. The dead no longer notice the living, a reversal of perspective that is also profoundly depressing. Against this backdrop, Scylla executes clever economies in her pantry, makes love to Picus, or deepens her relationship with her younger brother Felix. But however much the narrative insists on her mystical power to sustain the family, the memory of the trenches intrudes into the narrative at the level of the sentence and distorts it. Shell shock materially disrupts the beneficence of her magic.

Butts's narrative position thus allows civilian women to speak of modern violence with authenticity, because war experience is no longer confined to the physical experience of the battlefield. Even before Butts's heroines experience violence at the hands of shell shocked soldiers (a point I will discuss below), they live in a universe of war—against cruel mothers and late Victorian rigidity, against small mindedness and money troubles. Judy, for instance, has never seen a battlefield but is as callous as any army general moving troops into battles that (s)he knows to be futile. Van is in a mortal fight with her mother, as is Felicity, whose purity perishes under the strain of her psychological, spiritual, and economic battles with her mother and husband. Symbolic and actual war are presented on the same register as equally heinous.

Iterations of Shell shock: Peter, Clarence, and Picus

Looking closely at Butts's three shell shocked characters shows, first, the author's familiarity with emergent psychoanalytic theories about war-torn psyches. She presents the shell shocked vet with sympathy, in a parallel to the many contemporaneous newspaper editorials and reportage that show a popular support for soldiers' rights to better treatment and greater pension benefits, even though some medical establishments and governmental agencies continued to doubt the debilitating effects of war trauma. Thus, for instance, there is no hint of weakness or laziness about Picus or his friend Clarence, despite the prevalent association of shell shock with cowardice. Picus is repeatedly described as a tall bird with extraordinarily strong hands, and a visitor notes that Clarence is "tall and black, with close-set eyes and a walk affected to hide his strength" (14). Peter, who is the sickest of the three shell shocked men, is still of noble blood (which counts for much in Butts's world system) and physically powerful. All three men are physically imposing; further, although the narrative suggests that Clarence is gay, no stereotypical weakness is coded into descriptions of his character to distinguish him from the other two men. Despite her regressive place-based politics and social conservatism, Butts's novels display a paradoxical openness to non-normative experiences and desires that allow these three men a kind of liberty of spirit.

These descriptive features are significant at a time when cultural memory of the mistreatment of shell shocked soldiers during the war was still fresh. Leese writes of the "wartime courts-martial and execution of shell shocked soldiers" to public outcry and calls the treatment of shell shocked soldiers "a significant political issue during the postwar years" (125). Military officials' association of shell shock with physical weakness resulted in misdiagnoses and incarceration in asylums, as well as the denial of pensions. These issues were repeatedly discussed in newspapers and by politicians in the years 1920-1922, concurrent with the writing of *Ashe of Rings*. In this context, the absence of physical fear in these three men is a narrative feature as well as a political stance. Like shell shock, valor pervades Butts's view of interwar modernity, if only among the intelligentsia.

Picus, Clarence, and Peter constitute a range of damage by shell shock, and are differently capable of affecting their own cures. Butts proves wary of asylums and medical treatments, and indeed, doctors figure very rarely in her novels. The other curative authority figure in the novels is a sympathetic priest, with whom Clarence briefly considers seeking shelter when he leaves the Taverners at the end of *Armed with Madness*. He ultimately rejects the idea and starts out on his own. When Picus has a mental breakdown in a cemetery, he gropes his way towards "an old man in a nightshirt" who is presumably the warden or gatekeeper of the place, but not named as a church official (112). He also recovers himself seemingly without any direct interventions. Butts returned to Christianity in 1934 after she moved back to Dorset from Paris, but whatever the state of its author's faith, *Armed with Madness* resists narrating a psychological recovery through the intervention of holy men or other authority figures. The ex-soldiers are left responsible for their own development as an expression of their agentic abilities.

Picus is the least physically active of these men and yet is the most able to affect his own recovery. He is most often shown idle in *Armed with Madness*; later in *Death of Felicity Taverner*, he is again usually still, a silent emotional support for his wife, Scylla. This is a considerable development from when he is introduced in the first novel as the flighty and capricious friend of Clarence, who met him "in the war, wearing his shrapnel helmet" (26). At the outset, Picus is often malicious and inscrutable to the group of friends that Scylla and Felix draw together in their manor house in remote Dorset. He suffers from those recurrent physical complaints that remain unaddressed by the doctor (26). These symptoms could be explained by a direct reference to shell shock, but their cause is left unassigned. In keeping with the author's sense that the war is itself a symptom, and not a cause, of the modern world off kilter, Picus's response to physical and emotional violence is conflated and presented as aspects of the same psychic damage. Shell shock compounds other violent shocks to Picus's system, such as his mother's death by suicide when he was young, and his father's subsequent callousness towards him. Picus severs ties with his father and affects his own reconciliation with his losses in the graveyard scene referenced above, appearing in *Death of Felicity Taverner* as no longer given to the same internal complaints and external symptoms. Importantly, it is through his breakdown that Picus recovers—a sequence that refutes one Establishment view that soldiers suffering from shell shock ought to steel themselves against their demons. Also contrary to the paranoid view represented by Fenton and other psychologists of shell shocked soldiers as "cured for the purposes of everyday living, but always with the possibility of relapse," Picus effects a recovery that is perhaps medically unsound but nonetheless allows the character a measure of self-determination that is missing in other such representations.

Clarence, too, shows a great deal of self-sufficiency despite his violent breakdown. At the beginning of *Armed with Madness,* he has recurring bad dreams about losing Picus, with whom he lives in a remote cottage close to the Taverners. Like the others, Clarence mainly spends his time painting or sculpting, hunting game for food, carving wood into bowls and toys, and taking care of his little stone cottage. As with Picus, the narrative shows the impact of war on his psyche but elides placing the blame for his mental fragility solely on active service. For instance, the direct reason for his breakdown is jealousy of Scylla, who had just begun her love affair with Picus. In the middle of an obsessive fit, Clarence comes upon her alone and lassoes her to a life sized wooden statue of Picus that he had carved.

Operating according to an inverted logic, he shoots three arrows into her side to reenact the myth of Saint Sebastian. A visiting friend arrives just in time to find Scylla tied up and fainting from her wounds while Clarence bullishly roams the cottage grounds. Unable to bear the psychological weight of pain, Clarence falls asleep and wakes up with no memory of the day before, until Picus arrives and reminds him of what had passed. Even then, he does not quite believe his friend. It is only after he sees the dead body of a gull he shot to feather his arrows the day before, that the entire incident comes back to him.

The moment is crystalline in its affective power and emphasis on Clarence's emotional, human response. The body of the gull is caught in some bushes on the hillside where he had thrown it after plucking some feathers from the "torn white rags" (156). The man stops before this evidence of needless violence for "a long time while the dew dried" (156). He reflects on his (now forgotten) motivations: "I suppose I thought she [Scylla] was the bird." This emotional response is so powerful that it triggers the return of Clarence's memory: "The whole memory came back. The nut in his head [how he imagines his madness] dissolved like a drop of wax. His skull filled with pure memory. / The figure he had cut with his excuses. How save his reputation for sanity? With Picus. With all of them? / What does one do when one has done a thing like that?" (156). Clarence careens towards despair and suicide, determined to follow the trajectory of the bird's body, which just then is dislodged by the wind and falls into the sea. He takes "a last pull at memories . . . Of Picus. Of the band he had grown up with. Of war, whose issues he had found too simple" (157). He also imagines his death as a bit of revenge on his friends, and is almost hurtling over the cliff before Scylla sees him and pulls him away from the edge and inside the cottage. Clarence eventually leaves the band of friends but even though he is determined not to enter an asylum, the novel indicates that he does not commit suicide either.

Together with Picus's renewed and stabilized sense of self, Clarence's self-motivated recovery forms the emotional apex of the novel.

I have been arguing that the individuated psychological space and emotional agency accorded to Clarence makes this narrative unique among others in which women civilian writers consider shell shock. Also worth noticing is the closeness between Scylla and Clarence, for loving the same man and also for seeing the modern world in similar terms. As for Scylla (and Van Ashe and the author herself), the issues that lead to war are "too simple" for Clarence, and do not explain the fundamental changes he perceives in the world. This narrative closeness to the shell shocked character is in contrast with the distance generally accorded between the civilian narrator and the war-returned vet, evident in a representative novel like Woolf's *Jacob's Room*. For Butts's shell shocked veteran, the equivocal determination to remain alive is a marker of the humanity that links him to his generation and class in peacetime, despite their differences of experience.

An affective emotional response to a dead animal also stops Peter Amburton from losing his humanity in *Ashe of Rings*. Peter is the most damaged of the three men—not only his mind, but his body is analogously covered in "[u]gly shrapnel wounds. Pits of drawn skin, tight and blue" (204). Unlike Picus and Clarence who are part of a close circle of friends, Peter is an outsider in his family and misliked by his cousins through marriage, Van and her brother Val. His uncle, their stepfather, does not like Peter enough to leave him their family estate, and Van recalls that Peter was a "gloomy child" (149) even before his experiences in the army. The war is described as an event that exacerbated problems for an already damaged psyche that is altogether unlike the sensitive minds of Van and her brother. It is little surprise, then, that Peter readily falls under the sway of the conniving Judy, who becomes his fiancée and whom Van describes as getting "spirit-nourishing food out of the ruin of so much life" in wartime (149).

In a sense, Peter is the obverse of the other two shell shocked characters I've discussed. Whereas Picus and Clarence are drawn with narrative affection for their flaws, Peter is allowed hardly any interiority as a bit character in the larger drama of Van's life. There are no scenes of love or affection between him and Judy, only episodes in which she uses him for his money or physical power. Despite this, reading against the grain of narrative sympathy shows the similarity between Peter, Picus, and Clarence. Although Peter's epiphany is almost ignored in a scene from *Ashe of Rings* that is focused on Van's struggle and her magical collusion with place, his emotional response to the death of an animal remains an obstinate complication in the narrative. I suggested earlier that the materiality of shell shock interrupts the smooth functioning of magic in *Ashe of Rings*. Looking closely at Peter's altercation with Van reveals some of the inconsistencies and complexities of Butts's often regressive and limited narrative vision. The episode I now turn to, a scene in which Van is about to be raped by her cousin, tests the limits of readerly sympathy in an open-ended narrative experiment that throws surprising light on the place of the shell shocked veteran in interwar society.

Seeing Van alone one night out on the ancient earthworks known as the Rings, Judy (who wants to steal her inheritance) incites Peter to rape and ruin her. The provenance of their plan is unclear, but by the time Van appears, the couple have already killed Peter's dog on a large white stone that looks like a druidic altar. They declare they have performed blood sacrifice by killing the Airedale in a ritualized act that gives them access to the dark magic of the Rings—a site reserved for the Ashe family as the source of their priestly power, where no outsiders usually go. The narrative takes this invocation of magic entirely seriously. Van is terrified of her fate at their hands until she remembers her inherited place-based familial power. Confident that nothing can hurt her, she "[lies] back on the stone and open[s] her palms to the moon" (188). She remembers that Peter's eyesight is very bad, so she takes off her dark outer clothing and becomes still on the white stone in her white shift. The ruse seems to work: Peter is rebuffed and some pages later, the narrative declares that "the spell of Rings was wound up and worked out; and the Rings children [i.e., Van and Val] received the rewards of warriors" (207). The novel repeatedly suggests that the Rings and the moon defeated him to protect Van during this perilous episode.

Nevertheless, Butts's narrative is not blind to Peter's actions when Van is trapped almost naked on the altar stone poised to miraculously escape. The episode deserves close attention for details that subvert the stated resolution of the incident. Peter responds to Van's ridiculous ruse (of undressing to her white underclothes) by acknowledging that his eyesight is not good. Almost immediately, he also whispers that she should run away and abandon her inheritance to appease Judy and save herself. Van continues to lie as still as she can, hoping the white light of the moon on her body will blind Peter. He menaces her: "My mind's raw. I'll do what I said I'd do. It'll make Judy jealous. You wouldn't mind. I'll marry you" (189). Even in this regressive state, the shell shocked veteran of war is concerned for social niceties like the honor of his cousin, and promises to marry her. To a modern reader, his statement that Van "wouldn't mind" the rape makes it difficult to consider Peter as anything but a horrible cartoonish villain, and his ham-fisted attempt to reassure her is at odds with this villainy. Then, in an early iteration of the affective episode that Clarence experiences in *Armed with Madness*, Peter's hands grope blindly on the stone and touch the dead body of his dog. It had been "a great dog which had been so strong," a description that per the vocabulary of the novel confers nobility and positive strength on the animal that counters Judy's negative violence (189). Peter's affective reaction to the touch goes unrecorded; he only screams, "Oh, God!" and crashes back from the stone. Then he "crawl[s] away into the bushes, dragging with him the body of his dog" (191).

Although Van "fold[s] her hands on her breasts and watch[es] the moon" and wonders how she "could ever have been afraid of him," it is clear that Peter could have done serious harm to her if his hands had first encountered her body instead of the dog's (190). This minute but crucial detail rescues Peter from becoming a villain out of a child's fairytale. His real grief over the death of his dog is the polar opposite of the mad machinations of Judy and even the staunch belief that Van displays in the metaphysical power of place. In this sense, Peter is more human despite his shell shock than either woman because he is more sensitive to violence and more grief-stricken by the loss of his dog. At the end of the novel, Peter and Judy remain unhappily together and he does not affect a recovery of his humanity in the manner of Clarence and Picus. Nevertheless, Butts's first novelistic attempt to imagine a shell shocked ex-soldier bears within it the seeds of an emotional agentic response that counters established medical attitudes to the emotional damage suffered by soldiers in the First World War.

This then is the achievement of Butts's three versions of shell shock: despite many other regressive features that make her fiction difficult to read, she is able to restore the soldiers to their humanity by showing the emotional normalcy of their motivations. Each veteran responds to needless violence with pity and horror, despite one strand of cultural rhetoric that persistently presented the shell shocked soldier as immune to further violence and "home front" decencies. Butts does not imaginatively intrude into war zones, and she does not challenge the notion that experience of war is necessary to write directly about it. However, through her conviction that diseased modernity created the war (and that modernity cannot be redeemed from this decline), she denies the characterization of the First World War as an isolated, unrelated event in the history of European politics. In her admittedly problematic understanding of the social dynamics of the early twentieth century, violence is not confined to the war front, nor to soldiers or the masculine gender. But just as violence is pervasive, so is the ability of the human spirit to recover, and adapt, and love in isolated (classist and nativist) instances. Reading against the grain of Butts's narrative edifice, her careful constructions of myth and magic, reveals this surprisingly hopeful message from an era which had seen the end of one devastating conflict and did not yet anticipate the other.

Bibliography

Atkin, Jonathan. *A War of Individuals: Bloomsbury Attitudes to the Great War*. Manchester UP, 2002.

Bazin, Nancy Topping and Jane Hamovit Lauter. "Virginia Woolf's Keen Sensitivity to War: Its Roots and Its Impact on Her Novels." Hussey, pp. 14-39.

Butts, Mary. *Ashe of Rings and Other Writings*. McPherson and Co., 1998.

---. *The Crystal Cabinet: My Childhood at Salterns*. Beacon Press, 1988.

---. *The Taverner Novels*. McPherson and Co., 1992.

Eliot, T. S. "Mr. Milne and War [II]." *The Complete Prose of T. S. Eliot: The Critical Edition: Tradition and Orthodoxy 1934-1939*, eds. Iman Javadi, R. Schuchard, and J. Stayer, JHUP, 2017.

Garrity, Jane. *Step-daughters of England: British Women Modernists and the National Imaginary*. Manchester UP, 2003.

Hussey, Mark, editor. *Virginia Woolf and War: Fiction, Reality, and Myth*. Syracuse UP, 1991.

Leese, Peter. *Shell Shock: Traumatic Neurosis and the British Soldiers of the*

First World War. Palgrave Macmillan, 2002.

Levenback, Karen L. "Virginia Woolf's 'War in the Village' and 'The War from the Street.'" Hussey, pp. 40-57.

Radford, Andy. "The Enchantment of Place: Mary Butts, Wessex, and Interwar Neo-Romanticism." *National Identities* vol. 14, no. 2, 2012, pp. 157-172.

Rives, Rochelle. "Problem Space: Mary Butts, Modernism, and the Etiquette of Placement." *Modernism/modernity* vol. 12, no. 4, 2005, pp. 607-627.

Schaefer, Josephine O'Brien. "The Great War and the Late Age of World's Experience in Cather and Woolf." Hussey, pp. 134-150.

West, Rebecca. *The Return of the Soldier*. Penguin Classics, 1998.

Woolf, Virginia. *Jacob's Room*. Harcourt, 1922.

——. *The Letters of Virginia Woolf* vol. 2, ed. Nigel Nicolson, Hogarth Press, 1976.

Ria Banerjee is an assistant professor of English at Guttman Community College, CUNY. Her scholarly interests are in British and European modernism and post-World War II film. She has previously published on T. S. Eliot and Virginia Woolf, and is currently at work on a monograph on spatiality in interwar British fiction. She teaches undergraduate courses in developmental writing and literature, and graduate film courses with the Film Studies Certificate Program of the Graduate Center, CUNY.

10

"A WALKING PERSONIFICATION OF THE NEGATIVE"

African-American World War I Veterans in Ralph Ellison's *Invisible Man* and Toni Morrison's *Sula*

Jill Goad

Abstract

Ralph Ellison's *Invisible Man* (1952) and Toni Morrison's *Sula* (1973) feature African-American World War I veterans suffering from shell shock in a re-envisioning of a mental health history not often acknowledged immediately after World War I. During and after World War I, physicians, military personnel, and the public viewed shell-shocked soldiers who suffered both physically and emotionally as cowardly, infantile, and emasculated. Shell-shocked African-American soldiers' suffering was compounded by racial discrimination, since they were labeled in the military as unintelligent, undisciplined, and undeserving of quality medical care. Upon returning home, they received no acknowledgment of their service and no mental health treatment. In both Ellison and Morrison's novels, the veterans are relegated to the fringes of society upon their return, deemed damaged and inconvenient by dominant ideology. Through the shell-shocked veterans of the Golden Day, who can speak freely about racial discrimination because they are other and hidden away, *Invisible Man* comments on the ideology that upholds the narrative of irrational, immoral black men to keep them at a diminished status that overlooks their mental and physical sacrifices. *Sula* engages in an extended character exploration of a shell-shocked African-American soldier and includes scenes of other returning black soldiers, giving varied perspectives into the particular constraints facing them. Ultimately, African-American World War I veterans in *Invisible Man* and *Sula* are connected by the individual and collective impact of their coping behaviors and by what they reveal about the discriminatory ideology that shapes their communities. Through these fictional accounts, the extent of black soldiers' sacrifice can finally be more understood.

After World War I, American physicians did not classify the psychological and emotional condition of returning American soldiers as a mental disability. Instead, they called this state *shell shock*, believing that "soldiers' proximity to exploding shells" caused their condition.[1] Shell-shocked veterans who suffered physical symptoms, such as insomnia and digestive ailments, and psychological symptoms, such as anxiety and inability to control emotions, were labeled by physicians, military personnel, and the public as immoral cowards trying to avoid military tasks. A volume of the history of the United States army during World War I noted that neurotic soldiers were deemed malingerers and physicians treating these soldiers saw them as infantile, emasculated, and completely lacking in self-respect.[2] Dominant

---

1   Manuela Lopez Ramirez, "The Shell-Shocked Veteran in Toni Morrison's *Sula* and *Home*," *Journal of the Spanish Association of Anglo-American Studies* 38, no. 1 (2016): 131.

2   Pearce Bailey, Frankwood E. Williams, Paul O. Komora, Thomas W. Salmon, and Norman Fenton. *The Medical Department of the United States Army in the World War* X. (Washington, D.C.: U.S.

American ideology posited men, particularly soldiers, as physically and mentally strong and emblems of self-control to reinforce the image of American exceptionalism.[3] Consequently, people in the returning veterans' communities believed that shell shock was made up, viewed emotionally suffering veterans as weak, and shunned them. Trevor Dodman adds that shell shock was perceived as an amalgam of varied qualities that maintained the veteran's status as other: "a contagious disease, a genetic disorder, an inevitable byproduct of modern industrial warfare, a collection of physical ailments, a purely psychological matter, a sign of moral weakness, a lack of courage, a wound that would heal, a scar that would remain, an excuse, an accusation, a puzzle, a mystery."[4] Because shell shock was not viewed as a mental illness, veterans did not receive effective treatment.[5] Misperceptions of shell shock affected all soldiers, but African-American soldiers' suffering was compounded by racial discrimination.

In World War I, more than 350,000 African-American soldiers served in segregated units.[6] Compared to white soldiers, African Americans faced discrimination: they were drafted at higher rates, were more likely to serve support roles than combat roles due to fear that arming them would lead to their violent revolt, and received subpar medical care.[7] Military officials classified black soldiers as unintelligent, morally and physically undisciplined, and dirty, blaming the soldiers' illnesses on lax behavior.[8] While most other

---

Government Printing Office, 1929), 95, 511.

3   Ramirez, 131.

4   Trevor Dodman, "'Belated Impress:' *River George* and the African American Shell Shock Narrative," *African American Review* 44, no. ½ (2011): 153.

5   Ramirez, 131.

6   Library of Congress, "World War I and Postwar Society," last modified March 21, 2008, https://memory.loc.gov/ammem/aaohtml/exhibit/aointro.html

7   Jennifer D. Keene, "A Comparative Study of White and Black American Soldiers During the First World War," *Annales de Demographie Historique* 1 (2002): 71.

8   Keene, 76-78.

soldiers exhibiting signs of mental illness or disability were not permitted to serve the military in any way, African American soldiers referred to as "mental defectives" were used in labor battalions.[9] Conversely, military officials and medical professionals perceived African Americans as immune from neuroses due to historical stereotypes of uninhibited sexual and emotional expression.[10] Despite this perception of the soldiers' immunity, "shell shock was undoubtedly 'democratic' in its wide and unprejudiced reach, even if the American government, its armed forces, and many of its citizens at the time were not."[11]

Upon the black soldiers' return home, as they suffered from shell shock, "the unforgettable horrors of war persisted at the haunting center of their debilitating condition,"[12] often keeping them unable to acclimate to society. Beyond having no access to mental health treatment, African-American veterans returning home also received no acknowledgment of their service and sacrifice. Manuela Lopez Ramirez notes that black soldiers' shell shock was exacerbated by white society making the veterans feel invisible and prompting veterans' self-hatred through societal violation and denial of the black self.[13] This violation and denial perpetrated by white society, argues David A. Davis, was a reaction to seeing a military uniform, a marker of respect, on an African-American body; the uniform "distort[ed] . . . power dynamics . . . so to . . . prevent the assertion of equality the white hegemony forcefully subordinate[d] the African American veteran."[14] Because of

---

9   Bailey, Williams, Komora, Salmon, and Fenton, 70.

10 J. Bradford Campbell, "The Schizophrenic Solution: Dialectics of Neurosis and Anti-Psychiatric Animus in Ralph Ellison's *Invisible Man*," *NOVEL: A Forum on Fiction* 43, no. 3 (2010): 447.

11 Dodman, 151.

12 Ibid., 157.

13 Ramirez, 136.

14 David A. Davis, "Not Only War is Hell: World War I and African American Lynching Narratives," *African American Review* 42, no. ¾ (2008): 485.

historical refusal to honor African-American veterans' service, ongoing representational consequences persist. Ultimately, there are gaps in literary and historical representation and analysis of shell shock experienced by African-American soldiers because their war trauma has not been absorbed into America's collective memory of World War I.[15] This could be due in part to what James Baldwin refers to as "the American vision of the world," which "owes a great deal to the battle waged by Americans to maintain between themselves and black men a human separation which could not be bridged."[16] Additionally, perhaps due to the shame attached to shell shock and to the mistreatment of black soldiers serving their country equally and alongside white soldiers, "black histories from the period rarely mention the shell-shocked."[17] A small number of post-World War I literary works, however, attempts to recover these histories.

Ralph Ellison's *Invisible Man* (1952) and Toni Morrison's *Sula* (1973) feature African-American World War I veterans suffering from shell shock in a re-envisioning of a mental health history not often acknowledged immediately after World War I. In Ellison's novel, the black protagonist takes the white trustee of his college to a bar and brothel that local veterans, residents of a sanatorium, frequent weekly. The men subsequently taunt the trustee and riot in the bar, their actions leading to the narrator's expulsion from college and his subsequent painful journey of self-discovery. In Morrison's work, Shadrack, rendered emotionally bereft from the war, elicits fear from his fellow townsfolk who see him as erratic, perverse, and an emblem of death. Shadrack is at the center of three key scenes. At the novel's start, he hallucinates during his hospitalization and is unceremoniously released from care while his mental state is still fragile. Another scene

---

15   Dodman, 157.

16   James Baldwin, "Stranger in the Village," *Harper's Magazine*, 1953.

17   Dodman, 157.

includes him encountering Sula in his home, a moment that affects both characters through their lives. His final act in the novel is to ring a bell as the leader of a march that lures many of the townsfolk to their deaths. Minor characters in *Sula,* returning soldiers on a train and Plum, who becomes a heroin addict after the war, do not play central roles but nonetheless reveal aspects of the returning African-American soldier's plight. In both novels, the veterans are relegated to the fringes of society upon their return, deemed damaged and inconvenient by dominant ideology. As William Lyne notes, "They suffer not from the shell shock of war but from the shock of coming home."[18] Because of their race, they are not acknowledged or lauded for their service. To cope, the veterans find comfort in ways that translate to civilians as unstable, frightening behavior that justifies the veterans' isolation. Ultimately, African American World War I veterans in *Invisible Man* and *Sula* are connected by the individual and collective impact of their coping behaviors and by what they reveal about the discriminatory ideology that shapes their communities.

In *Invisible Man,* the first mention of the African-American veterans portrays them as an inconvenience and even as criminal. This is an idea shared by the military medical establishment of the World War I era who argued that mentally ill soldiers, particularly black soldiers who were more likely to be intellectually inferior than their white counterparts "wasted the time of those endeavoring to instruct them, interfered with the training of their brighter or better-adjusted comrades, and occupied hospital beds which often were urgently needed for others."[19] Seen as a drain on resources and generally useless to the military, these soldiers were classified as takers who never compensated with service. The narrator, frantically driving his

---

18 William Lyne, "The Signifying Modernist: Ralph Ellison and the Limits of the Double Consciousness," *PMLA* 107, no. 2 (1992): 327.

19 Bailey, Williams, Komora, Salmon, and Fenton, 57.

college's wealthy, white trustee, Mr. Norton, to the closest bar for a drink to alleviate his shock after a prior encounter, sees the veterans blocking the road as they also journey to the bar: "Ahead of the radiator's gleaming curve they looked like a chain gang on its way to make a road."[20] By equating African-American veterans with criminality,[21] the narrator, a young black man intent on staying in the good graces of the white power structure, implies that the veterans have committed some act against society; simply existing as symbols of sacrifice for a country that wants to forget their efforts could be this act.

Perhaps their consistent status as apart and even immoral is what makes the veterans internalize their institutionalized domination. Yonka Krasteva points to the Golden Day chapter of *Invisible Man* as expressing the "effects of the asylum upon the mad in terms of their internalization of the values of the dominant structure that marginalizes and excludes them."[22] For example, at the chapter's beginning, to remove the veterans from the road, the narrator tells the "leader" of the group to step aside for General Pershing, the leader's white World War I commander, pretending that Mr. Norton is the general. Upon the veteran hearing this name, "the wild look changed in his eyes and he stepped back and saluted with stiff precision."[23] This reaction can be connected to internalized military training but can also indicate the veteran's inclination to obey a white authority figure even though the veteran exists outside of "normal" society.

Supercargo, the veterans' attendant, a black man, also depends on the veterans' internalized deference to authority to keep them docile. Intent on preserving the status quo, he yells to the increasingly-agitated men in the

---

20   Ralph Ellison, *Invisible Man* (New York: Vintage Books, 1947), 71.
21   Campbell, 451.
22   Yonka Krasteva, "Chaos and Pattern in Ellison's *Invisible Man*," *The Southern Literary Journal* 30, no. 1 (1997): 63.
23   Ellison, 72.

Golden Day who have been affected by Mr. Norton's presence, "I want order down there . . . and if there's white folks down there, I wan's *double* order."[24] Serving as dominant culture's proxy, Supercargo, referred to repeatedly by the bar's owner as a "stool-pigeon" and by the veterans as "the white folks' man," accompanies the veterans "to see that the therapy [at The Golden Day] fails."[25] Since Supercargo acts as a representative of dominant ideology in ruling the veterans through fear instead of treating or humanizing them, one confides to the narrator, "Sometimes I get so afraid of him I feel that he's inside my head."[26] This connects Supercargo to the superego, because even when Supercargo is absent, his specter of authority looms over the men, keeping their behavior in line with what society expects. Other veterans see Supercargo as a frightening father figure who infantilizes them by consistently threatening punishment with a brandished straitjacket. His threats are consistent with the punitive and entrapping pre-World War I treatment of soldiers suffering from mental illness that seemed not quickly curable: although some men were hospitalized, most were put into prison wards and some were even put into portable steel cages.[27] Patients were often imprisoned and untreated for weeks or months. During World War I, the first plans created for neuropsychiatric wards in military hospitals called the wards "isolation-insane" and buildings consisted of barred windows and cell-like spaces. However, later plans referred to the wards as psychiatric wards and included open and airy spaces with no bars on windows.[28] Supercargo as an extension of the medical establishment uses threats as a quick way to establish order, a method fitting with military physicians who saw black soldiers' hysteria as a relatively simple defect; this defect, coupled

---

24   Ibid., 82.

25   Ibid., 81-84.

26   Ibid., 84.

27   Bailey, Williams, Komora, Salmon, and Fenton, 39.

28   Ibid., 39-40.

with natural intellectual inferiority, required simple and dehumanizing methods of control and cure.[29]

The veterans' fear of their attendant or "censor"[30] appears justified when Supercargo, summoned to maintain order, drunkenly stands on the Golden Day's staircase and viciously kicks men running up to him. The men's ultimate beating of him into unconsciousness, therefore, seems a revolutionary act, resulting in the complete shedding of their fear-motivated "good" behavior: "Some made hostile speeches at the top of their voices against the hospital, the state and the universe. The one who called himself a composer was banging away the one wild piece he seemed to know on the out-of-tune piano, striking the keyboard with fists and elbows and filling in other effects in a bass voice that moaned like a bear in agony."[31] The cacophony of sound coming from the soldiers is a release and reaction against authoritarian opinion that emotional expression and lack of cheer in soldiers must be combated for them to become normal and functional.[32]

The history and nature of the black-only bar, named the Golden Day, contribute to the idea that dominant ideology seeks to make the veterans hidden away if not entirely invisible. The bar's name, implying that being there is a pleasure and reward, is a misnomer, since war trauma and racial discrimination prevent the veterans from experiencing postwar ease. One of the veterans tells Mr. Norton of the bar that doubles as a brothel, "We're patients sent here as therapy."[33] The veterans being shuttled here from the sanatorium indicates the skewed post-World War I view of shell shock as a weakness with a simple cure. Although alcohol and sex were not sanctioned treatments for shell-shocked veterans, the men's belief that these outings

---

29   Bailey, Williams, Komora, Salmon, and Fenton, 213, 384.
30   Ellison, 81.
31   Ibid., 85.
32   Bailey, Williams, Komora, Salmon, and Fenton, 102.
33   Ellison, 81.

serve as their "therapy" speaks to the American societal perception of black men as sexually uninhibited and undeserving of traditional medical interventions. Reports from military physicians during and after World War I perpetuate this perception by placing emphasis on black soldiers' high rates of venereal disease compared to white soldiers.[34] Additionally, the reports claim that black men are practically immune from negative effects of alcohol consumption, syphilis, and nervous introspection; as a result, black soldiers warranted less medical care than their white counterparts.

Aside from its name, the Golden Day's history represents racial discrimination endured by the veterans. According to the narrator, "the [historically black college in the town] had tried to make the Golden Day respectable, but the local white folks had a hand in it somehow and [college officials] got nowhere."[35] It is not sufficient for the town's African Americans to simply have a bar separate from whites; the bar also must be a site of degradation and chaos to both keep its patrons at a lower status and justify racial segregation. A similar upholding of degradation is present with Jim Trueblood, a black farmer from the novel's previous chapter. Guilty of incest, Trueblood is shunned by the black community yet financially compensated by the white power structure who wants him as a visible symbol of the black community's moral delinquency, providing justification for racial discrimination and separation. The Golden Day has been through many incarnations, the building once a church, then a bank, and then an upscale restaurant and gambling house, and the bar's owner notes that it may have also once been a jailhouse. Marc Singer's contention that "The building's history recapitulates a fall from spirituality into crass commercialism and social anarchy" ties the structure to both the destruction

---

34 Bailey, Williams, Komora, Salmon, and Fenton, 211.

35 Ellison, 73.

of war and historical African-American oppression.[36] While the church has long served a central role in the black community, religion has been used to justify racial segregation, discrimination, and even violence. The bank and the prison system are two institutions long posited as maintaining disparate racial treatment.

Outside of the nature and history of the bar, the constrictions affecting the veterans are evident through the Golden Day chapter. The narrator notes of the veterans, "Many . . . had been doctors, lawyers, teachers, Civil Service workers; there were several cooks, a preacher, a politician, and an artist. One very nutty one had been a psychiatrist."[37] Placing the former psychiatrist in a separate sentence and calling attention to his occupation highlights the tragic nature of his particular situation. He has knowledge that could help shell-shocked veterans, but it is inaccessible because he lacks a healing support system to break through his trauma and he is instead dismissed as "nutty." Despite their pasts in often aspirational jobs, the post-World War I period began the veterans' loss of any significant status. The veterans may have once enjoyed a certain status in the black community, but their mental illness is an emasculating force compounding black men's historical attempted emasculation by the white power structure. Considered less than men and with no political power to speak out against their oppression, the veterans belong to no community except their own marginalized group. Because dominant ideology, represented by white society, purports to embody reason, it uses black veterans' behavior as justification to keep them under control, and black citizens of the same town are seemingly complicit in this domination because they cannot identify with the veterans. The narrator notes, "Sometimes it appeared as though [the veterans] played some vast and complicated game

---

36   Marc Singer, "'A Slightly Different Sense of Time:' Palimpsestic Time in *Invisible Man*," *Twentieth-Century Literature* 49, no. 3 (2003): 395.

37   Ellison, 74.

with me and the rest of the school folk, a game whose goal was laughter and whose rules and subtleties I could never grasp."[38] The veterans exist in their own community as a result of having greater insight into the black American experience than the narrator. In classifying the veterans' behavior as a game, the narrator, who mentions feeling uncomfortable in their presence, blames them for being separated from their community, a strategy that fits with dominant society's minimization of the effects of war on soldiers, especially African-American soldiers. If the veterans are separate from others, this is consistent with World War I military medical personnel's beliefs that black soldiers are different than white soldiers: more prone to hysteria, unable to engage in complex mental processes, more frank in their speaking and behavior with no regard for social mores.[39] The narrator also uses the metaphor of the game to render the veterans "other" in their separate language and behaviors that fall outside the norms of behavior he has been told is proper for black men.

Rebellion against the dominant order from the veterans in the form of their aggression in the Golden Day results from Mr. Norton's presence in the bar. Mr. Norton, overcome by his conversation with Jim Trueblood that confronts him with his deep-seated incestuous feelings for his daughter, is in and out of consciousness before arriving to the Golden Day and repeatedly faints while inside. Despite his physical weakness, however, his presence has an authority that James Baldwin in "Stranger in the Village" attributes to white men who "cannot be, from the point of view of power, strangers anywhere in the world." Baldwin might argue that the veterans' responses to Norton stem from the internal rage black men carry as they push white men to see them as human instead of "exotic rarit[ies]":

---

38   Ibid.

39   Bailey, Williams, Komora, Salmon, and Fenton, 213, 246.

since white men represent in the black man's world so heavy a weight, white men have for black men a reality which is far from being reciprocal; and hence all black men have toward all white men an attitude which is designed, really, either to rob the white man of the jewel of his naiveté, or else to make it cost him dear.

Mr. Norton's feeling that he is connected to black men, has a responsibility to help them succeed, and, therefore, cannot be their enemy is "the jewel of his naiveté" and going to the Golden Day sets him up to be disavowed of his blindly idealistic notions. Although the Golden Day is a place of vice that "respectable" black men and women want nothing to do with, it is the veterans' place, and an authoritarian white man brought in upsets the only refuge they have. J. Bradford Campbell's claim that "Ellison embraces a dialectical understanding of neurosis that figures it as both disabling and enabling"[40] applies to the reactions Mr. Norton elicits in the veterans. When the narrator carries him in, "Some [veterans] were hostile, some cringing, some horrified; some, who when among themselves were most violent, now appeared as submissive as children. And some seemed strangely amused."[41] The men unable to speak and shrinking from Mr. Norton are disabled by what he represents confronting their neurosis, while those who are hostile and amused seem to be prompted into a state of control previously out of their reach. Later, other veterans become franker and more philosophical as a reaction to Mr. Norton. Overall, what the veterans say and do in Mr. Norton's presence initially appears to be a product of madness yet gives insight into dominant ideology: the "vets' mad babble bears too many incisive commentaries to be taken lightly . . . alludes to

---

40   Campbell, 446.

41   Ellison, 81.

matters clos[e] to home . . . is . . . a mode of social commentary"[42] and "contain[s] the deepest truths."[43]

The veterans' verbal responses to Mr. Norton's entrance into The Golden Day give insight into the trauma of the society they have returned to from war and the trauma that has been the foundation of their history. As the narrator and veterans usher Mr. Norton in, they discuss his identity: "Gentlemen, this man is my grandfather!...He's Thomas Jefferson . . . That ain't no Mister Eddy, man, that's John D. Rockefeller . . . Here's a chair for the Messiah."[44] By labeling him as various historical figures, they associate whiteness with political, economic, and religious power. Thomas Jefferson relates to hidden miscegenation, speaking to the shame white society associates with blackness and implying that Mr. Norton brings that shame into the Golden Day. Mentioning the Messiah implies that white society wants to "save" the veterans while knowing nothing about the constraints they face. Mr. Norton as Messiah is an ironic commentary on a man who feels he can elevate all black men to a status he sees as acceptable only because he abstractly feels a fatalistic connection to them. Of course, Mr. Norton is no Messiah, with his unwillingness to truly sacrifice to help others and his underlying lust for his daughter. By referencing these figures in identifying Mr. Norton, the veterans show what they know about the trustee, knowledge that comes to the narrator as a frightening epiphany: "He was like a formless white death, suddenly appeared before me, a death which had been there all the time and which had now revealed itself in the madness of the Golden Day."[45] The narrator realizes what the veterans have experienced for years, that dominant culture represented by wealthy

---

42   Campbell, 452.
43   Lyne, 327.
44   Ellison, 78
45   Ibid., 86.

and powerful white men is an omnipresent threat that subsumes instead of supports those unlike them. Whiteness for the veterans always connotes the consistent threat of destruction at the hands of the power structure who finds them different, less-than, and dehumanized.

Other veterans contribute to the cacophonous dialogue in the bar with seemingly nonsense statements that carry deeper truths, defined by James Baldwin as an expression of rage. One who tells Mr. Norton that he is a student of history proclaims, "The world moves in a circle like a roulette wheel. In the beginning, black is on top, in the middle epochs, white holds the odds, but soon Ethiopia shall stretch forth her noble wings! Then place your money on the black!"[46] Within his short speech lies the hope that black men and women will gain societal power but his awareness that whites are currently dominant. Another veteran named Burnside screams that his idea to change blood into money was stolen by John D. Rockefeller. Although his raving is dismissed by Mr. Norton and other veterans, "[Burnside's] paranoia is rooted in a belief that rich whites are somehow capitalizing on him—that they have 'stolen' something from him."[47] Since Burnside presumably saw his medical career end due to shell shock, he could argue that he has been capitalized on by giving his sanity and livelihood to the war effort for a country that does not value that effort.

A veteran who helps the narrator carry the unwell Mr. Norton upstairs to recover on a bed is even more direct about the degradation he has experienced from dominant culture. The narrator sees the veteran "acting toward the white man with a freedom which could only bring on trouble."[48] Although the prostitutes at the Golden Day speak freely of drinking and sex to and around Mr. Norton, the narrator sees them as inconsequential because they

---

46 Ibid., 81.

47 Campbell, 453.

48 Ellison, 93.

are both black women and sex workers. In contrast, the veteran speaking candidly to Mr. Norton is frank to the extent of frightening the narrator:

> They might realize that you are what you are, and then your life wouldn't be worth a piece of bankrupt stock. You would be canceled, perforated, voided, become the recognized magnet attracting loose screws. Then what would you do? Such men are beyond money, and with Supercargo down, out like a felled ox, they know nothing of value. To some, you are the great white father, to others the lyncher of souls, but for all, you are confusion come even into the Golden Day.[49]

The veteran warning Mr. Norton against going downstairs into the chaos of the Golden Day emphasizes the danger the white man is in because of what he symbolizes. Mr. Norton as a wealthy and influential white man embodies ambivalence, where he professes to nurture the growth of young black men, but his status and methods make him complicit in black men's degradation. White men like Mr. Norton are complicit in the veteran's inability to remain a doctor, for example, because they deny his dignity and humanity. The veteran, therefore, like many of his compatriots, blames white men's superior social status and violence for his current status and can only react in anger to the presence of a white man. However, what is truly enraging to the veteran is that Mr. Norton is actually nothing, a sick, immoral old man who by virtue of his race and money alone angers and frightens those denied access to political and social power.

Aside from bluntly confronting Mr. Norton about what he represents to the veterans, he addresses the problematic connection between Norton and the black students Norton claims to be invested in. When speaking on what the narrator and Mr. Norton mean to each other, the veteran says to

---

49   Ibid.

the white man, "To you he is a mark on the scorecard of your achievement, a thing and not a man; a child, or even less—a black amorphous thing. And you, for all your power, are not a man to him, but a God, a force."[50] In effect, the veteran argues that Mr. Norton's function in the lives of young black men is to render them automatons for the cause of white superiority. Singer agrees that "African-Americans must always linger in the ashes of slavery if they are to continue to receive [Norton's] helping hand."[51] Mr. Norton, shaken by the conversation, proclaims the veteran insane, but both Norton and the narrator in this interaction have been confronted with societal truths about racial disparity and the perpetuation of white power that they had previously been unable or unwilling to understand.

Ultimately, "Invisible Man thus demonstrates ... that African Americans are ... 'full of the tensions of modern man' (Shadow 297) and suffer them more acutely because their social conditions are more oppressive and their access to quality treatment is largely denied."[52] Through the shell-shocked veterans of the Golden Day, who can speak freely about racial discrimination because they are other and hidden away, *Invisible Man* comments on the ideology that upholds the narrative of irrational, immoral black men to keep them at a diminished status that overlooks their mental and physical sacrifices.

Toni Morrison's *Sula* engages in an extended character exploration of a shell-shocked African-American soldier, Shadrack, and includes scenes of other returning black soldiers, giving varied perspectives into the particular constraints facing them. Overall, according to Ramirez, "Morrison seems to use the tribulations and emotional turmoil that these returning soldiers had to cope with back home to express the tensions of the society they returned to live in as well as the ensuing breakdown of social patterns."[53]

50   Ibid., 95.
51   Singer, 393.
52   Campbell, 454.
53   Ramirez, 130.

Shadrack both opens and closes the novel, his story is the focus of the sections titled "1919" that covers the end of World War I and "1941" that covers the start of World War II.[54] Vashti Crutcher Lewis points out the allusion of Shadrack's name, referring to the Biblical figure who defied dominant ideology, was thrown into a fiery furnace, and "walk[ed] out of the furnace unscathed, untouched, and unburned."[55] Shadrack's name, then, could be ironic, since at no point in the novel does he emerge from a killing force without being marked in some irreparable way. The novel introduces Shadrack as "blasted and permanently astonished by the events of 1917 . . . handsome but ravaged,"[56] a man in his early twenties whose last memory before waking in a hospital is a fellow soldier's head being blown off. Shadrack's shell shock manifests itself in fear of the unstructured and fear of losing control. His food, soft in color and texture, cannot hurt him by "explod[ing] or burst[ing] forth" because "[its] repugnance was contained in the neat balance of the triangles [on his tray]—a balance that soothed him, transferred some of its equilibrium to him."[57] The act of looking for his hands so that he can eat prompts caution because, still focused on the horrors of war, he worries that "anything could be anywhere."[58] Shadrack's preoccupation with lack of boundaries and control leads to a terrifying hallucination where "his fingers . . . began to grow in higgledy-piggledy fashion like Jack's beanstalk all over the tray and the bed."[59] Hands are a powerful body part, exhibiting, among many qualities, strength, stability,

---

54 Patricia Hunt, "War and Peace: Transfigured Categories and the Politics of *Sula*," *African American Review* 27, no. 3 (1993): 446.

55 Vashti Crutcher Lewis, "African Tradition in Toni Morrison's *Sula*," *Phylon (1960-)* 48, no. 1 (1987): 93.

56 Toni Morrison, *Sula* (New York: Plume, 1981), 7.

57 Morrison, 8.

58 Ibid.

59 Ibid., 9.

hospitality, friendship, and acceptance. In effect, the hands "speak" for the body. Since verbally expressing his distress that nowhere is safe would make him a difficult patient and subject to punishment, Shadrack feels his repressed lack of control elsewhere. Additionally, that his hands, such a strong symbol and essential part of communication, labor, and individual power and control, betray him, indicate the far-reaching horrors of war.

Shadrack's hands feeling alien, disconnected, and unstoppable symbolize his body not being his own: it has always belonged to the white power structure, the military, and now, medical authorities, but his life before he suffered shell-shock may have kept him in the illusion of bodily autonomy. Living in a society where male fear is seen as weak, "alternatives to combat . . . [are] viewed as unmanly," and verbalizing feelings of vulnerability is taboo, Shadrack, like other soldiers of his time, "express[es] conflicts through the body."[60] Because his panic over his hands prevents him from feeding himself and leads him to push a nurse, Shadrack is restrained by hospital staff, but his confinement places him within the structure he craves: "When they bound Shadrack into a straitjacket, he was both relieved and grateful."[61] Shadrack's need to be under control speaks to an internal conflict between the security and powerlessness of having authority exerted over him, a conflict stemming from his time in the military. Unlike the veterans in *Invisible Man*, Shadrack embraces containment to prevent the same chaos he saw in the war. This does not mean, however, that the way the hospital staff, the authority in control of him as long as he is a patient, generally treats him provides him with any comfort.

When Shadrack is in the hospital, the nurse seems to think of him as a petulant child and an emblem of shame instead of as a mentally-ill man in

---

60   Elaine Showalter. *The Female Malady: Women, Madness, and English Culture, 1830-1980*. (New York: Pantheon Books, 1985), 171.

61   Morrison, 9.

need of psychiatric treatment, reflecting post-World War I sentiment about shell shock. According to a history of the U.S. army during World War I, patients with shell shock "were made to realize that a personal interest was taken in their welfare, that things were done for them, and that much was expected from them in return" (102). In effect, aside from electrotherapy and hydrotherapy, physicians focused on placing the emotional burden of healing on patients by emphasizing that patients "owed" the doctors who were sacrificing time and effort for them. Shadrack's treatment by the nurse through his stay is also reflective of Dr. Lewis Yealland's approach to treating shell shock through "blatant use of power and authority," a strategy "at the most punitive end of the . . . spectrum."[62] Yealland would order unresponsive patients to speak but had no concern for listening to the men in his care, and he threatened soldiers who displayed any "negative" emotions of sadness or anger with severe disciplinary action. Acting in a fashion much more extreme than Shadrack's nurse, Yealland shocked mute soldiers who were fastened down, and he considered his treatments a success if soldiers began having nightmares about him rather than the war.[63] Ultimately, Yealland was part of a movement at the time that sought quick cures and used shame and physical pain to achieve these supposed cures. In contrast, at the same time, Dr. W. H. R. Rivers, who was engaged in "the most enlightened, probing, humane, and sensitive studies of wartime neuroses," was a benign figure who understood how societal expectations of men contributed to the effects of shell shock.[64] With his patients, Rivers focused on listening and bringing them to a sense of self-understanding. Men like Shadrack, largely unable to access this non-shaming treatment, suffered from those who embraced the authoritarian approach of Yealland.

---

62 Showalter, 176, 177.

63 Ibid., 176-178.

64 Ibid., 184.

When the nurse first enters the room after Shadrack yells about his hallucinations, he refers to Shadrack's behavior condescendingly as "trouble," implying that Shadrack's fright is an inconvenience and a way to get attention. The nurse orders Shadrack to pick up his spoon to eat, angry that his patient seemingly refuses to do so, seeing this resistance as a strategy to be coddled by hospital staff. To make Shadrack focus, the nurse repeatedly calls him Private, perhaps assuming that invoking the white power structure of the military will lead to obedience. In contrast, Shadrack is left confused: "'Private' he thought was something secret, and he wondered why they looked at him and called him a secret."[65] His question could relate to all African-American veterans of World War I whose contributions were actively overlooked. To eliminate the "human remove" black men have long been placed in by white men, Baldwin argues, would mean Americans must acknowledge an ugly history of enslavement and racial violence that defeats the image of American exceptionalism, particularly in having a moral high ground.

Shadrack's departure from the structure of the hospital is marked with panic and fear and gives insight into the way shell shock affects the veteran's acclimation to society. Upon seeing the various cement paths, "each one leading clearheadedly to some presumably desirable destination," Shadrack is uneasy at their presence and opts to cut through grass "in a direction of [his] own."[66] Despite his desire for structure, Shadrack resists taking predetermined paths because no neat exit from his trauma exists for him, and, based on previous experience, he has reason to fear paths created by authority figures for him to take. As he makes his way toward the exit of the hospital grounds, Shadrack sees milling groups of people he was not aware of before. To him, "they were thin slips, like paper dolls floating down

---

65   Morrison, 10.

66   Ibid.

the walks,"[67] insubstantial because his trauma separates him from them and makes him feel apart from their world. As he walks down a road, weak and dizzy, people in cars look away from him, and the narrator attributes this behavior to Shadrack appearing drunk. Additionally, ignoring this man could indicate the larger urge to render African American veterans invisible to avoid acknowledging their sacrifices. Military doctors labeling black soldiers as fit for labor but not for intellectual pursuits and prone to knee-jerk hysteria was part of sanctioned efforts to label them as troublesome and other.

Shadrack's thin veneer of control breaks when his uncoordinated fingers cannot loosen the shoelace knots the nurse double tied as though assisting a child. So invested in being able to complete this simple task and gain some control, he feels that "his very life depended on the release of the knots."[68] The closing passage of this scene, before Shadrack is picked up by police for vagrancy and intoxication, sums up both his plight and the plight of many returning soldiers:

> Twenty-two years old, weak, hot, frightened, not daring to acknowledge the fact that he didn't even know who or what he was . . . with no past, no language, no tribe, no source, no address book, no comb, no pencil, no clock, no pocket handkerchief, no rug, no bed, no can opener, no faded postcard, no soap, no key, no tobacco pouch, no soiled underwear and nothing nothing nothing to do . . . he was sure of one thing only: the unchecked monstrosity of his hands.[69]

Maureen Reddy argues that the rootlessness Shadrack experiences is a connecting thread between war and slavery, both brutal efforts to leave

---

67 Ibid., 11.
68 Ibid., 12.
69 Ibid.

black men with nothing to call their own.[70] Hunt concurs that Shadrack is utterly bereft at this point in the novel and notes that this marks a birth of sorts for him.[71] However, Shadrack could be considered born (or reborn) when, in a jail cell, he finally sees his face after a year and marvels at the "black so definite, so unequivocal"[72] that there is no doubt he exists. As soon as the sight of his face reassures him that he is real, Shadrack no longer hallucinates his monstrous hands and he can sleep the deep sleep of "his new life."[73] This scene is particularly significant because it marks Shadrack feeling a sense of bodily autonomy—he is present, concrete, so his hands, long put to work for others, finally belong to him, even though he is still restricted by the authority of the law. Seeing his face is reifying, as Shadrack's face is presumably the only thing that has ever been his own. Soon after, the sheriff sends Shadrack to Medallion, Ohio, where he exists as both part of and separate from a black community within the town called the Bottom.

Aspects of Shadrack's life in Medallion represent the struggle of the returning shell-shocked veteran to make sense of his post-war existence and cope with being disconnected from people who do not understand his experiences. Upon starting his new life, Shadrack continues to struggle with fear about the unexpected and unstructured, so in a "futile attempt to control death and chaos,"[74] he creates National Suicide Day, one day a year when people can kill themselves or each other. In his perspective, when death is expected, the rest of the year is safe. To mark this day, Shadrack marches through the Bottom with a hangman's rope and cowbell; the first

---

70 Maureen T. Reddy, "The Tripled Plot and Center of *Sula*," *Black American Literature Forum* 22, no. 1 (1988): 33.

71 Hunt, 451.

72 Morrison, 13.

73 Ibid., 14.

74 Reddy, 31.

year, community members are frightened, but after years of encountering Shadrack's encouragement to use this single day for death, the people absorb the day as part of their lives. Moving from fear of Suicide Day to accepting it as "part of the fabric of life"[75] mirrors the townsfolk's changing feelings toward Shadrack and, broadly, how communities may transition from fear of the returning shell-shocked veteran to wary acceptance of his presence. To become accustomed to the traumatized veteran means not having to put in the work to make the community more hospitable and supportive for him.

Shadrack's not-quite-complete integration into the Bottom is likely helped by its status as a solely black community separate from and all but forgotten by white society; Cedric Gael Bryant notes that men like Shadrack would be ostracized "in the larger world."[76] Shadrack's main obstacle to being a full part of the community, therefore, is their perception of his mental state, not his race. The people of the Bottom initially fear Shadrack because they do not know what he is capable of. They see that "[he] was crazy but that did not mean that he didn't have any sense or, even more important, that he had no power."[77] In spite of their initial perceptions of him, as Shadrack continues to live in the Bottom, his consistency of routine, a way for him to maintain control of his life, helps the community see that his madness is not unpredictable: "On Tuesday and Friday he sold the fish he had caught that morning, the rest of the week he was drunk, loud, obscene, funny and outrageous. But he never touched anybody, never fought, never caressed. Once the people understood the boundaries and nature of his madness, they could fit him, so to speak, into the scheme of

---

75   Morrison, 16.

76   Cedric Gael Bryant, "The Orderliness of Disorder: Madness and Evil in Toni Morrison's *Sula*," *Black American Literature Forum* 24, no. 4 (1990): 732.

77   Morrison, 15.

things."[78] Alternating between indifference toward him and embarrassment of him,[79] the townsfolk see him as part of the Bottom while comfortable that he lives quite separately from them in a shack on the riverbank.

Fittingly, Shadrack recedes into the narrative until one key scene with the novel's titular character, Sula Peace. After she and her friend Nel drop a child into the water and he drowns, Sula runs to Shadrack's shack to see if he witnessed what they had done. When heading to the shack, Sula sees that "there was no path. It was as though neither Shadrack nor anyone else ever came this way."[80] Simply, the lack of path indicates Shadrack's loneliness with a lifetime of no visitors, but the lack of path also mirrors Shadrack's departure from the hospital in the novel's opening section. Having no walkways represents the surface impressions of Shadrack that the people of the Bottom rely on while they overlook the deeper motivations behind his behavior. Having no walkway could be his way of continuing to resist prescribed pathways. The neat, orderly, and restful atmosphere of Shadrack's home also belies Sula's perception of him as the terrible Shad who behaves shockingly. "The sharp contrast between his disorderly physical appearance and behavior and the inner tranquility of the neatly arranged interior of his house"[81] is the line between what Shadrack shows to his community and what he keeps to himself until Sula comes to his home and he sees her as a friend. The neat home, his way of maintaining a refuge and keeping chaos at bay, is not an aspect of his life that many will both see and understand. Upon encountering Sula and identifying her as a friend who needs something from him, Shadrack says to her, "always," intended to comfort her "so she would not have to be afraid of the change—the falling away of

---

78   Ibid.
79   Bryant, 735.
80   Morrison, 61.
81   Bryant, 735.

skin, the drip and slide of blood, and the exposure of bone underneath."[82] He wants to make her reassured of permanency in a way he never could be and "[assure] Sula of the inability of death to conquer all."[83] Instead, Sula, like the other people for whom Shadrack will always be a man apart, flees in fear, not understanding the intention behind his words, though he sees enlightenment in her facial expression and long after finds comfort in her brief presence. Her left-behind belt for years reminds Shadrack that he once had a visitor and could have company again, though this promise is never again fulfilled. Overall, Shadrack's encounter with Sula and its implications for surface perception versus reality speaks to the distance between a shell-shocked veteran and his community.

The novel's final scene involving Shadrack marks a deceptively positive and drastic change in him that turns to tragedy. After Sula's death and with it the end of the promise of anyone being his friend, Shadrack's behavior shifts from outward chaos and inward control to the opposite. He stops drinking "to forget whatever it was he could not remember," he allows his home to become messy, and "the messier his house got, the lonelier he felt, and it was harder and harder to conjure up sergeants, and orderlies, and invading armies; harder and harder to hear the gunfire and keep the platoon marching in time."[84] For those in the community who never see Shadrack's home and rely only on his behavior to gauge his state of mind, this transformation would appear positive. Although the narrator notes that Shadrack "improve[s] enough to feel lonely,"[85] according to Dodman, "for shell-shocked veterans, the tasks of remembering and forgetting often

---

82   Morrison, 157.

83   Lorie Watkins Fulton, "'A Direction of One's Own:' Alienation in *Mrs. Dalloway* and *Sula*," *African American Review* 40, no. 1 (2006): 70.

84   Morrison, 155-156.

85   Ibid., 155.

overwhelm all efforts at recovering themselves whole."[86] The final scene, taking place on National Suicide Day, indicates that despite the changes in Shadrack, he does not undergo recovery, which represents the shell-shocked black soldiers who remained bereft and disconnected through their lives.

Although Shadrack is prepared for his final Suicide Day march, "it was not heartfelt this time, not loving this time, for he no longer cared whether he helped [the townsfolk take control of their lives] or not."[87] With Sula's death comes the realization for Shadrack that Suicide Day cannot keep the unexpected away, so instead of a call to control death, the march becomes "an exhortation to chaos and madness."[88] Unlike every other Suicide Day, the townsfolk of the Bottom for the first time receive Shadrack with joy, following him in a line of dancing and taking a break from their lives marked by poverty and oppression. He ultimately becomes a pied piper to death, leading the townsfolk through the white part of town to attack one of the main symbols of their dashed hopes: a tunnel project that promised jobs and stability to the Bottom's residents yet never came to fruition, what Marie Nigro calls "the monument to the White world's refusal to let them in."[89] When the townsfolk minus Shadrack attack this visible sign of their deprivation and discrimination at the hands of dominant culture, most of them are killed when the tunnel collapses. The deaths of many townsfolk is "fitting and ironic [as] a final act of defiance for promises unkept, committed on National Suicide Day, a holiday intended to allay fears of death so that people could get on with their lives."[90] As many die, Shadrack continues ringing his bell, "his ritualistic role bring[ing] about the sacrifice

---

86   Dodman, 152.

87   Morrison, 158.

88   Bryant, 743.

89   Marie Nigro, "In Search of Self: Frustration and Denial in Toni Morrison's *Sula*," *Journal of Black Studies* 28, no. 6 (1998): 734.

90   Nigro, 734.

of the black community to the oppression of a racist white-dominated society."[91] Shadrack staying alive does not provide a message of hope but one of cynicism: the figure of the shell-shocked soldier is there to remind us that the oppressors often triumph and that those affected by the trauma of war may not ever get better and may, in fact, get worse.

Although Shadrack's story is the central shell-shock narrative of *Sula*, the novel includes two other brief narratives of returning black soldiers to make points about the tyranny of shell shock and of the communities to which the soldiers returned. In an early scene, Nel Wright travels with her mother Helene on a train bound to New Orleans; when Helene accidentally boards the white instead of the colored car and is berated by a conductor, "four or five black faces were watching, two belonging to soldiers still in their shit-colored uniforms and peaked caps. [Nel] saw their closed faces, their locked eyes."[92] The color of the soldiers' uniforms represents their status after returning stateside. Instead of heroes, they are excrement, and because they are nothing to the verbally-abusive conductor, they do not intervene and risk being harmed. After Helene inexplicably smiles at the conductor who calls her "gal" and angrily pulls her along, "the . . . soldiers, who had been watching the scene with what appeared to be indifference, now looked stricken. [Nel] saw the muscles of their faces tighten, a movement under the skin from blood to marble. No change in the expression of the eyes, but a hard wetness that veiled them as they looked at the stretch of her mother's foolish smile."[93] The tension present in the soldiers' faces could be contained rage at a black woman treating with coquettish charm a man who represents the power structure that keeps black men and women separate and treated as less than. Though the soldiers' presence in the novel is brief, they serve

---

91 Ramirez, 143.

92 Morrison, 21.

93 Ibid., 21-22.

as a symbolic reminder that "their war service, like Shadrack's, has done nothing to alter the 'restricted zones' of Jim Crow America."[94]

Plum, Eva Peace's son, has a narrative that encompasses more postwar trauma than post-war racial discrimination. When he returns from the war, he copes with his experiences and tries to return to his same loving and lovable self by using heroin, but his family can see that he is a shadow of himself, poorly groomed, thin, and secretive. Reddy contends that Plum's heroin use is a "futile, self-defeating [attempt] to reorder [his] world, to make it less chaotic and less terrifying" and "to effect the regression to a comparatively safe childhood he so desperately desires."[95] When Eva and her daughter Hannah discover Plum's drug use, Eva shortly after burns him alive in his bed, holding him first in his filthy room before "baptizing" him with kerosene. Asked why she killed her son, Eva argues that her act saved him from regressing to infancy, from relying on his mother to birth him again: "There wasn't space for him in my womb. And he was crawlin' back. Being helpless and thinking baby thoughts and dreaming baby dreams and messing up his pants again and smiling all the time."[96] Because of the war, Plum cannot stand on his own and doesn't want to be a man but a dependent child. Eva's act preserves his dignity as a man even as dominant ideology does not lend him the same dignity for being both a man and a soldier.

In arguing that "shell-shocked [African American] soldiers are the ultimate example of the fractured black self in relation to its own community and society in general," Ramirez pinpoints the need to study this historically elided group.[97] Accounts of shell-shocked post-World War I black soldiers

---

94   Dodman, 150.
95   Reddy, 33.
96   Morrison, 71.
97   Ramirez, 143.

have historically been limited, only a small number addressing the mental anguish of the returned soldier combined with racial discrimination and violence he faced when back in America. *Invisible Man* and *Sula*, both published decades after World War I, explore what happens to shell-shocked black soldiers whose experiences leave them in emotional and mental limbo; they are unable to process the world around them in a logical and acceptable way and are kept separate from their communities and the rest of their society as a symbol of shame instead of heroism. Through these fictional accounts, the extent of black soldiers' sacrifice can finally be more understood.

Bibliography

Bailey, Pearce, Frankwood E. Williams, Paul O. Komora, Thomas W. Salmon, and Norman Fenton. *The Medical Department of the United States Army in the World War* X. U.S. Government Printing Office, 1929.

Baldwin, James. "Stranger in the Village." *Harper's Magazine*, 1953.

Bryant, Cedric Gael. "The Orderliness of Disorder: Madness and Evil in Toni Morrison's *Sula*." *Black American Literature Forum*, vol. 24, no. 4, 1990, pp. 731-745.

Campbell, J. Bradford. "The Schizophrenic Solution: Dialectics of Neurosis and Anti-Psychiatric Animus in Ralph Ellison's *Invisible Man*." *NOVEL: A Forum on Fiction*, vol. 43, no. 3, 2010, pp. 443-465.

Davis, David A. "Not Only War is Hell: World War I and African American Lynching Narratives." *African American Review*, vol. 42, no. ¾, 2008, pp. 477-491.

Dodman, Trevor. "'Belated Impress:' *River George* and the African American Shell Shock Narrative." *African American Review*, vol. 44, no. ½, 2011, pp. 149-166.

Ellison, Ralph. *Invisible Man.* Vintage Books, 1947.

Fulton, Lorie Watkins. "'A Direction of One's Own:' Alienation in *Mrs. Dalloway* and *Sula.*" *African American Review*, vol. 40, no. 1, 2006, pp. 67-77.

Hunt, Patricia. "War and Peace: Transfigured Categories and the Politics of *Sula.*" *African American Review*, vol. 27, no. 3, 1993, pp. 443-459.

Keene, Jennifer D. "A Comparative Study of White and Black American Soldiers During the First World War." *Annales de Demographie Historique,* no. 1, 2002, pp. 71-90.

Krasteva, Yonka. "Chaos and Pattern in Ellison's *Invisible Man.*" *The Southern Literary Journal*, vol. 30, no. 1, 1997, pp. 55-72.

Lewis, Vashti Crutcher. "African Tradition in Toni Morrison's *Sula.*" *Phylon (1960-)*, vol. 48, no. 1, 1987, pp. 91-97.

Library of Congress. "World War I and Postwar Society." *African American Odyssey,* last modified 21 March 2008, https://memory.loc.gov/ammem/aaohtml/exhibit/aointro.html.

Lyne, William. "The Signifying Modernist: Ralph Ellison and the Limits of the Double Consciousness." *PMLA*, vol. 107, no. 2, 1992, pp. 318-330.

Morrison, Toni. *Sula.* Plume, 1981.

Nigro, Marie. "In Search of Self: Frustration and Denial in Toni Morrison's *Sula.*" *Journal of Black Studies*, vol. 28, no. 6, 1998, pp. 724-737.

Ramirez, Manuela Lopez. "The Shell-Shocked Veteran in Toni Morrison's

Sula and *Home*." *Journal of the Spanish Association of Anglo-American Studies*, vol. 38, no. 1, 2016, pp. 129-147.

Reddy, Maureen T. "The Tripled Plot and Center of *Sula*." *Black American Literature Forum*, vol. 22, no. 1, 1988, pp. 29-45.

Showalter, Elaine. *The Female Malady: Women, Madness, and English Culture, 1830-1980*. Pantheon Books, 1985.

Singer, Marc. "'A Slightly Different Sense of Time:' Palimpsestic Time in *Invisible Man*." *Twentieth-Century Literature*, vol. 49, no. 3, 2003, pp. 388-419.

Jill Goad is an assistant professor of English and the director of the online writing lab at Shorter University in Rome, Georgia. She has published articles on Natasha Trethewey in *South* and *Irish Studies South,* articles on Toni Morrison in *Motherhood in Toni Morrison's Novels* (Demeter Press) and in *New Academia,* and an article on psychoanalytic theory in Gloria Naylor's work in *The New Union,* among others. She is currently working on a chapter for a book on new readings of *Gone with the Wind* (Transatlantica Press).

PUNITIVE/ANALYTIC DICHOTOMY AND ANTIWAR COMPLEXES

in Pat Barker's *Regeneration* and
Dalton Trumbo's *Johnny Got His Gun*

Arsev Ayşen Arslanoğlu Yıldıran

Abstract

Shell shock, a term used to describe soldiers' psychological breakdown, originated when the British physician Charles S. Myers defined the underlying reason behind trauma as proximity to shell explosions. However, it was observed in time that those who had not been exposed to any explosion suffered the symptoms of shell shock as well. The potential heroism began to fade in time and the number of shell-shocked soldiers increased enormously. Actually it was not the content but the scale that worried military and medical authorities. Among the values related to shell shock, seen as a neurological disease or a social disease, manliness took the first place. The unity of body and mind as well as moderation and self-control was essential for being a "true man." War was considered as a test of manliness and shell-shocked men seemed to fail this test. Treatment regimens were shaped by how authorities saw shell shock. Within this context, I will focus on the English novelist Pat Barker's *Regeneration Trilogy* and Dalton Trumbo's

Johnny Got His Gun and discuss how Barker updated the long tradition of shell-shock treatment while analyzing how Trumbo questioned the legitimacy of war in a broader context.

In the broadest sense, shell shock was a term used to describe soldiers' psychological breakdown. Among its wide-ranging symptoms were mutism, stammering, twitching, paralysis, nightmares, and hallucinations. The designation of shell shock originated when the British physician, Charles S. Myers, defined the underlying reason behind the trauma as proximity to shell explosions. However, it was observed in time that those who had not been exposed to any explosion suffered these symptoms as well. What was actually surprising for the medical and military authorities was not the disorder's content, but its scale. Furthermore, it is worth noting that there was no such thing as shell shock, specifically, when the war began. In previous wars, war trauma was designated weak-heartedness, and any soldier suffering from war trauma was considered unable to bear the pressures of war. While all soldiers were seen as potential heroes at the beginning of the Great War, the potential heroism of battle began to fade in time and the number of those afflicted by the disease increased enormously. Under these circumstances, shell shock got a great deal of attention from both military and medical authorities because its treatment was crucial for nations in need of manpower. As Mark Micale and Paul Lerner point out, "[i]n light of the insatiable, European-wide need for military and economic manpower, the treatment of shell shock became a matter of urgent national concern, as different communities mobilized to explain, prevent, and counteract these debilitating symptoms" (18). In time, as Lilian R. Furst demonstrates, the problem of distinguishing the disorder from a physical illness became a great concern as well because of the absence of any visible pathology (x). Lacking an organic cause, shell shock was widely seen as a mode of converting fear into bodily symptoms. As such, it also determined the physicians' approach and the authorities' way of handling the problem. Jay Winter defines shell shock as a term of mediation "with a quicksilver and shifting character" and adds that "[i]t stood between soldiers who saw combat and physicians behind the lines who rarely did, between pensioners and medical boards, between veterans and families often unable to comprehend the nature of the injuries that men bore with them in later years" (7). One of the crucial things to understand is how people's perspectives on shell shock affected the formation of relationships among different groups. As Winter elaborates in his article, shell shock has turned from a diagnosis into a metaphor (7).

The relation of shell shock to hysteria or neurasthenia was noted from the very beginning; yet, social norms prevented, under many circumstances, authorities from expressing this explicit relation. Shell shock was seen either as a neurological disease or a social disease that threatened society's values in general. Among these values, "manliness" took first place. It was believed by European societies that "a true man was a man of action who controlled his passions, and who in his harmonious and well-proportioned bodily structure expressed his commitment to moderation and self-control" (Mosse 101). The unity of body and mind as well as moderation and self-control was essential for being a "true man." Those who could not fulfill these requirements were labeled as outsiders and seen as nervous and ill-proportioned. Most importantly, it was believed that their will-power was gone. In such an environment, war was presented as a test of manliness and shell-shocked men seemed to fail this test. Treatment regimens for shell shock were shaped by how authorities saw the disorder. While the analytic approach focused on the psychodynamics behind shell shock, the punitive approach made the treatment harsh so the shell-shocked person could return to the front as soon as possible. In this chapter, composed of two parts, these two different treatment regimens will be evaluated; in the first part, I will focus on English novelist Pat Barker's *Regeneration* trilogy (1990-95), discussing how Barker updated the long tradition of shell shock treatment by comparing Lewis Yealland's and W. H. R. Rivers's approaches respectively. In the second part, a broader perspective will be adopted and the legitimacy of war will be questioned through an analysis of an American antiwar masterpiece, Dalton Trumbo's *Johnny Got His Gun* (1939).

In a 1920 article, American author C.P . Cary draws attention to the fact that "shell shock is not a term to be taken too literally. It means various forms of breakdown of a nervous sort and from any cause that results in a strain too great for the nervous system to withstand" (61). For Cary, any nervous breakdown with the same symptoms as the failure to cope with actual fire on the battlefield could be called shell shock. The broadening of diagnosis to include psychological distress with no organic cause resulted inevitably in revising the national mood dominant at the beginning of the war. While stern determination seemed to be "the keynote of a national mood" for most people in 1914 (Fletcher 40), the aftermath of the war witnessed the shattering of the Victorian ideology of manliness that formed the basis of the national mood. It is worth noting that reactions to such a change determined the way people conceptualized shell shock to a considerable degree. In this respect, it may well be claimed that Pat Barker depicts Lewis Yealland as a physician who harshly advocates Victorian codes of masculinity while portraying W. H. R. Rivers as recognizing that all men were susceptible to mental breakdown.

Another key point is that shell shock was not an entirely new condition for medical authorities although the term was not used before. The disease called neurasthenia, characterized by a physical weakening and exhaustion of the nerves, was widely observed by neurologists before the war. Its symptoms, such as mental exhaustion, memory troubles, indifference, sadness, hypochondria, muscle spasms, headaches, cardiovascular and digestive troubles, just to name the most common, led medical authorities to question if it was a form of hysteria. The birth of the term "shell shock" can be seen as a result of an effort to express trauma peculiar to the Great War. As Jay Winter points out, the term "denoted a violent physical injury of a special kind" and this kind of injury enabled "many people and their families to bypass the stigma associated with terms like 'hysteria' or 'neurasthenia' connoting a condition arising out of the psychological vulnerability" (9). Yet, the underlying doubts about the reasons why "strong men" suffered from such a psychological breakdown continued to shape approaches to treatment throughout the war and its aftermath.

Victorian masculinity emphasized the importance of moral purity in young men above physical characteristics. However, the "evangelical" men of the early Victorian era gave way to those who valued physical courage and morality. Accordingly, the education system in Victorian schools emphasized these characteristics and incorporated the cult of athleticism. Sport was seen as a way of strengthening both moral character and the body and was also considered a way to cultivate a sense of subordination to the group. Victorian masculinity was indeed a form of reinterpretation of medieval chivalry. In this context, sacrificing oneself for the country and repressing emotions were key components. These ideals dictated the fact that men were "noble, fearless heroes" ready to devote themselves to the British empire. However, what they faced at the Western Front was entirely different from their expectations and they were in no way ready for its realities. It was under these circumstances that shell shock emerged as a new diagnosis. As Anthony Fletcher explains:

When the war began, there was no such thing as 'shell shock'. In the course of it, shell shock provided an honourable explanation for the failure of Victorian manliness. When it ended, doctors had been working for four years to understand a condition which made nonsense of the old code of manhood, revealing the male self in an entirely new guise. (Fletcher 50-51)

While the essence of Victorian masculinity was based on the repression of emotions above all, shell shock shattered this very essence. As Elaine Showalter explains, shell shock was, in a sense, a protest against Victorian masculinity: "If the essence of manliness was not to complain, then shell shock was the body language of masculine complaint, a disguised male protest not only against the war, but against the concept of manliness itself" (172). While wrestling with shell shock, both military and medical authorities were led to reconsider their conceptualization of masculinity, as well. In January 1916, The Royal Society of Medicine accepted that shell shock included a number of nervous disorders which might or might not result from soldiers' proximity to shells. A soldier's loss of control of his nerves was seen to be the common feature in all forms of nervous disorders.

Social expectations determined the way people defined these war neuroses. Many social commentators considered "neurosis" and "malingering" as synonyms. In general, homosexuals, pacifists, and the mentally ill were seen as failures. In his reading of Pat Barker's work, Greg Harris points out that Siegfried Sassoon proved a "troubling" case for Rivers (294) because he could not classify Sassoon under the existing codes. Although Rivers educated himself on pacifism, he could not leave his position as a medical figure; instead, he applied a new medical term, antiwar complex, to Sassoon's condition. As Samuel Hynes notes, "[a]ll feelings about war were valid, and were better expressed than suppressed, though in the end men should control those feelings, and should return to the fighting" (186). Under this circumstance, the disciplinary and psychological treatments of Yealland and Rivers reflected the two doctors' different reactions to the changing concept of masculinity. It is these two approaches and the dilemmas and problematics experienced by their founders that Pat Barker explores in detail. Disciplinary therapists had the mission "to make the consequences of the symptom painful and to persuade the patient to relinquish it and resume his official, soldierly, and manly function" (Leed 171). On the other side, analytic therapists saw shell shock as an unconscious product of conflicting psychological pressures. For them, shell shock was an unconscious defense against the terrors of the ongoing war. Ankhi Mukherjee points out that "the analytic method regarded the neurotic soldier as one who was helplessly divided between his instinct for survival and the social-moral imperatives that force him to repeatedly risk it" (50). By placing Rivers at the center in the novel, Pat Barker shows how the doctor applying the analytic method might well become divided between treating shell shock over a longer period, compared to the disciplinary method, and returning the soldier to the front as soon as he becomes functional whether the underlying conflicts have been resolved or not.

In his article in *The Lancet* (1918), one of Pat Barker's sources, Rivers focused on the problem caused by repression in the original formation of shell shock. Emphasizing that repression did not cease on the battlefield but continued at the hospital and at home, he expressed that the most distressing symptoms "[were] due to the attempt to banish from the mind distressing memories of warfare or painful affective states which have come into being as the result of a war experience" (3). In *Instinct and the Unconscious*, Rivers identified three kinds of war neurosis. The first one resulted in physical manifestations such as blindness, paralysis, and mutism; the second kind led to lassitude, enervation, and various disorders of sleep;

the third kind caused mental instability and restlessness (232). Rivers's treatment for all kinds of war neurosis rested on encouraging the patient to remember what had been repressed voluntarily or involuntarily. The only case for which Rivers avoided applying this method was that of an officer "flung down by the explosion of a shell so that his face struck the distended abdomen of a German several days dead" (Rivers 7). In this officer's case, Rivers believed remembering was "extreme" because the trauma was too severe. Rivers incorporated three components to his therapeutic approach: remembering, re-education, and faith and suggestion. By means of these additional components, he helped the patient to reframe painful memories and to overcome their disabling effects.

Pat Barker depicted Rivers' method in detail by including Siegfried Sassoon as a major figure. Rivers' treatment of Sassoon, who was shell-shocked but not disabled, led both men to question what they had taken for granted. It was after Sassoon had been invalided home a second time and had written his famous statement "A Soldier's Declaration" to be read in the House of Commons that he met Rivers in the hospital. In his declaration, Sassoon expressed that the war "upon which [he] entered as a war of defence and liberation ha[d] now become a war of aggression and conquest" (173). In *Regeneration*, after Sassoon fails to attend his first medical board, a second one where he is made to accept the treatment is arranged. During his stay at the hospital, Sassoon continued expressing his beliefs about the war explicitly. Yet, there was an important point that made him different from an ordinary pacifist: he would cease opposing the continuation of the war if valid reasons were presented. However, there was no one, including Rivers, who could persuade Sassoon that his judgment about the prolongation of the war by the selfish motives of political authorities was invalid. What made matters more complicated was that Rivers started to get lost in his own dilemmas about the war:

Rivers was aware, as a constant background to his work, of a conflict between his belief that the war must be fought to a finish, for the sake of the succeeding generations and his horror that such events as those which had led to Burns's breakdown should be allowed to continue. This conflict, though a constant feature of his life, would certainly have been strengthened by his conversations with Sassoon" (47)

Rivers's inner conflicts seem to be caused by his dilemmas on not only war but also the essence of masculinity he has been taught: "In advising his young patients to abandon the attempt at repression and to let themselves feel the pity and terror their war experience inevitably evoked, he was excavating the ground he stood on" (48). In his sessions with the patients, he was leading them to understand that their feelings and their responses to the trauma of the war were nothing to be ashamed of, which was against the teachings of their upbringing. His patients had also been trained to see those who broke down or cried as weaklings and failures. The repression of emotions was a necessary condition for a "successful and manly" adult life. On the other hand, Rivers was becoming increasingly aware that there was no such man who could face the horrors of war without being traumatized. Besides, his sessions with Sassoon were strengthening his doubts about the legacy of the war. It was during this period that Rivers wrote his well-known article "The Repression of War Experience."

As they approach the end of the treatment period, Rivers finds himself in another dilemma: "Rivers knew the full extent of the dilemma that would face him if Sassoon had deserted and did make another public protest. He would be asked to take part in declaring him insane; they would never court-martial him. Not now. The casualty lists were too terrible to admit of any public debate on the continuation of the war" (211). The medical authority's declaring Sassoon insane would solve the problem for the political authority but it would only deepen the matter for Rivers himself because he would then be in the critical position of questioning what being insane means under the present circumstances. On the other hand, Sassoon seems somehow relieved and directs all his anger and sorrow into poetry. He also makes up his mind about returning since he cannot leave his comrades alone at the front. However, Sassoon's new stance is a source of another anxiety for Rivers: "At the back of Rivers's mind was the fear that Craiglockhart had done to Sassoon what the Somme and Arras had failed to do. And if that were so, he couldn't escape responsibility" (221). Rivers's mind is occupied by such turbulent feelings and fears when he leaves Craiglockhart on November 14, 1917.

Rivers was one of the respected medical figures in the treatment of shell shock in London at the time. He was due back at Craiglockhart on November 25 but he had been invited to visit Queen Square where he would get the chance to meet Lewis Yealland, the prominent name in applying the disciplinary approach in the treatment of shell shock. As opposed to Rivers' approach, Yealland was not interested in the psychological dynamics behind shell shock although he had accepted their presence (Yealland ix). He was known for his harsh attitude towards the soldiers. Rivers was critical about Yealland's approach and increasingly identified with the soldiers. When he went to visit Yealland, he found himself in an uncanny, empty corridor where he felt completely insecure. While expecting to be met by a nurse, Rivers met a strange figure whose portrayal seemed to be exemplary of the patients in Yealland's book *Hysterical Disorders of Warfare*:

> ... a creature—it hardly resembled a man—crawled through the door and began moving towards him. The figure made remarkably rapid progress for somebody so bent, so apparently deformed. His head was twisted to one side, and drawn back, the spine bent so that the chest was parallel

with the legs, which themselves were bent at the knees. In addition one arm, the left, was pulled away from the body and contracted. The right hand clung to the rail, not sliding along it, but brought forward step by step, making slapping sounds on the wood. (223)

The physical appearance of the patient demonstrates that he has not only lost his physical abilities but also his subjectivity as a man at the front. However, having no time to contemplate this shocking figure, Rivers finds himself before Yealland who thinks the best introduction would be a round of the ward. As opposed to Rivers, who is full of doubts and dilemmas, Yealland is depicted as utterly sure of himself: "Yealland was an impressive figure. In conversation he did not merely meet your eye, but stared so intently that you felt your skull had become transparent" (224). This posture was actually seen as the necessary doctor stance in treating shell shock in *Hysterical Disorders of Warfare*. The real historical Yealland writes that the doctor "must possess sympathy, understanding, tact, imperturbable good temper and untiring determination, in addition to a sense of humour and the ability to meet unlooked for situations as they arise with ready decision" (vi). These characteristics are entirely different from those in Rivers' psychoanalytic method; Yealland posited the doctor as the sole authority in the treatment process. In the novel, Barker depicts Rivers through his conversation with the patients. He does not present himself as an authority figure but tries to help them by getting them to share their troubles resulting from the war. The most significant difference between Rivers and Yealland is that Yealland was so sure of himself that he claimed that the patients they were seeing with Rivers would be out within a week (224). In addition, the patients' lack of organic disease indicated to Yealland that he would be triumphant for sure. On the other hand, Yealland's God-like tone while talking to the patient and the patient's explicit fear alarm Rivers.

Barker's inclusion of the case of Callan is very effective in presenting Yealland's approach. This case also reflects the historical Case A 1 who cannot speak in Yealland's original work. Yealland invited Rivers to witness Callan's treatment as if he were inviting a person to a performance. Yealland chose this case because previous treatments had failed (227). He saw shell shock as an enemy to be defeated no matter what. Thus, the feelings of the patient had no importance for him; all he required was strict obedience. For instance, Callan's smiling, which implied he wanted to be cured, was not sufficient for him and his response seemed to leave no subjective space for the patient. After telling Callan that he seems very indifferent to his condition, Yealland emphasizes that Callan's condition makes no difference to him and he must recover his speech immediately (227). The treatment was traumatic not only for Callan as the patient but also for Rivers as the witness. Here, the patient was in an entirely helpless position in a locked room with no chance to get out except by full recovery. What was striking was that Yealland was using pain as a means of controlling the patient. After reminding him of the expected heroic behavior from a soldier, he says there were two keys to the door: one in his pocket and one in Callan. It was a key that Callan could use if only he recovered. As Tobi Smethurst points out, pain becomes deconstructive of the self in the disciplinary approach: "Pain, in this sense, is deconstructive of the self; it effects an abrogation of civilized impulses and behaviors, such as voluntary speech, in order to reconstruct the victim—the voice of the victim—in line with expectations of the regime. As a disciplinary therapist, Yealland—most explicitly Barker's Yealland—is the agent of this de- and reconstruction" (417). The destructive effect of pain was so great that even Rivers could not help the patient, with whom he had identified. He wanted to speak for him from time to time but it was impossible even for him to speak under that condition. Yealland's insistence on full recovery in one session alone was turning treatment into a form of torture, indeed.

Pat Barker gives the profound effect of witnessing such a session in a chapter where Rivers experiences hallucinations. That evening when he is trying to work on a paper, Rivers is haunted by "the man in the corridor at Queen Square, Yealland's hands, Callan's open mouth, the two figures, doctor and patient, walking up and down" (234). The vividness of the image causes him to feel ill and lost in the depths of neuroticism. His meeting with Yealland had been a confrontation for him that led him to question his treatment method and his position as a doctor. The content of the dream he saw that night deepened the conflict present since the beginning: "From the beginning he'd felt a tension between, on one hand, his sympathy for the patients, his doubts about the quality of the treatment they were receiving, and on the other, the social and professional demands on him to be reasonably polite" (236). Although he uses none of the brutal means of Yealland's treatment, the dream seems to suggest that there is no essential difference between the two. They were silencing people and removing the possibility that they could oppose the war:

> Just as Yealland silenced the unconscious protest of his patients by removing the paralysis, the deafness, the blindness, the muteness that stood between them and the war, so, in an infinitely more gentle way, he silenced his patients; for the stammerings, the nightmares, the tremors, the memory lapses, of officers were just as much unwitting protest as the grosser maladies of the men. (238)

In addition to this problem of "silencing," Rivers experiences the dilemma arising from the fact that those who had been saved from death and cured were being sent back into the midst of war where there was a high possibility of death. In this case, the meaning of recovery was becoming questionable. Rivers tried to cope with the questions in his mind by considering the fact that nobody is a free agent in the war; yet, this palliative approach apparently did not solve any problem.

Focusing on the perspective of Rivers from the beginning of the first volume of her trilogy, Pat Barker touches upon the questions regarding the legacy of the war and shell shock in detail. The fact that Sassoon is not only shell-shocked but has a logical argument against the continuation of the war puts into question both the social conditions leading to the war and the way those conditions shaped the reception of shell shock. As noted above, the Victorian conceptualization of masculinity was one of the most effective factors in shaping the perception of shell shock. As George L. Mosse points out, shell shock was a condition that could be understood within an existing cultural context (101). A firm image of masculinity shaped the approach of not only ordinary people but also military and medical authorities. As a result, the treatment approaches differed in relation to their understanding of Victorian masculinity as well as other factors. Pat Barker posits Rivers as a witness to Yealland's treatment of Callan both to reflect her critical stance against Yealland's disciplinary method and to give the reader an opportunity to evaluate the problematics caused by the war in a wider context. Yealland's continuous emphasis on being a "true man" during his session is a clear indicator of the degree to which his method was grounded in the traditional conception of masculinity. On the other hand, Rivers becoming skeptical about almost everything he has learnt during his sessions with Sassoon shows how fragile all these teachings are. Thus, Pat Barker does not only present a doctor-patient relationship in this first volume; rather, she opens a window towards the social conditions and their effects on the understanding of shell shock through this exemplary relation.

The American novel, *Johnny Got His Gun*, questions the legitimacy of the war by telling the story of a terribly-wounded soldier who has lost all except his consciousness. Written in 1938 and published in September 1939, the novel reflects author Dalton Trumbo's hatred of the popular World War I song "Over There" (Doctorow vii): "Johnny get your gun, get your gun, get your gun / Take it on the run, on the run, on the run / Hear them calling you and me / Every son of liberty." Trumbo depicts the protagonist, Joe Bonham, in a way that represents every single soldier traumatized heavily by the war and leads the reader to question the legitimacy of war in general. In his "Introduction," Ron Kovic—a Vietnam War veteran who had then spent twenty-two years in a wheelchair—expresses the novel's effect on him: "It led not to sleep or comfort, but kept me wide awake and agitated—making me thinking, and in thinking see, and in seeing act, powerfully and with others against what was frightening me" (xvi). Seeing the novel as the most revolutionary document against war and injustice ever written, Kovic concludes that "the enemy is the government in all its greed and corruption, in all its scheming and manipulations, in its endless desire for profit at the expense of human lives" (xxiv). To contextualize what this means in *Johnny Got His Gun*, it is helpful to understand the period before the war in the United States.

The initial reaction in the United States to the outbreak of World War I was to let European nations fight their own battles (Volo 313). There had been nearly a century of noninvolvement policy and many Americans were unwilling to join battles in Europe. At the beginning of the war, the United States tried to continue safe trade in Europe but the sinking of the Lusitania and several other boats made staying out of war impossible. Although Wilson called the war "the most terrible and disastrous of all wars," he could not wait for people's feeling for war to grow (Schaffer 4) and followed policies that would make every person believe in the legitimacy of the war. The propaganda stressed the importance of national unity and those who did not cooperate with the government were depicted as the "enemy." Despite strong governmental propaganda, American entry into

World War I in 1917 generated a great deal of war resistance (Schaffer 3). Although many favored ties with the British and believed that the Allies had the moral high ground, public opinion was against entering the war. Those in favor of intervention insisted that "the nation's defenses were inadequate and proposed that military training would toughen American youth and help Americanize foreign immigrants" (Volo 315). On the other hand, war resisters and pacifists "denounced preparedness as 'a scheme to fatten the pockets of big business' and to enrich armament manufacturers, financiers, and international bankers" (Volo 315). While there were lively debates between the two parties, most young Americans were unaware of what was going on. War was presented to young boys as a chance to prove their masculinity. Many young boys, like Trumbo's protagonist, Joe Bonham, went to war under the effect of propaganda and developed critical insight only when they were badly hurt and left alone. Wilson's reelection slogan in 1916, two years after the war had begun, "He Kept Us Out of War," shows the public inclination to remain neutral at first. However, Wilson's stance changed later and he established George Creel's Committee on Public Information whose task was to promote the United States's entry into the war. Creel promoted the idea that the world must be made safe for democracy. From this new perspective, Wilson was considered the man who could set a hysterical continent aright, and he symbolized healing and recovery for many Europeans (Stagner 256). However, the result was a disaster for both Europeans and Americans as neither Europe was set aright nor the world made safe for democracy. Nearly 120,000 Americans perished in the war. Many veterans suffered from mental and physical wounds. The illusion that the world would be safe for democracy and that this was the war to end all wars collapsed. There remained many vivant mortes (living deads) who had lost in a fight which was not theirs, and Joe Bonham represents them all:

> He lay and thought oh Joe Joe this is no place for you. This was no war for you. This thing wasn't any of your business. What do you care about making the world safe for democracy? All you wanted to do was to live. You were born and raised in the good healthy country of Colorado and you had no more to do with Germany or England or France or even with Washington D.C. than you had to do with the man in the moon. (25)

Johnny Got His Gun is a masterpiece of anti-war literature. As Dalton Trumbo points out in his "Introduction," the novel "held a different meaning for three different wars. Its present meaning is what each different reader is gloriously different from every other reader, and each is also changing" (xxviii). In the "Appendum" he wrote eleven years later he emphasizes how numbers dehumanize people: "Over breakfast coffee we read of 40,000 Americans dead in Vietnam. Instead of vomiting, we reach for the toast" (xxix). Combined with the propagandist discourse, normalized violence in war causes people to feel as if what happens is normal. However, only the degree of individual suffering, which reaches the extremest point in Joe Bonham's case, shatters the illusion that war must go on. At the beginning of the novel, a telephone rings endlessly; yet, Joe cannot answer. It is not clear whether he is in a dream or not. However, what is certain is that the machine that connects people does not work for him any more: "With each ring it seemed to get lonesomer. With each ring he got more scared" (9). From this point onward, Joe gradually discovers his own condition. While not knowing what makes war necessary, being reduced into an object makes it utterly unjustifiable no matter what the gains are. War deprives Joe of his body and his right to communicate with others. The following quotation summarizes Joe's living dead condition in a striking way:

You couldn't lose that much of yourself and still keep on living. Yet if you knew you had lost them and were thinking about it why then you must be alive because dead men don't think. Dead men aren't curious and he was sick with curiosity so he must not be dead yet. (63).

Shell shock, which is war trauma specific to the First World War, is not sufficient to express Joe's condition, clearly. What is significant in shell shock is that it is some form of somatization since the soldier cannot express his fears and anxieties at the level of consciousness because these are not acceptable in terms of social norms. What makes *Johnny Got His Gun* unique is that Trumbo goes a step further and creates a character who has nothing left except consciousness. As Susan Kingsley Kent points out, "the sights and experiences of war could not be integrated into customary patterns or meaning systems that organized the ordinary rhythms of life; they traumatized people" (11). Traumatic experiences do not fit into the system over which we make sense of ourselves. In Joe Bonham's case, losing the ability to use his body ends in developing a more critical understanding of war. While theoretically the war victim cannot face reality and develops some form of amnesia, Joe confronts what he has experienced and tries to create a coherent pattern which will become his life from now on. In order to do this, he has to find out what state he is in. First, he realizes that his arms are gone. It's not only his arms but the ring given by Kareen that signifies their future together: "There was a ring on my hand. What have you done with it? Kareen gave it to me and I want it back. I can wear it on the other hand. I've got to have it because it means something it's important" (29). Joe tries to think about what has happened but all he gets is the realization that he has lost much of his body. At this point, he thinks of killing himself by holding his breath; yet, he cannot stop the air his lungs are pumping. So he can neither live nor die and gradually he comes to understand that this is no dream but the reality of his life. At this stage, Joe is still incapable of separating day and night, reality and dream. Yet he feels he has to do it because in his words this makes him less than nothing. And here we see the complete collapse of the illusion that one must fight for liberty:

> If there could be a next time and somebody said let's fight for liberty he would say mister my life is important. I'm not a fool and when I swap my life for liberty I've got to know in advance what liberty is and whose idea of liberty we're talking about and just how much of that liberty we're going to have. And what is more mister are you as much interested in this liberty as you want me to be? . . . and I've already decided that I like the liberty I've got here the liberty to walk and see and hear and talk and eat and sleep with my girl. I think I like that liberty better than fighting for a lot of things we won't get and ending up without any liberty at all. Ending up dead and rotting before my life is even begun good or ending up like a side of beef. Thank you mister. You fight for liberty. Me I don't care for some. (115)

While idealists confidently claim there are ideals are worth fighting for, Joe is lying there helplessly as just one consequence of the desire to fight for those ideals. His life is taken from him and all he wants is just to live and know. He thinks of himself as the nearest thing to a dead man on earth and he now knows that there is no word for one's life:

> You take the words. Give me back my life. I'm not asking for a happy life now. I'm not asking for a decent life or an honorable life or a free life. I'm beyond that. I'm dead so I'm simply asking for life. To live. To feel. To be something that moves over the ground and isn't dead. I know what death is and all you people who talk about dying for words don't even know what life is. (122-23)

His mind is the only thing left to him and he has to find some way to express what he thinks and feels. When he senses the presence of a person in the room, he hopes it will be his mother and his sisters and Kareen. However, his delight soon turns into shame and he does not want anyone to see him in his current condition. Ironically, some men come into his room and the reader learns that they are there in order to give him a medal, which drives Joe into fury: "They could afford to couldn't they the dirty bastards? That was all they ever had time to do just run around putting medals on guys and feeling important and smug about it. How many generals got killed in the war" (166)? Then a feeling of sickness pervades his existence; yet, he feels obliged to find a means of communication since it is the only way for him to feel alive. From this point on, all his life will be tapping out morse code with his head but this does not solve the problem as the only person who can help him has no idea what he is doing. Besides losing most of his body, he is now kept as a prisoner in his consciousness, wishing to get the relief of death as soon as possible. Instead of giving up, Joe insists on tapping and expressing what is in his mind. Those who talk about the virtue of joining the war are nowhere to be found in Joe's condition; they consider themselves having performed their duty when they give him a medal. Now it is only silence that is all around:

> It was something like the silence you hear when you put a seashell to your ear the silence of time itself that is so great it makes a noise. It was a silence like a thunder in the distance. It was silence so dense that it ceased to be silence. It changed from a thing to a thought and in the end it was only fear. (195)

What is worse is that he does not belong to either the living or the dead; he is something in between. He thinks he is there forgotten and abandoned but with the coming of a new nurse he finds a new chance to communicate when a nurse traces letters on his chest: "Each time she paused he shook his head and then she repeated the design once more and in the midst of this patient repetition the barrier between them suddenly broke down" (206). The first thing the nurse draws is "Merry Christmas" which gives Joe a sense of time even if he cannot know what year it is. He now feels like a god as he has found a way to communicate and prove that he is a person, not an object. The fact that his mind is unaffected causes him to feel strong and to keep his critical stance. It may well be said that his case is the opposite of shell shock in that his mind is intact while his body is almost completely lost. He cannot use his body but his mind works well and all his effort is to communicate with the nurse. The first question the nurse asks is what he wants. This question leads Joe to wonder what others can give him, and he realizes they cannot give him what war has taken from him. They cannot give him his body and life back. Still, their presence is important since a man needs to be among his own kind and feel he is a person: "Every living thing needed to be among its own kind. He was a man a part of mankind and he wanted to be taken out so that he could sense other men around him" (230). The first thing the medical team asks him is what he wants; however, his wish to be outside and to be presented to others as what war makes of man in reality is considered to be against regulations. He realizes that he is at their mercy and there is no hope for him because these people keep their minds closed to any alternative critical view about the war and its legacy. Yet, Joe considers himself as a perfect picture of a future full of wars, and considers that these people are afraid to face the future they have themselves created.

In conclusion, the questions regarding the nature and legitimacy of war are more explicitly posed in *Johnny Got His Gun* than in *Regeneration*. While neither Rivers nor Sassoon can explicitly state that war is meaningless and unacceptable, Joe sees himself in a position to tell all about war because it has deprived him of everything except his consciousness. However, Dalton

Trumbo is aware of the fact that such an antiwar stance will not be accepted without serious opposition. The response of the doctors in the novel shows how difficult it is to see the illegitimacy of war. Ironically, as a result of government policies, common men who go to war and risk their lives do not question the policies behind the war. It seems normal that men go to war and fight for the ideals taught them by the authorities. Their defending these ideals so strongly makes authorities more powerful, causing people to consider war as inevitable and normal. When the majority shares these views, people who oppose them are seen as outcasts. Sassoon and Joe question whose ideals they are expected to defend and even to die for. Since defending these ideals is presented as proof of being loyal to the country, Sassoon and Joe are considered outcasts by the majority. Sassoon's return to the army and Joe's being ignored by others at the moment when he can finally communicate with them show how thoroughly indoctrinated people are to accept war. Under these conditions, it seems that war will continue and those who question its legitimacy will remain a minority.

Bibliography

Cary, C. P. "Educational Morale and Shell Shock". *The Journal of Education*, vol. 92, no. 3, 1920, pp. 61-62, https://www.jstor.org/stable/42829809

Fletcher, Anthony. "Patriotism, the Great War and the Decline of Victorian Manliness." *History: The Journal of Historical Association*, 99, January 2014, pp. 40-72. http://eds.a.ebscohost.com/eds/pdfviewer/pdfviewer?vid= 2&sid=25889164-dc36-4dfc-8fe4-d01c6696aea4%40sessionmgr4008.

Furst, Lilian R. *Idioms of Distress: Psychosomatic Disorders in Medical and Imaginative Literature*. State University of New York Press, 2003.

Harris, Greg. "Compulsory Masculinity, Britain and the Great War: The Literary- Historical Work of Pat Barker." *Critiques: Studies in Contemporary Fiction, vol.* 39, no. 4, Summer 1998, pp. 290-304, https://doi.org /10.1080/00111619809599537.

Hart-Davis, Rupert, ed. *Siegfried Sassoon Diaries 1915-1918, Vol.1.* Fabre, 1983.

Hynes, Samuel. *A War Imagined: The First World War and English Culture.* Athenaeum, 1990.

Kent, Susan Kingsley. *Aftershocks: Politics and Trauma in Britain 1918-1931.* Palgrave Macmillan, 2009.

Kovic, Ron. "Introduction." *Johnny Got His Gun,* Dalton Trumbo, Bantam, 1984, pp. xiv-xxiv.

Leed, Eric. "Fateful Memories: Industrialized War and Traumatic Neuroses." *Journal of Contemporary History,* vol. 35, no. 1, 2000, pp. 85-100, https://www.jstor.org/stable/261183.

Micale Mark S. and Paul Lerner. *Traumatic Pasts: History, Psychiatry and Trauma in the Modern Age, 1870-1930.* Cambridge University Press, 2001.

Mosse, George L. "Shell Shock as a Social Disease." *Journal of Contemporary History,* vol. 35, no. 1, 2000, pp. 101-8, https://www.jstor.org/stable/261184.

Mukherjee, Ankhi. "Stammering to Story: Neurosis and Narration in Pat Barker's Regeneration." *Critiques: Studies in Contemporary Fiction,* vol. 43, no.1, 2001, pp. 49-62, https://doi.org/10.1080/ 00111610109602171.

Rivers, W. H. R. "The Repression of War Experience." *Proceedings of the Royal Society of Medicine,* 1918, No.11.1-17.

Schaffer, Ronald. *America in the Great War: The Rise of the War Welfare State.* Oxford University Press, 1991.

Smethurst, Toby. "The Making of Torture in Pat Barker's Regeneration." *Critique: Studies in Contemporary Fiction*, vol. 55, no. 4, 2014, pp. 406-421, https://doi.org/10.1080/00111619.2013. 783781.

Showalter, Elaine. *The Female Malady: Women, Madness and English Culture, 1830-1980.* Penguin Books, 1987.

Stagner, Annessa C. "Healing the Soldier, Restoring the Nation: Representations of Shell Shock in the USA During and After the First World War." *Journal of Contemporary History*, vol. 49, no. 2, 2014, pp. 255-274, https://www.jstor.org/stable/43697299.

Trumbo, Dalton. *Johnny Got His Gun.* New York: Bantam, 1984.

Volo, James M. *A History of War Resistance in America.* Greenwood, 2010.

Winter, Jay. "Shell Shock and the Cultural History of the Great War." *Journal of Contemporary History*, vol. 35, no. 1, 2000, pp. 7-11, https://www.jstor.org/stable/261177.

Yealland, Lewis R. *Hysterical Disorders of Warfare.* Macmillan and Co., Limited, 1918.

Arsev Ayşen Arslanoğlu Yıldıran is an assistant professor at the Department of English Language and Literature at Artvin Çoruh University, Turkey. She has published essays and presented papers on experimental Canadian and American literature, graphic medicine, and modernist American literature. Currently she is working on a book project on hysteria and literature.

www.ingramcontent.com/pod-product-compliance
Lightning Source LLC
Chambersburg PA
CBHW041312240426
43669CB00023B/2964